BROKEN BENEFITS

What's gone wrong with welfare reform

Sam Royston

D0963924

P

First published in Great Britain in 2017 by

Policy Press
University of Bristol
1-9 Old Park Hill
Bristol
BS2 8BB
UK
t: +44 (0)117 954 5940
pp-info@bristol.ac.uk
www.policypress.co.uk

North America office:
Policy Press
c/o The University of Chicago Press
1427 East 60th Street
Chicago, IL 60637, USA
t: +1 773 702 7700
f: +1 773 702 9756
sales@press.uchicago.edu
www.press.uchicago.edu

British Library Cataloguing in Publication Data
A catalogue record for this book is available from the British Library.

Library of Congress Cataloging-in-Publication Data
A catalog record for this book has been requested.

ISBN 978-1-4473-3326-5 paperback
ISBN 978-1-4473-3328-9 ePub
ISBN 978-1-4473-3329-6 Mobi
ISBN 978-1-4473-3327-2 ePdf

Cover design by Lyn Davies
Front cover: image kindly supplied www.alamy.com
Printed and bound in Great Britain by CPI Group (UK)
Ltd, Croydon, CR0 4YY
Policy Press uses environmentally responsible print
partners

To Mum and Dad,

Sarah and Alfie

"A superb and deeply knowledgeable analysis of how our benefit system really works – and sometimes doesn't – for those in need. Benefits too often confuse, conflict, are wrongly sanctioned and wrongly denied; claiming them even leaves some people worse off. Yet a sane and decent benefit system, both for those in and out of work, is the most effective path out of poverty. Clear-eyed, compassionate and compelling, this book is a must-read, and must-keep, for all who care about the poverty and insecurity of our fellow citizens."

Rt. Hon. Baroness Hollis of Heigham, former Social Security Minister

"Gives expert, accessible exposure of social security provision in the UK – its past, its cuts, its future plans. It strongly calls for better benefits."

Terry Patterson, National Association of Welfare Rights Advisers

Contents

List of figures and tables

Figures

Tables

About the author

Sam Royston is Director of Policy and Research at The Children's Society and chair of the End Child Poverty coalition, and spends much of his time trying to make the benefits system work a little bit better for children and families. He regularly gives evidence to parliamentary committees on welfare reform issues, and his work often appears in the national press.

Prior to this he worked as a welfare rights advisor, in which role he spent many frustrating days on the phone with the DWP and HMRC, trying to help fix people's broken benefits.

Broken Benefits has an accompanying website available at www. brokenbenefits.uk where you can find updates on some of the topics discussed in the book, and an online calculator illustrating the impact of key welfare changes on personal finances.

Acknowledgements

Thank you first and foremost to those who spent time talking to me about their personal, and very difficult, experiences of the benefits system. Thanks also to those who have worked with these people (and helped by putting me in touch with them), including Stevenage Citizens Advice Bureau (CAB), Craven and Harrogate Districts CAB, and The Trussell Trust.

While writing this book I have continued in my role as Policy and Research Director at The Children's Society – an amazing organisation packed full of people doing good things for children and young people facing the most difficult of circumstances. Thank you to everyone at the charity (and particularly everyone in the Policy, Research and Public Affairs team, and Peter) for your understanding, support, flexibility (and occasional active interest!) over the last year and a bit.

Thank you to Alison, Rebecca, Laura, Kathryn and Jess at Policy Press for thinking this wasn't such a bad idea for a book, and for your help and support throughout the process of writing and publishing it. Thanks also to those who reviewed the initial book proposal and the first draft of the text.

Thank you to Andrew Hood and Tom Watson at the Institute for Fiscal Studies for permission to reproduce two of their graphs.

Also thanks to what was Ripon and District CAB (now part of Craven and Harrogate Districts CAB) for my lengthy apprenticeship while I worked there, learning how the benefits system works in practice. Welfare rights advisers are amazing and deeply under-appreciated professionals currently facing an incredibly difficult job.

Talking of which, thanks to my mum for showing me what a sprawling, complicated machine the benefits system is, how the different parts work together and separately, and just how poorly understood it all is. I know of no one else with anything close to your practical knowledge of the system, as clear an idea of how it needs to change, and the consequences if it does not.

Thanks also both to my mum and dad for teaching me that numbers are really, really important. Many bad things in the world happen because people don't think that they matter that much.

Thank you finally to my wife Sarah, for her constant help and advice while writing the book, and for reading and improving the whole text. As with all things in life, it is much better because of you.

Part I
Introducing the benefits system

1

Introduction

'There are few more entrenched problems than our out-of-control welfare system and few more daunting challenges than reforming it.' (David Cameron, Bluewater, Kent, 25 June 2012)

The benefits system is broken. It is broken when people take on additional hours of work with little or no reward, when they pay their National Insurance Contributions but seem to get nothing in return, and when they get paid the wrong amount – or nothing at all.

The system wasn't working when the coalition Government took office in 2010 promising *"welfare that works"*[1], and despite – and in many cases because of – reforms to the system, it has become still more dysfunctional since then.

Somehow, despite the hardship caused by half a decade of benefit cuts for the poorest families, the UK spent more on benefits in 2015 than it *ever has before*. By the end of the decade, the country is still expected to spend more on benefits than it did at the start.

Despite failing to reduce the overall cost of the system, there are severe social consequences to some of the cuts which have been introduced over the course of the decade. Projections suggest that the number of people in poverty will have risen by more than two and a half million over the course of the decade – mostly due to increases in child poverty. By 2020, 15.6 million people – including 5 million children – are expected to live in poverty across the UK. [2]

Benefits matter. Yet rather than a smooth, well-oiled machine, the system feels like a disjointed, hulking iron beast. Its cogs are sticky, and its gears are jammed. It has few friends, certainly fewer than in the past. It lost some by getting too big, or not being big enough; it lost others by being too complicated.

Regardless, the creaking wheels continue to turn, and the system continues to do its job – just about. But something inside *seems broken*. This book is about why that is, why it is getting worse, and what can be done to put things right.

What exactly are 'benefits'?

Let alone resolving how to make the benefits system work, it is something of a challenge to define exactly what benefits *are*.

At a basic level, benefits are *cash transfers*, from either national or local government, to either individuals or households (a claimant household typically being an adult, and a partner if they have one, and any dependent children), in order to promote their economic wellbeing.

There are many things that are *not* cash transfers that nonetheless help with living costs for families – a free education system and national health service, and the provision of social housing at low rates of rent being particularly obvious examples. While these are crucial contributors to living standards, they are not benefits.

Similarly there are many forms of cash transfer that are not benefits – payments made to employees, for example, are not part of the benefits system since they are transactional payments for delivery of goods or services rather than made in order to promote people's economic wellbeing.

There are inevitably a number of grey areas. For example, in some parts of this book we talk about so-called 'benefits in kind', such as free school meals, which are forms of support often associated with the benefits system but not paid in cash; these are normally closely linked to the benefits system, for example, through entitlement being gained on account of receipt of certain other benefits (a process known as 'passporting').

There are also cash transfers that may be provided by institutions other than the state. For example, some charities make small grants to families facing financial difficulties. We do not consider these in detail in this book (although the following chapter does discuss non-state provision of financial support, in the context of providing a historical background to poor relief in Britain).

In this book a few terms are used interchangeably, in particular, 'benefits', 'social security' and (on occasion) 'welfare'. While this makes life much simpler, I appreciate that reference to the welfare system also often covers non-cash provision of state support (including education and healthcare), in addition to cash payments.

What is 'broken' about the benefits system?

There are many reasons why the benefits system can seem broken – from its cost, and its failure to support working families, through to the sense that it no longer rewards those who make a contribution, and that its administration is a mess. All of these issues are addressed in detail through the course of the book.

Cost of benefits

Perhaps the most frequently mentioned cause of dissatisfaction with the benefits system is the cost. We all pay a great deal of money towards the benefits system each year – an average of around £8,000 from each household in the country in 2016.[3] Indeed, the UK spends much more on social security than on the NHS, or substantially more than on schools, the police, and defence combined.[4]

The cost of the system has created discontent on all sides of the political spectrum – on the right, because it is said to drive dependency on the state and a culture of entitlements; on the left, because it is said that 'poverty pay' in the private sector requires top-ups from taxpayers in order to provide a decent standard of living.

In the course of this book we will see how what have been framed as cuts to the benefits system to reduce the cost have, to a great extent, represented a 'rebalancing' of the system. At least in part, this rebalancing has been away from children and those of working age, and towards pensioners.

While most benefits for children and those of working age have suffered from a series of freezes and cuts in recent years, the State Pension has increased rapidly. This has been the result of a 'triple lock' – a guarantee that the Basic State Pension will rise each year in line with whichever is the highest of inflation, increases in earnings or 2.5%. Original forecasts from the Treasury in 2010 suggested that the triple lock would cost £450 million per year by 2014-15; in reality, it cost *over five times more*. In fact, overall, the rising cost of the State Pension consumes pretty much all of the savings achieved by radical cuts to benefits for children and those of working age.

There may be some justification for this. It has historically been the case that pensioner poverty rates have been unacceptably high, and additional support targeted at low-income older people since the start of the century has led to dramatic improvements in their lives. However, because of the interaction with benefit payments, it is not the lowest-income older people who principally gain from the triple lock, and despite its introduction in 2010, pensioner poverty rates have not budged.

Furthermore, a large group of low-income people in their sixties are being reclassified as 'working age' and denied a key pensioner benefit (Pension Credit), which is targeted at those on low incomes. Despite having the slowest rise in life expectancy, it is low-income older people who are seeing their effective retirement age increase the fastest – making it less and less likely that they will live to see a significant period of healthy retirement. Instead, many are spending much of their later life in receipt of sickness or unemployment benefits. At the time of writing in 2017, there are around 350,000 Employment and Support Allowance and Jobseeker's Allowance claimants over 60 years old.

Failing to support working families

Much of the rhetoric around the failures in the benefits system has been around its unfairness to working families. For example, in 2013, the then Chancellor George Osborne introduced changes to limit increases in benefit and Tax Credit payments to just 1% for three years (later extended into a further four-year freeze on entitlements). He said this was about "being fair to the person who leaves home every morning to go out to work and sees their neighbour still asleep, living a life on benefits ... we have to have a welfare system that is fair to the working people who pay for it."[5]

But these changes cut the support received by working claimants just as much as for non-working claimants. As we will see, some groups of hard-working families could be left as much as £9,000 per year worse off by 2020 as a result of changes to provision over the course of this decade.

While the benefits system is often presented as something that only really affects non-working families, the reality is that without support from the system, many workers would simply be unable to make ends meet. In Chapter 12 I give the example of a single parent with one child with rent and Council Tax of £150 per week, working 16 hours per week and earning £120, who would receive £259 in benefits to help top up her earnings. Without this top up, her earnings on their own wouldn't even be enough to pay her rent.

While the former Chancellor was wrong that cutting the benefits system was fair for working families, he was right that the benefits system can seem broken for this group. For many of the lowest-paid workers in particular, on earning an additional £1, they get to keep just 4p because of the way in which benefits are reduced as earnings increase. This means that for many in this group, if they take on some extra hours, or work for a promotion, they keep next to nothing from any additional pay.

Upcoming decisions about the future of the benefits system threaten to compound these risks – creating tipping points for low-paid workers, where, on earning more money, they would actually be left worse off.

National Insurance Contributions scam

The post-war social security system was originally intended to be built around a contribution-based benefits system – people paid in their contributions in order to provide protection for themselves in periods of sickness and unemployment, and for their retirement.

However, for many of the lowest-paid workers today, the provision of contribution-based benefits may have very little impact on their overall income. Indeed, as we will see in Chapter 14, it has reached the point where many working people paying National Insurance Contributions find themselves left *worse off* as a result of making payments – in some cases by hundreds of pounds – in what I can only describe as an appalling insurance scam. Such an approach to 'rewarding' those who make a contribution can only serve to undermine faith in the system as a whole.

Dysfunctional administration

When you flick a light switch, you don't necessarily need to know how the power is generated or transmitted, but you do need to be confident that the light will turn on. Similarly, while claimants do not necessarily need to know the ins-and-outs of how the benefits system works, they do need to know what they might be entitled to, how to claim, and to be assured that they will receive the correct payments on time. However, too often this simply isn't the case. Many people are not aware of what they are entitled to. Others face problems with the claims process – particularly with errors and delays in processing and decision-making about an application.

This is particularly the case with disability and sickness benefits, where failures in assessments and lengthy delays in processing applications are leaving people without support for months on end. And increasingly, when wrong decisions are made, people are facing new barriers that make it hard to challenge them.

Even when benefits start to be paid, this doesn't mean that they are paid correctly. For example, billions of pounds per year are being wrongly paid in Tax Credits – largely at no fault of the people claiming the money – simply because of the way the system is structured. This is causing hundreds of thousands of families to get into debt on their benefits, without being able to do anything to prevent it.

The benefits system is changing

For all of the reasons outlined above – and many more – people see a benefits system that simultaneously costs a lot, yet has apparently poor outcomes, giving an overall impression of being *bad value for money*.

Governments both past and present have recognised the problems facing the benefits system, and have sought to address them in their different ways. At the time of writing in 2017, social security is going through its biggest upheaval since the post-war system was first put in place. *Broken Benefits* particularly focuses on reforms introduced since 2010 – when the coalition Government took office, and began the process of policy change that would culminate in the 2012 Welfare Reform Act.

The changes come in two main parts. The first is simple – at the time of writing, the government is introducing major cuts to working-age benefits, which come on top of cuts that have been put in place in the first half of the decade. The scale of these cuts is simply astonishing. The former Chancellor George Osborne, who put in place many of the measures to deliver them, believed that they represented a 'new settlement' – a large-scale shift from being a "low wage, high tax, high welfare economy" to a "higher wage, lower tax, lower welfare" country.[6]

However, many of the cuts just serve to entrench – rather than mitigate – some of the problems that run at the heart of the benefits system. Despite the promises to make the 'new settlement' one that works for working people, many of the heaviest cuts have fallen on exactly this group. As this book will show, many of these cuts haven't just affected the amount of support working families receive; they also undermine incentives to work and cause administrative chaos, including Tax Credit overpayments reaching £1.7 billion per year. The rate of overpayments is at a similar level to a decade ago, when the then Shadow Chancellor George Osborne questioned whether the Labour minister responsible should resign.

The cuts have also been targeted at many of those who are least able to respond – in particular, children and people with disabilities. Some of the most vulnerable and socially isolated people with severe disabilities will lose the most through the process of welfare reform.

However, it is not cuts alone that are causing the benefits system to change. At the same time as delivering tens of billions of pounds of reductions in support, the benefits system is facing large-scale structural change. Old benefits are being scrapped; new ones are being introduced. Perhaps the most significant of the changes is the introduction of the new Universal Credit.

Universal Credit brings together six different means-tested benefits into a single payment. This book will show how, while it does help to address *some* of the problems in the benefits system, with work incentives and administration, it is simultaneously introducing new ones. Its introduction in the context of spending cuts is undermining its potential, making it less and less likely to achieve what it was designed to.

Another significant 'structural' change is the new disability benefit called the Personal Independence Payment that has also started to be introduced – in a way that one parliamentary committee described as a "fiasco" that "has let down some of the most vulnerable people in our society." [7]

At the same time, much provision is being 'localised', with responsibility being passed across to local authorities. This includes support with Council Tax bills, and providing families with emergency financial support in a crisis.

Some of the structural reforms that have been introduced over the course of this decade have been well intentioned but corrupted by the prioritisation of reductions in provision over the effectiveness of reform.

Fixing the benefits system

I hesitate to suggest further radical change to the benefits system. People in receipt of support are already struggling to keep up as it is, and the process of change introduces further complexity (even if the changes are designed to eventually simplify the system). For example, families who currently receive benefits for their children could end up on one of *three* different benefits systems, because the transition from the first to the second hadn't been completed before the third was introduced;[8] and a fourth might just be a step too far.

This book does not suggest we build a new benefits system, which is in keeping with reform of welfare across Britain's history. Even when he began drafting plans for the post-war benefits system, one of its principal founders, William Beveridge, argued that it was more a continuation from the past than a radical change – what he called a 'British revolution'.

However, there is so much that we can do to *fix what we already have*. To make sure that it supports the most vulnerable; to make sure that it responds to the individual and varying needs of claimants; to make sure that when people do the right thing, they are clearly and consistently rewarded by the system – not punished by it.

Such servicing and repair of the benefits system could be done in a way that, to the claimant, would seem largely invisible, but would simply make the system function more smoothly, and more fairly.

What next?

Broken Benefits has six parts. The remainder of this first part is introductory, and asks *where did the UK[9] benefits system come from, and what is it for?* It looks at the history of the benefits system (from its foundations not only in the wide-scale changes introduced after the Second World War, but also in the Elizabethan Poor Law and before), highlighting how many of today's difficulties and decisions are just the same as those that have faced policy-makers for hundreds of years. It also considers the reasons why benefits are paid, making the case for three main grounds: to provide a safety net for those most in need, to address inequalities in need between households (and particularly those that can't be addressed through the labour market), and to 'reward' socially desirable behaviours.

Part II asks *how does the benefits system operate today?* This looks at how different benefits combine to provide an overall entitlement, how means-tested and contribution-based benefits work together (or separately), and how entitlements reduce as earnings increase.

The third and fourth parts of the book ask *what's changing?* They consider some of the key reforms being introduced between 2010 and 2020, which include both cuts to provision (Part III) and changes to the way the system is administered (Part IV).

The fifth and final parts ask *how will the benefits system look in 2020 compared with 2010, and what needs changing to fix it?* The cumulative impact of benefit reforms on spending on the system, and on incomes for different household types is considered. Having explored this, some of the potential social impacts of the changes are also reviewed.

The book concludes with recommendations for change built around four key themes: providing an effective safety net, responding to variations in household needs, supporting socially desirable behaviours, and creating a system that is simple from the claimant's perspective. There is an accompanying website at: http://brokenbenefits.uk

Reforming the benefits system is a complex job – there are no two ways about it. It is a job that requires a detailed understanding of the different parts that make up the system, and how they interact. But too often among policy-makers, researchers and lobbyists, this understanding can be missing. While it is right to look at the system as a whole and how this fits into a broader socioeconomic context – how it needs to respond to economic cycles, an ageing population and changes to the gender composition of the workforce – this will only get us so far. When fixing a broken machine, nothing can replace a detailed look at its gears and cogs and levers, how they work separately, and how they run together.

This book aims to bridge that gap, and show that with such understanding, as well as effort and commitment, it *is* nonetheless possible to make benefits work better.

2

The makings of a 'British revolution': A brief history of benefits

The provision of financial support is far from new in Britain. Systems of poverty relief can be traced back to at least the Middle Ages, well before the first statutory provision of financial support was put in place through the Elizabethan Poor Laws. Looking back, although it may be difficult to see the similarities between provision made in the distant past and the benefits system today, many of the issues that they sought to address were just the same as those that come up now.

One of the principal architects of the new benefits system that emerged after the Second World War, William Beveridge, said that he saw his proposed scheme of social security as in some ways a 'revolution', but 'in more important ways it is a natural development from the past.' He called this 'a British revolution'.[1]

Before we go on to consider the contemporary benefits system – and the problems it currently faces – it is worth reflecting on the development of this 'British revolution', and how an ongoing process of both continuity and change has brought us to where we are today.

Poor relief before the Poor Law

In the Middle Ages, the provision of welfare (so far as it existed) was largely through the Church.[2] Attitudes towards the poor were somewhat different – the idea of giving away one's possessions (among certain groups) as a step towards salvation meant that poverty retained a certain amount of status and social acceptability.[3] Reflecting this, alms tended to be given by the

Church to all those in need, irrespective of 'desert' (which was later to become a major issue in discussions around support for the poor, right up to the present day).

There were also some forms of secular provision – including from private foundations – which set up almshouses and hospitals.[4] Trade guilds also provided some charitable assistance (these were also involved in mutual insurance of a sort, which existed even at this time among merchant and craft guilds, a precursor of the 19th-century mutual insurance societies). This secular welfare provision was to become more widespread through the 16th century.

Despite this, the dissolution of the monasteries under Henry VIII destroyed many of the most formalised institutional means for welfare provision by religious organisations. As one historian has noted:

> In 1536 and 1539 Henry VIII expropriated the monasteries and turned their properties over to his followers. This action, like the Black Death in the fourteenth century, gave dramatic point to an already bad situation. A social resource, inadequate at its best, was now substantially diminished.[5]

However, it is not universally agreed that the dissolution of the monasteries had a significant negative impact. A large proportion of donations to the church went not into welfare as such, but rather to religious purposes such as church improvements and masses for the dead; it has been argued that so little was devoted to social welfare that the dissolution had little impact on overall provision.[6]

Furthermore, the dissolution was accompanied by a trend away from philanthropic donations being used for religious purposes, and towards more secular and 'socially useful' ones such as the building of hospitals and schools and the creation of workhouses. As a result, some have found that although philanthropic disposition may have declined between the Reformation and the early 17th century, the amount of such contributions used for the benefit of society increased.[7]

The 16th century also saw a focus on the creation of a legal distinction between 'deserving' and 'undeserving'. Although this may be traced back to a 1349 prohibition on dispensing alms to 'able-bodied' beggars, it was revived in 1495, when all local authorities were ordered to track down 'vagabonds', place them in stocks and then send them on their way.[8] In the second half of the 16th century, the law set in place the difference between the 'impotent poor' and 'vagabonds', with the latter outlawed 'under pain of whipping and boring through the ear for a first offence, unless the culprit would enter service for a period of one year'.[9]

The Poor Law

At the same time, across the course of the 16th century, the 'deserving' poor were given some entitlements in law to welfare provision, initially (in 1531) by being given entitlement to beg, then in 1536 by alms collected by 'every preacher, parson, vicar, curate of this realm' who 'shall exhort, move, stir and provoke people to be liberal and bountifully to extend their good and charitable alms and contributions'.[10]

By 1563, the collection of alms was legally enforceable, with (as one historian put it) the provision of support for the poor moving from 'social pressure' to 'police power' – voluntary giving having failed, 'the law now inserts a "must"'.[11] A Poor Law was introduced in Scotland around the same time. The Poor Law in England was essentially finalised by Acts of 1597-98 and of 1601,[12] and would remain in its basic form for the next 300 years. The Beveridge Report describes the 1601 Act as 'the starting point of state provision of social security'.[13]

The Poor Law was, at least in part, an attempt to reintroduce the kind of semi-formal welfare system that had been provided prior to the dissolution of the monasteries. However, there were economic causes as well – including higher rents and prices and enclosures of common land leading to larger numbers of severely poor people.[14] It has been suggested that it was 'the triad of wet summers and bad harvests between 1594 and 1597, with food riots in 1596, that brought the Poor Law in its final form'[15] – perhaps it is reasonable to suggest that (both then and now) the provision of welfare is not entirely driven by humanitarian concern, but also by the risk of social disorder being threatened by large numbers of severely poor people.[16]

The Poor Law created fundamental differences in philanthropy between Britain and many continental European countries that had no such counterpart and where, if taxes were used to provide relief, this would be as a temporary expedient.[17] While in Britain philanthropy still remained the major force in welfare until the 20th century, the Poor Law showed, not necessarily the first, but certainly an early and marked intention to assert some kind of state involvement in the field.

However, in the initial period of its existence, the Poor Law was unpopular and not regularly invoked, with parishes relying instead on charitable donations to poor relief. 'In almost every parish where rates were levied there was a swarm of angry and outraged complaints regarding the rating methods, the probity of overseers, and urgent denials that the poor were not already well provided'.[18]

Rather than the Poor Law, the vast majority of welfare was provided by un-coerced philanthropy aided by the emerging wealthy middle class. It has been estimated that in no year prior to 1660 did more than 7% of the money spent on care for the poor come from taxation.[19]

Welfare from 1800 to 1945

At the start of the 19th century, state provision for the poor was still provided under the old, Elizabethan, Poor Law,[20] with parish poor relief subsidised by charitable giving. However, the old system came under a lot of pressure during the course of the century. It was felt by many that poor relief encouraged irresponsibility, including (according to the economist Thomas Malthus) irresponsible breeding.[21] Much unemployment was seen as voluntary, and it was believed that it could be reduced by encouraging able-bodied men to find work.[22] As a result of this, by the middle of the century, the old Poor Law system had been replaced by a new and notoriously repressive system of dealing with poverty, through the Poor Law Amendment Act of 1834.

The Act renewed the focus on the distinction between the 'deserving' and 'undeserving'. The 'deserving' poor – including the sick, elderly and children – were those who 'could not be expected to support themselves by work, and could not be described as work-shy dependents upon the public purse'.[23] These people would be granted a dole with which they could support themselves (known as 'outdoor relief'). However, in order to discourage the seeking of relief by anyone other than the truly destitute, the able-bodied poor would not be able to claim 'outdoor relief' but would rather face the 'workhouse test' – only being able to claim support if they entered the workhouse.[24] While reforms to the law made it more humane from 1848, for lack of an alternative, the basic structure remained the same for several decades afterwards.[25] The distinction in Scotland was, if anything, even sharper, with statutory poverty relief under the Poor Law not extended to the able-bodied poor at all. It was not until well into the 20th century that statutory poverty relief was extended to the unemployed in Scotland.[26]

This re-focusing of poor relief was not restricted to provision from the state under the Poor Law. A similar 'problem' was perceived with regard to charitable giving, and in response, in the second half of the 19th century, the Charity Organisation Society (COS) was formed with the intention of reorganising philanthropic efforts (and administration of the Poor Law). It was the view of COS that rises in poverty in the 1860s were the result of 'lax' implementation of the Poor Law, and of 'indiscriminate almsgiving'.[27] Their 'harsh' and rigid' approach to the poor has given not just themselves, but perhaps Victorian philanthropy more generally, something of 'a bad name'.[28]

The approach of both the COS and the Poor Law reformers has been described as a 'muddled' rather than 'malevolent' approach caused by the need to deal with complicated issues of an unprecedented kind.[29] Regardless of the reasons for it, the approach made scapegoats of the poor, framing them as lazy and dependent, whereas others believed there existed more pernicious problems causing poverty in Victorian England. As Beatrice Webb[30] summed up her view, the main cause of 19th-century poverty was 'a deeper and more continuous evil than unrestricted and unregulated charity, namely unrestricted and unregulated capitalism.'

Throughout the 19th century, protest about poverty was increasingly expressed by the poor themselves. Certainly by the 1880s this had resulted in increased activity among the working classes in economic and political issues, particularly at times of economic depression and social unrest.[31] Towards the end of the century, concerns about militancy resulting from unemployment, combined with inadequate charitable support to relieve the unemployed poor, led to a number of reforms aimed at increasing state provision of welfare (beyond the Poor Laws). Between 1870 and 1900 central government action to address social problems significantly increased, but it remained inadequate to deal with the scale of the problems presented, and the level of demand for action.[32]

Continuing the trend towards increased state intervention in the provision of welfare, a number of key welfare reforms were introduced by the liberal governments of the start of the 20th century. These included the school meals Act of 1906 (which enabled schools to provide free meals),[33] and the Old Age Pensions Act of 1908 (which provided a non-contribution-based pension to low-income pensioners[34]), the latter of which Beveridge describes as 'the first real departure from the Poor Law'.[35] Later reforms introduced additional provisions for workers in periods of sickness and unemployment.[36]

These reforms created a new atmosphere of state involvement in welfare provision. The reforms of 1908 and 1911 in particular took a big step towards securing the welfare of workers and pensioners, areas that had traditionally been the province of voluntary action. However, this role was set to step up considerably following the Second World War.

The Beveridge Report, 1942

At the point in 1941 when Sir William Beveridge was asked to chair an interdepartmental committee on coordinating social insurance, Nicholas Timmins describes him as being 'an egotistical sixty-two year old civil servant who believed his destiny was to organise key parts of Britain's war effort'.[37] The task of the committee was seen by the Treasury as a 'tidying up operation', to sort out the 'mess of sickness and disability schemes' that provided protections to workers by that point. The terms of reference of the committee were said to be 'as harmless as they could be made'.[38]

However, the report that the committee was to produce – the snappily titled *Social insurance and allied services report* (but now much better known as simply the 'Beveridge Report'), was far more than a tidying up operation of any description. It set the foundations for the creation of the post-war welfare state.

The report proposed a system of National Insurance by which, in return for a contribution, workers and certain adult dependents would receive (non-means-tested) support in times of unemployment or sickness and in old age. Further, it proposed a 'national assistance' scheme to provide rigorously means-tested support for those who hadn't made sufficient contributions to receive insurance-based assistance. It also proposed non-means-tested, and non-contribution-based, 'family allowances' to assist with the costs of children. Other forms of support were also proposed, including maternity and funeral grants, as well as the creation of a free national health service.

Beveridge insisted that the rates of payments through the benefits system were made at a minimum subsistence level[39] (and the rates that were later introduced have been criticised as inadequate for even that). The intention was that this would provide a basic standard of living, which would not discourage people from working and saving in order to achieve something more.

Immediately after the Second World War came to an end, many of the provisions outlined in the Beveridge Report were brought into being. The Family Allowances Act of 1945 established a universal child allowance giving 5 shillings for second and subsequent children (although, notably, none for the first child), which by 1949 was being paid to nearly 3 million families, costing £59 million per year.[40] As an official report of the time put it, 'The state now accepted the responsibility of making a financial contribution to the cost of bringing up every family of two or more children, regardless of the parents' means'.[41]

The National Insurance Act of 1946 gave workers, in return for a weekly contribution, entitlement to seven kinds of benefit: sickness and unemployment benefit, an old age pension, maternity and widows' benefits, a guardian's allowance for orphans, and a death grant to cover funeral expenses.[42] The National Assistance Act of 1948 then 'created a single, national means-tested allowance available to all those not in employment whose financial resources fell below a standard set by Parliament'.[43]

Not everything was as Beveridge had proposed. For example, he had suggested that contribution-based unemployment and sickness benefit should be paid without a time limit, emphasising that 'to reduce the income of an unemployed or disabled person, either directly or by application of a means-test, because the unemployment or disability has lasted for a certain period, is wrong in principle'.[44] Instead of time limits, Beveridge felt that maintaining manageable levels of claims should be achieved through two key mechanisms. First, that after a limited period of time, unemployment benefit claimants would need to look for work outside of their previous occupation, and attend a 'work or training centre'.[45] Those refusing suitable employment, dismissed for misconduct or leaving work voluntarily could be disqualified from benefit receipt. Second, Beveridge's system was predicated on the government managing the economy to achieve low rates of unemployment. Overall he argued that,

> … payment of unconditional cash benefits as a right is satisfactory provision only for short periods of unemployment; after that, complete idleness even on an income demoralises. The proposal of the Report accordingly is to make unemployment benefit after a certain period conditional upon attendance at a work or training centre. But this proposal is impracticable, if it has to be applied to men by the million or the hundred thousand.[46]

Third, the creation of a free health service would reduce the length and frequency with which the provision of sickness and disability benefits were required. As Beveridge put it, 'it is a logical corollary to the payment of high benefits in disability that determined efforts should be made by the state to reduce the number of cases for which benefit is needed'.[47]

While the post-war government agreed that contribution-based sickness benefits should be paid indefinitely, the period for which unemployment benefit could be paid was extremely contentious. Concerned about the costs of provision (and after much disagreement in Cabinet),[48] the Chancellor Hugh Dalton successfully argued that it should be limited to 30 weeks.[49] This is an important point, since for Beveridge, the social security system should be based fundamentally on contribution-based provision. A limited period for claims made this considerably harder to achieve, since the long-term unemployed would need to rely on means-tested support instead.

One problem for both Beveridge and the post-war government was what to do about regional variations in rent. Even at the time of the Beveridge Report, levels of rents had a great deal of geographical variation, with the report noting that 'for food, clothing, fuel and light, the percentages [of average expenditure] for the separate divisions [regions] all lie in a narrow range, between 94.2 and 104.9. For rent, the range is much greater, from 70.4 per cent in Scotland to 148.1 per cent in London in industrial households'.[50]

However, in the end, the report did not recommend varying the payment of benefits to reflect different levels of rent, arguing that 'the principle that a flat rate of insurance contribution should lead to a flat rate of benefit has a strong popular appeal and is much easier to defend than any departure from it'[51] (although the report did go on to note that if it was seen as 'desirable and practicable' to adjust provision according to rent, this could be made without affecting the main structure of the system).

In the end, the post-war government decided not to vary national contribution-based benefit rates to reflect differences in regional rents. However, national assistance support for the unemployed did vary – with assistance allowances normally including provision for the rate of rent actually paid.[52]

This is likely to have contributed to the reasons why, by the early 1950s, large numbers of benefit claimants were relying on national assistance payments to 'top up' contribution-based benefits. One memorandum from a National Insurance minister in 1952 found that of the 1.5 million cases of national assistance being paid out, two-thirds were supplementing National Insurance pensions or benefits.[53] Again, this necessity to 'top up' inadequate insurance-based payments undermined the principle of an insurance-based benefits system.

Some things change, some things stay the same

It is remarkable just how many of the rules proposed in the *Social insurance and allied services* report remain in place today. First, a non-means-tested and non-contribution-based benefit to support the needs of children remains (to a degree) in the form of Child Benefit. However, this is now supplemented in significant part by the provision of means-tested support for children (in particular, through Child Tax Credit). Beveridge was against the provision of means-tested support for children partly because he felt that this would make it much harder to ensure that people were better off in work than out of work. A graduated approach to the tapering of in-work benefits, together with additional benefits paid to working claimants, helps to avoid this problem today – although, as we will see in Chapters 12 and 13, the problem of work incentives remains a core problem within the benefits system.

A notable difference is that Beveridge proposed (and the post-war government agreed) that additional benefits should not be paid for the first child when the family is working, on the basis that a single worker's earnings should be sufficient to cover the needs of themself, their partner and one child. The circumstances are very different today, where higher rates of payment are made for the first child, and (as discussed in Chapter 8) limitations are imposed on support for families with more than two children.

Second, we retain a combination of out-of-work benefits provided through contribution-based support for those who have made sufficient National Insurance Contributions (including contribution-based benefits paid during periods of unemployment and sickness, as well as – through the State Pension – in retirement), and means-tested benefits to those in need who have not paid sufficient contributions, and to 'top up' inadequate contribution-based provision.

Today, contribution-based Jobseeker's Allowance can be paid for around the same time as when first introduced in 1946, with a six-month limit on claims. However, it is notable that in the last few years a one-year time limit has been introduced for many claimants in receipt of contribution-based sickness benefits (contribution-based Employment and Support Allowance), which was not previously time-limited, representing a significant step away from the principally insurance-based system first introduced.

This is not the only respect in which the contribution-based benefit system no longer offers a significant safety net for workers. As we will see, flaws in the system mean that it can even be the case that households are left significantly *worse off* when they have paid to receive 'insurance'-based support.

Third, as in the past, rates of means-tested national assistance were varied to reflect variations in rent; today, Housing Benefit is a means-tested benefit that can be paid as a supplement to contribution-based entitlements, and that varies according to local rents and household needs (although, as discussed in Chapter 7, particularly for those in private rental housing, it is no longer 'normal' for it to reflect the rent paid by a household – increasingly falling well short of this).

Despite many similarities, there are many other ways in which the benefits system has changed considerably since these foundations were set in the post-war years. For example, while non-means-tested support for children was introduced immediately after the end of the Second World War, similar non-means-tested provision to assist with the additional costs of disability were not introduced until Attendance Allowance and Mobility Allowance were created in the 1970s.[54] For working-age claimants, these benefits have since been merged into Disability Living Allowance, and then further transformed with the recent (and much troubled) introduction of the Personal Independence Payment (discussed in more detail in Chapter 15).

The approach to ensuring that claimants are always better off in work has also changed significantly. Beyond non-means-tested support for children, neither the Beveridge Report nor the post-war reforms made significant allowance for in-work support to 'top up' earnings. It was assumed that earnings, with some additional support for larger families through family allowances, would be sufficient to meet people's needs.

Since this was not always found to be the case, there was a problem that a national assistance rate that met minimum needs might outstrip the wages that a household could expect to make in employment – leaving the family better off out of work than in work. In such circumstances, a 'wage stop' was applied to assistance levels, leaving them below minimum subsistence levels in order to ensure that work incentives were maintained. In 1963, around 25,000 households (with 100,000 children) had a wage stop applied to their national assistance provision.[55]

Today, the problem of ensuring that (a) adequate allowances are provided for those out of work while (b) people are better off in than out of work is principally addressed through payment of in-work benefits to top up insufficient earnings.

In-work provision – through a range of benefits including Tax Credits, Housing Benefit and increasingly, Universal Credit – is now a core component of the benefits system. This both helps to ensure that out-of-work benefits aren't higher than in-work provision, and also (as discussed in the following chapter) helps to address differences in levels of household need that cannot be met through the labour market. However, the payment of means-tested in-work benefits also raises significant problems for incentives to progress in employment. These are further discussed in Chapters 12 and 13.

Conclusion

It sometimes seems like there is nothing new under the sun. Over time the same issues have come up over and again in determining how best to provide financial support in Britain. What is the right level of support to provide? How do you distinguish support for those who need it from those who should be able to provide for themselves? How do you make sure that incentives to move into work are maintained while still making financial provision for those without any earnings to rely on?

Given this, it is perhaps unsurprising that by the time that Beveridge drafted the *Social insurance and allied services* report, he saw the scheme as more of an ongoing development from the past than a revolution in provision.[56] The state of the benefits system today may be seen as much the same. The strengths of it – the safety net for those most in need, and some level of responsiveness to individual circumstances – are strengths that have existed for some time. Similarly, many of the difficulties – how to properly assess and respond to differences in need, how to encourage work and reward saving, how to ensure that the system as a whole is fair and consistent – are by no means new problems either.

The benefits system needs repairing and improving, not building anew. Ideally, it needs doing so from the same position of hopefulness and optimism that marked the post-war period, but if that's not possible, the British response must be to stoically get the job done anyway.

In the concluding chapters of the book we look at some of the changes that could be made to improve the benefits system in the future. However, before we come on to some of the solutions, or even to fully understanding the problems, we need to understand in more detail what the benefits system is for and how it operates today.

3

What are benefits for?

A common misconception is that there is one reason, and one reason only, for paying benefits – to alleviate poverty by providing a minimum 'safety net' of support for those in need. If this was the case, it would make little sense to pay in-work benefits to those whose earnings exceed that minimum level; it would make no sense at all to pay non-means-tested benefits to those with disabilities, or in retirement.

A more sophisticated understanding of the social security system is needed. I argue during the course of this book that there are three main reasons for paying benefits:

1. to ensure a 'safety net' of minimum provision;
2. to 'level the playing field' (in particular, by addressing variations in need that cannot be met through the labour market);
3. to promote socially desirable behaviours.

This chapter outlines how the benefits system can serve each of these three objectives. It also shows how these different aims may come into conflict, creating undesirable, or even perverse, outcomes.

Providing a 'minimum' safety net

One of the greatest things that people can do for each other is to provide support when times are difficult. This can be done in many ways, from neighbourly help (through what might have been called the 'Big Society' in recent times), to systematised provision (provided through the state or some other organisation, such as a religious group or charity). Over time, the nature of provision has changed significantly, gradually becoming more ordered and systematic (although its generosity has varied).

As seen in Chapter 2, until the late 19th or early 20th century, such 'safety net' support was principally provided through philanthropic aid – either through the church or more secular routes. From the 16th century charitable provision was supplemented by the first statutory provision under the Poor Law, but state support didn't replace charity as the principal form of support until much later. Since the post-war settlement, the provision of such a safety net has been placed firmly on a statutory footing.

The reasons for state provision of social security are broadly the same as for the provision of other key public services – a social security system principally provided through philanthropy, voluntary personal saving or other non-compulsory means is likely to be inequitable, inadequate and inefficient. There are a number of reasons for this.

Provision other than that regulated by the state is likely to be inequitable since everyone benefits from a universal safety net, but without compulsion through taxation, 'free riders' may take advantage of the benefits of this, without contributing towards them. The more people are concerned that others are free riding, the more likely they are to do so themselves – further undermining provision.

This free rider problem is likely to contribute to the inadequacy of non-compulsory provision of social security. Another factor contributing to this may be a very human tendency not to make sufficient personal plans for the future – we may be underprepared for future periods of unemployment, ill health or old age because we prioritise the present day, underestimate the risks of difficulties occurring, or simply don't have the resources needed to plan ahead.

Certainly, welfare provision without state involvement has historically been found to be inadequate. The Poor Law was introduced because, even in a pre-industrial society, non-compulsory provision proved to be insufficient to meet the level of need. The 1536 legislation requiring certain religious persons to 'move, stir and provoke' people to provide alms proved a flop. It was only after this (and faced with civil disorder) that the Poor Law was introduced in its final form. Similarly, through the course of the 19th century, it seemed that despite this being the 'golden age of philanthropy', charity was wholly inadequate to meet the needs of the industrial age – and the foundations of the welfare state began to be set in place.

Finally, unless it is made a central function of the state, social security provision is likely to be deeply inefficient. A patchwork of provision across the country through charities and other bodies is likely to be poorly joined up and potentially difficult to access.

On the assumption that we accept the need for some kind of statutory safety net (as has been the case in England since Elizabethan times), some determination needs to be made about the level at which this safety net should be set. The Beveridge Report suggests that the system 'should aim at guaranteeing the minimum income needed for subsistence'.[1] In the report itself, Beveridge takes a kind of 'shopping basket' approach – asking how much would different household types require for a minimum subsistence in Britain at the time.

A similar approach could be taken for setting benefit entitlements now. For example, the Joseph Rowntree Foundation 'Minimum Income Standard' project takes a similar – although notably more generous – shopping basket approach; working out what level of income would be necessary to purchase the goods and services that people think necessary to achieve a socially acceptable standard of living.[2] Of course a 'socially acceptable' standard of living may be considerably more generous than a minimum income needed for subsistence, but the approach taken (of considering a basket of 'necessary' goods in order to establish a minimum income standard of one description or another) is the same.

One challenge to this fixed 'basket of goods' approach to understanding minimum living standards is that it relies on a complex, subjective account of household needs, which also requires frequent updating to reflect social change.

Another approach could be to set a minimum income level, not according to a required 'basket of goods', but relative to typical incomes in Britain. The 'relative' poverty line is set according to this approach – a household is considered to be living in 'relative' poverty if they have less than 60% of median household income (varied to take account of household composition).

This approach simplifies the shopping basket approach. Rather than saying that a minimum income is an amount needed in order to purchase a fixed set of goods, it may be assumed that living on an income somewhere close to the average (varied for household size) is enough for a minimum standard of living in line with normal social standards.

In reality, rates of benefit do not appear to be established according to either a basket of goods approach or relative to typical incomes. While in some cases initial benefit rates may be set with some underlying logic, this tends to be lost as benefit rates are changed over time. In fact, out-of-work benefit rates for working-age households are typically well below the relative poverty line – for example, a non-working couple without children can expect a minimum income that is around half the level of the poverty line for their household type.[3]

In practice, one key factor determining the level at which the safety net is set is the extent to which the claimant is seen as 'deserving' or 'undeserving' of support. A higher 'minimum' safety net may be set for those seen as deserving of support, while those who are seen as undeserving may be provided with a bare minimum (or nothing) for sustaining basic living needs. In Chapter 2 we noted how, during the course of the 16th century, provision was introduced for the 'deserving' poor, while those who were considered to be able to work were punished with physical violence. Similarly, the distinction made in the 19th century between those eligible for 'outdoor' relief, and those for whom support was only available on entering the workhouse, related to how deserving of support the claimant was seen as being.

There are a number of reasons why certain cases may be considered 'deserving' of a higher minimum standard of living than others. For example, those who make personal contributions (through National Insurance) may be considered deserving of a higher safety net to fall on when times are hard (because they have paid for it). As we will see in Chapter 14, however, this is by no means always the case, even to the point where people who have made such contributions may receive a lower level of support than those who have not.

Regardless of the approach taken to determining the nature of the 'minimum' safety net, consideration also needs to be given to how this minimum should vary to take account of differences in 'need' between households. Such variations may include (for example) the number of people in the household, whether anyone has a disability likely to incur additional costs of living and the level of housing costs faced.

Varying support on the basis of the number of people within the household don't necessarily mean that the same amount needs to be provided for each person – for example, a couple living together are likely to have a lower level of need than two people living separately, simply because they don't need to pay for and maintain two homes – efficiencies are likely to result in savings on a range of items including rent, fuel and food costs. The means-tested benefits system reflects this, with a lower level of support normally provided for a joint claim for benefit than for two individuals living separately.[4]

Variations on account of disability raise particular questions about how such disabilities are assessed – which experience has shown is not an easy matter. This issue is discussed in some detail in Chapter 15.

Rents vary a great deal on account of household size and (crucially) where in the country people live. As highlighted in the last chapter, even at the time of the Beveridge Report, levels of rents had a great deal of geographical variation.[5] In the present day, Housing Benefit responds to the problem of variation in rents differently for households in the social and private rental sectors, but in both cases it has some flexibility to provide for different levels of support to respond to geographical variations in rents – as described in detail in the following chapter.

Variations in need occur not only between households, but also change within an individual household over time. At the start of the 20th century, Seebohm Rowntree[6] illustrated how changing levels of need and income across a life course can result in a 'cycle of poverty'. He suggested that a typical labourer at that time faced three periods in their life when higher levels of household need or lower ability to generate income resulted in poverty. These were childhood, when they are unable to earn and the family income is stretched as a result of more people to support, in adulthood when they have to care for their own children, and in old age, when they are no longer able to work. In those periods when a household's income would be unacceptably low relative to need, minimum 'safety net' provision should ensure that the basic living standards are secured.

'Levelling the playing field' between households with different levels of need

So far, we have discussed the role of the benefits system in providing people with a 'safety net' to guarantee a minimum standard of living. However, there are also circumstances in which it might be considered desirable for benefits provision to go beyond a minimum. One reason for doing so is to 'level the playing field' between households with different levels of need – and in particular, additional needs that cannot be met through the labour market.

Household earnings reflect a number of things, including skills, hours worked, experience and consumer demand. Levels of household wealth are similarly determined by a number of factors, including levels of earnings, savings habits and inherited wealth. However, neither pay nor savings normally reflect the *financial need* of a household. Even in circumstances where earnings do reflect such variations (such as in the case of differences in pay reflecting living costs across different parts of the country), the differences are frequently inadequate. As a society we may believe that there are some kinds of need that should be reflected in provision – which skills and inheritance shouldn't be required to cover.

For example, disabled people frequently incur significant additional costs as a result of their condition. Leaving aside that some will be unable to move into work, in circumstances where they do so, they aren't likely to receive higher pay in order to reflect the additional costs they face as a result of their condition. So their additional level of need will not be provided for through the labour market.

The benefits system can, however, respond to this increased level of need by providing a correspondingly increased level of support. One approach that could be taken to this – the 'safety net' approach discussed above – would be to make some allowance for the additional costs faced as a result of a disability in calculating the level of income disabled people need in order to have a basic minimum standard of living. However, once a person's independent income exceeds this minimum level, the safety net is withdrawn, since the person is thought to have sufficient income in their own right to cover these additional costs.

An alternative approach might be favoured, which aims at levelling the playing field between disabled people and non-disabled people. This approach is similar to the provision of a 'safety net' in that the additional costs of disability are added to the minimum level of support that someone is thought to require. The difference is that the claimant retains that support *even after their independent income would be sufficient to cover those additional costs in full.*

The argument for such an approach may be that the costs of disability are incurred *regardless of income or wealth*, and as a result, the support provided should be paid on the same basis. As described above, such an approach is about levelling the playing field – disabled people should be entitled to the same standard of living as an equivalent person without a disability, and this applies regardless of how much money they have.

If two people each earn £100,000 per year, but one has a disability that incurs additional personal costs of £5,000 per year, then (while they are both likely to be well above a level of income needed for a 'minimum' standard of living) one is still significantly worse off than the other. A 'needs'-based approach to benefits provision would provide some correction or levelling of their positions (which a 'safety net' approach would not).

In fact, the current benefits system does exactly that. Disability Living Allowance and the Personal Independence Payment provide support for the additional costs of disability regardless of the level of the claimant's individual or household income. Another example of such an approach is Child Benefit, which until recently was paid to all families with children, regardless of income. In recent years full payment has been restricted to families with no one earning more than £50,000.

Benefits can be constructed in such a way as to provide a balance between safety net provision to support the least well off, and universal provision to 'level the playing field' between households with different levels of need. The new lower earnings threshold for Child Benefit (which remains well above the level needed for a minimum living standard for most families) could be seen as such an approach.

Similarly, Child Tax Credit as originally introduced was a particularly good example of what has been called 'progressive universalism' – the core idea, as the social policy analyst Donald Hirsch rather neatly puts it, being, 'something for everyone but more for the poor.'[7] While the bulk of provision through the Tax Credit system was paid to lower-income households, the £545 family element was paid in full to families with children with incomes up to £50,000 – a much higher threshold. What's more, for those with incomes above that level, entitlement reduced very slowly (by £6.67 for each extra £100 of earnings), meaning that families could receive some benefit until their earnings reached around £58,000 per year.[8]

In 2010 around 1.6 million families received only the family element, including nearly 150,000 claimant families with incomes over £50,000 per year.[9] Since 2011, this additional provision for higher-income families has gradually been removed.

Recent changes (as we shall see) have increasingly imposed sharp limitations on the ability of the benefits system to respond to variations in household need (particularly in terms of the ability to respond to variations in household size and in variations in rent by location). These limits are discussed in Chapter 8.

Promoting socially desirable behaviours

In addition to providing a minimum safety net, and responding to variations in household need, the benefits system can also be used as a means to promote behaviours seen as socially desirable (and to discourage undesirable behaviours). This is not a new approach; it was certainly not one that Beveridge himself was averse to. For example, he argued that the provision of support for children through family allowances could help to improve the birth rate in Britain since:

> ... with its present rate of reproduction, the British race cannot continue ... children's allowances can help to restore the birth rate, both by making it possible for parents who desire more children to bring them into the world without damaging the chances of those already born, and as a signal of the national interest in children, setting the tone of public opinion.[10]

Similarly, Beveridge's proposals were built on the importance of encouraging saving. Such saving was in part ensured through the introduction of compulsory insurance as a means of funding provision. However, Beveridge also wanted to encourage voluntary saving. For this reason, he proposed avoiding means testing of insured claimants; in this way, voluntary savings could also be encouraged (since savings that had been built up wouldn't affect the amount that a claimant could receive).

> This objection [public objection to means-testing] springs not so much from a desire to get everything for nothing, as from resentment at a provision which appears to penalise what people have come to regard as the duty and pleasure of thrift, of putting pennies away for a rainy day (emphasis added).[11]

In the present day, while many of the behaviours seen as socially desirable have changed, the idea of using the benefits system to promote certain outcomes has not.

Children

Attitudes that favoured using the benefits system to actively encourage parents to have more children have disappeared entirely since the 1940s. Where Beveridge wanted to make it possible for parents who wanted more children to do so, in 2015 the then Secretary of State for Work and Pensions, Iain Duncan Smith, announced that the introduction of a limit of two children on the child element of Child Tax Credit was about 'bringing home to parents the reality that children cost money'.[12]

In Chapter 8 we raise questions about the appropriateness of such an approach, not on the grounds that we need to actively encourage parents to have more children, but on the grounds that Child Tax Credit is paid as support for a child, not for their parents, so the use of withholding support in order to ensure that parents make the 'right decisions' seems inappropriate.

Work

Governments (both past and present) have been keen to use the benefits system to encourage people to work. Such an intention has always been relatively uncontroversial in its own right.

The benefits system can provide two kinds of so-called 'work incentive'. The first is to provide adequate support to encourage the move into work, and the second is to provide incentives to progress in employment (by working longer hours or getting a promotion).

Providing incentives to move *into* work means looking at the difference between income in work and income out of work for an equivalent family type. One challenge here is that out-of-work households are likely to receive significant support through the benefits system. If this support is removed in entirety on moving into work, it is likely that the claimant will be left much worse off in work than they were out of work.

Suppose Angela and Simon are a couple with two children, paying £118 per week for rent, and £20 per week for Council Tax.[13] In 2017/18 their out-of-work benefit entitlement (a combination of Jobseeker's Allowance [JSA], Child Tax Credit, Housing Benefit, Council Tax Reduction and Child Benefit) was £404 per week.

Angela finds a job, where she work 30 hours per week on the National Living Wage (of £7.50 per hour). In total she earns £225 per week before tax (and £216 per week after tax). If Angela and Simon lost all of their benefit entitlement on moving into work, their income in work would be little more than half what it was out of work.

This risk of working families being left worse off in work than out of work was a key reason for Beveridge's proposal that family allowances should be paid regardless of family income, saying 'it is dangerous to allow benefit during unemployment or disability to equal or exceed earnings during work. But without allowances for children during earning and not earning alike, this danger cannot be avoided'.[14]

An alternative is to make pound for pound deductions from entitlements on the basis of additional earnings, so on earning £216 per week, Angela and Simon have £216 deducted from their benefit entitlement. This means that their income remains at £404 per week, but is made up of £188 benefit entitlement and £216 earnings. This maintains the 'safety net' minimum income level that Angela and Simon receive, but doesn't provide them with any additional financial reward for Angela's 30 hours of work each week. If the system worked in this way, she would essentially be working for nothing.

Today, in reality, despite deductions from some of the household's benefits, overall income for Simon and Angela's family would be around £468 per week in work – making them about £64 per week better off in work than out of work. The mechanism by which the benefits system maintains some level of incentive for families in receipt of benefits to move into work is explained in the following chapters.

As a result of in-work support paid through the benefits system, there is normally some incentive for people to move into low-paying work, although these incentives can often be relatively small (in the example above, Angela is effectively being paid a little over £2.10 per hour for her work[15]). However, there is a second challenge to promoting work incentives through the benefits system – improving incentives to *progress* in work. This is not necessarily the same as incentives to move into work in the first place, and (as shown in later chapters) the incentives for working claimants to take on additional work – or to look for another job with higher pay – can be minimal, non-existent or even negative in some cases.

The government has recently sought to improve incentives to both move into and progress in work through the introduction of Universal Credit. However, as we will explore in Chapter

13, the introduction of the new benefit in the context of cuts to provision has deeply undermined its effectiveness in achieving this goal.

Saving

We may want to use the benefits system to promote incentives for people to save for the future, and to insure themselves to protect their standard of living. There are two ways of encouraging this – one is through compulsory insurance and savings, and the other is through voluntary approaches.

The current tax and benefits system attempts to do both. National Insurance Contributions provide a compulsory insurance scheme, which can be accessed in times of unemployment (through contribution-based JSA), sickness (through contribution-based Employment and Support Allowance [ESA]) and old age (through the State Pension). However, as we will see in Chapter 14, this system is deeply flawed – in many cases, contribution-based benefits may not only be worthless, but they can even cost claimants money.

The benefits system also encourages small amounts of voluntary savings through ignoring them for the purposes of means testing (although larger savings lead to significant reductions in means-tested benefit entitlements). Wanting to further encourage benefit claimants to save, the government recently announced the introduction of a 'Help to Save' scheme to provide an additional payment to some low-income households who choose to save from their benefits over a period of two years.

'Couple formation'

Another, and more controversial, area that policy-makers may seek to encourage (or at least to avoid penalising) through the benefits system is 'couple formation'. As discussed in Chapter 9, the government has explicitly warned of the risks of the benefits system penalising partners who want to live together as a single family, stating that new policies in development should be 'tested' against such risks.

Unfortunately, at the same time, strict limits on benefit receipt (including the 'benefit cap' and the 'two-child limit' for Child Tax Credit) have actively introduced large couple penalties into the benefits system, to the point where a coalition of religious leaders called the two-child limit 'fundamentally anti-family'.

We will discuss why this problem exists later, but for now, it is worth noting that this shows how different objectives within the benefits system (in this case, wanting to reduce its flexibility to respond to different levels of household need) can conflict with other policy intentions (in this case, it conflicts with wanting to avoid the benefits system penalising couple formation).

Conclusion

The benefits system serves three key ends. It provides a basic safety net, it corrects for variations in household needs (and particularly those that cannot be addressed through the labour market), and it is used to reward behaviours seen as socially desirable.

The priority given to these different ends will likely depend on policy-makers at a particular time. Some governments are likely to see the benefits system as principally providing a safety net to protect those in dire need, and not see it as the state's role to intervene to address inequalities of need above a 'minimum' level. Others may see a more significant role for the state in intervening in labour markets to promote equality of outcomes between groups.

All governments are likely to use the benefits system as a lever to promote socially desirable behaviours – although the things they seek to encourage will vary.

In some cases policy-makers can face tensions between different objectives – for example, a government may see the benefits system as principally providing a minimum safety net for those with no independent income to rely on (and nothing more), but also want to promote work incentives. As we have seen (and Beveridge understood), these two objectives can severely conflict, leaving low-income workers effectively working for nothing, or in the worst cases, even paying to work. Similarly, we have noted how government policies that seek to reduce variation in the amount of benefit paid according to household need can conflict with ensuring that the benefits system doesn't penalise couple formation.

In Chapter 2 we considered the historical roots of the benefits system; in this chapter we have considered why we might want a benefits system at all. We haven't yet looked in detail at how the benefits system actually operates today, which is the subject of the next part of *Broken Benefits*.

Part II
Mapping it all out – The mechanics of the benefits system

The following three chapters give an overview of how the benefits system hangs together (or tries to). This is not intended to tell you everything you could possibly need to know about the system, and there will always be inconsistencies, special rules and exemptions. I am also conscious that for simplicity, some very important benefits (including certain forms of employment-linked support, such as statutory maternity pay and statutory sick pay) are not discussed. Also excluded are the often very complex entitlements for those not able to receive all mainstream benefits as a result of their immigration status, or because they are not permanently resident in the UK. The recent decision to leave the European Union (EU) may well have further implications on entitlements for EU migrants – which are not fully known at the time of writing in 2017.

However, the chapters should provide an idea of some of the core mechanics through which the benefits system works – including the way in which different benefits combine to give an overall maximum entitlement, and how earnings, savings and other income reduce this.

Broken Benefits addresses the benefits system that exists in practice across the UK. It should be noted that Northern Ireland has its own benefits legislation[1], but in reality this largely mirrors the UK system. Some differences have been introduced recently (such as provisions to protect some groups affected by the benefit cap – mentioned later in this Chapter), so whilst the content of *Broken Benefits* largely applies to Northern Ireland as much as the rest of the UK, it should be read with a little caution. Whilst Scotland does not have fully devolved responsibility over welfare provision, it has started to have some devolved powers (for example over Discretionary Housing Payments – mentioned in Chapter 18). At the point of writing in 2017, further changes (such as the replacement of the Sure Start Maternity Grant with the 'Better Start Grant' mentioned in Chapter 9, and reform of the Personal Independence Payment), are expected to be introduced in Scotland in the near future.

Chapter 4 starts out with the simpler kinds of case – households that aren't working, don't have any other independent income or savings to live off, and that aren't entitled to receive any contribution-based benefits. It builds up a picture of the different kinds of support such claimants may receive – including help for their own needs, and those of a partner if they have one, help with the additional costs of children or a disability, and help with housing costs.

Chapter 5 then looks at the impact of a claimant (or their partner, if they have one) being entitled to 'contribution-based benefits' – paid on account of having made sufficient National Insurance Contributions. It shows how the contribution-based benefits system is 'layered' over equivalent entitlements in the income-based system – resulting in many households receiving both contribution-based and income-based benefits simultaneously.

Chapter 6 considers how benefit entitlements are affected by a claimant, or their partner, moving into work and earning money independently. It shows how certain benefits are only paid to households not in full-time work (so-called 'out-of-work benefits') and others are only paid to households *in work* – while still others may be paid to those both in and out of work. It explores how benefits are 'means tested', and how this means that a benefit claimant's *maximum* entitlement is not necessarily the same as their *actual* entitlement, since deductions are made from the maximum on account of other income. It also shows how, in addition to means-tested and contribution-based benefits, some people may be entitled to receive so-called 'universal benefits' that are not normally affected by income or savings.

Throughout the three chapters, all benefit values are given at their 2017-18 rates, as these were current at the time of writing. However, the exact rates don't really matter – they are given to exemplify the underlying structure of the system. If the structure of provision is changing significantly between 2010 and 2020, this is indicated.

It is also worth noting from the start that two different structures of provision are presented – what we will call the 'old system' and Universal Credit (the new system that replaces a number of key benefits, and has very gradually been introduced since 2012). We will see how the introduction of the new system significantly changes how benefits are means tested, and reduces (although does not abolish) the distinction between in-work and out-of-work benefits.

These chapters form the most technical part of this book. Rather than read them through, some readers may prefer to skip to the next part and refer back to this as necessary.

4

Benefit entitlements for people with no other income or savings

As discussed in previous chapters, one of the principal objectives of the benefits system is to provide a safety net against destitution – providing support in circumstances where claimants have no other income or savings to fall back on.

This chapter looks at the social security safety net for those in exactly this kind of situation. In this chapter we will also assume that households haven't made any National Insurance Contributions that might entitle them to receive contribution-based benefits (although we will address the difference this makes in the following chapter).

We look at this in five key parts – support for a claimant's own needs, extra help if they have a partner, support for their children, help with housing costs, and extra help if they have a disability, or are caring for someone.

The chapter also considers the impact of the introduction of Universal Credit for this group. Notably, with some very important exceptions, the new system doesn't typically make an enormous amount of difference to entitlements for claimants with no other income or savings, but in the following chapters, where earnings and other income are considered, the difference becomes much more profound.

Support for personal living costs: the 'personal allowance'

If the benefits system was a create-your-own pizza, the personal allowance would be the base. It is the money a claimant gets for their own basic needs – intended to cover their day-to-day living costs (leaving aside housing costs, which we will come to shortly). This personal allowance can be paid as part of a number of different benefits.

The personal allowance for a single claimant depends on their age. If they are 25 or over, it would be £73 per week. Under-25s normally get a lower rate of £58 per week, although exceptions apply. The personal allowance for those over pension age is £159 per week.

A claimant might get a personal allowance as part of the following benefits: Jobseeker's Allowance, Income Support, Income-based Employment and Support Allowance, and Pension Credit.

Income-based Jobseeker's Allowance

Jobseeker's Allowance (JSA) can be paid to those available for and actively seeking work. As we will see in later chapters, the requirements placed on people claiming this benefit can be strict, with sanctions applied on those who fail to meet these conditions.

If a single claimant is 25 or over, their personal allowance would be £73. Under-25s normally get £58 per week (unless they are a lone parent or have a disability, and are aged between 18 and 24, in which case they receive the higher rate).

As we will see in the following chapter, there are two 'forms' of JSA – income-based (also known as 'income-related' or 'means-tested') and contribution-based. The differences between the two types of payment are explored further in Chapter 5; this chapter assumes claimants are not entitled to any contribution-based benefits.

Income Support

Some groups of people can claim Income Support instead of JSA. This includes people who are providing care for someone with a disability, and single parents with very young children. People in receipt of Income Support do not have to be available for and actively looking for work (although they may often have some work-related requirements, such as attending interviews with an adviser to discuss their plans around moving into work, and the support they might need in order to do so).

Rates of support (including personal allowances) are the same as for JSA; principally it is the work requirements that are different.

Income-based Employment and Support Allowance

If someone is unable to work as a result of illness or disability, they may be entitled to receive Employment and Support Allowance (ESA). ESA has two 'phases' – the assessment phase, while the claimant's illness is assessed, and the 'main phase', after the assessment has been completed.

As with Income Support, the personal allowance for ESA is broadly the same as for JSA (although claimants under 25 who have been assessed as having 'limited capability for work' can receive the higher £73 rate). However, ESA claimants may receive additional components on top of their personal allowance, which we will come to in a moment.

As with JSA, ESA can be paid in both a 'means-tested' and 'contribution-based' form. As noted above, for this chapter, we assume no contribution-based benefits are payable.

Pension Credit

Some older claimants are entitled to receive Pension Credit instead of JSA or ESA. The allowance for the claimant's own needs in Pension Credit (called the 'minimum guarantee') is £159.[1] Receipt of Pension Credit doesn't come with any requirements to seek work.

Since 2010, the age at which someone would be entitled to claim Pension Credit has been rising in line with increases in the State Pension age for women, so that in 2018 claimants will need to be 65 before they can make a claim, and by 2020 they will need to be 66.

For example, Emma is a 23-year-old with no illness or disability. She receives JSA, with a personal allowance of £58. When Emma reaches 25 her personal allowance increases to £73.

Emma has a baby and is a single parent. Her personal allowance doesn't change (she continues to receive £73), but for a while she receives Income Support instead of JSA, and doesn't have to actively seek work. When her child reaches the age of five she moves back on to JSA but her personal allowance doesn't change.

James is a single man aged 63. He has a heart condition that means he is not able to work at this point. He receives ESA with a personal allowance of £73. When he turns 66, James moves on to Pension Credit and receives a 'minimum guarantee' of £159.

Extra help if you have a partner

If a claimant has a partner with whom they are cohabiting, and neither have other income or savings (and assuming, as above, they aren't entitled to contribution-based benefits), they should make a claim for support as a couple.[2]

For income-based JSA, income-based ESA and Income Support, as long as both claimants are over 18 (the amounts can be different if one or both are under this age), their joint personal allowance is paid at the 'couple' rate of £115 per week. This amount is less than the sum of their personal allowances as single claimants, since it is assumed that a couple need less money together than two single claimants living separately would.

For example, Roopa, aged 23, moves in with her partner Jack, aged 26. Individually Roopa has a personal allowance of £58 and Jack £73 (a higher rate since he is over 25). When they move in together they have a joint personal allowance of £115 (since they are both over 18).

Had Roopa lived on her own, her personal allowance would have increased to £73 at 25, but since she lives with her partner, their allowance doesn't change.

It is worth noting that only one partner in a couple needs to meet the rules around having limited capability to work as a result of sickness or disability to make a claim as a couple for ESA.

For Pension Credit, the personal allowance for a couple is £243. Importantly, only one of the couple needs to be above pension age to make a joint claim for Pension Credit.

> For example, Ian, aged 67, and his partner Ruth, aged 60, could put in a joint claim for Pension Credit and receive £243. Separately Ian would receive £159 Pension Credit, and Ruth £73 in JSA (or equivalent).

Notably, this is an unusual circumstance under which their joint income as a couple is *higher* than their individual incomes as two single claimants.

The rules around whether someone has a partner for their benefit claim can be quite complicated and revolve around the couple living together 'as a married couple'. A decision about this can look at things like how frequently they are staying overnight in the same house, whether they are in a sexual relationship, and whether they share bills and financial commitments.

Most claimants are likely to receive significantly more where two partners live separately (for example, two JSA claimants over 25 who are living separately are entitled to a total of £146; if they are living together, this is £115). The difference between support when living together and separately can be considerably greater where one partner is in work.

As a result, claiming the wrong type of support (for example, claiming as a single person, when the rules say a claim should have been made as a couple) can often be a cause of benefit problems, including benefits being overpaid.

Support for children

In addition to a personal allowance, the benefits system provides for additional support for children in the household who are cared for by the claimant. The key forms of support include Child Benefit and Child Tax Credit. As above, we continue to focus in this section on the level of support provided for a household with no other income or savings.

Child Benefit and Child Tax Credit

The claimant receives Child Benefit for the oldest child in the household at a rate of £21 per week, and £14 for each additional child. Only one person responsible for a child can make a claim for Child Benefit (so that this does not get paid more than once on account of the same child), and it is normally paid to the mother.

In addition to Child Benefit, someone responsible for a child may receive Child Tax Credit to provide further support for the child's needs.[3]

Tax Credits (Child Tax Credit and Working Tax Credit) are paid together as a single entitlement. Child Tax Credit is paid to support those with children (whether or not they are working), while Working Tax Credit is paid to support those in work (whether or not they have children). The provision of Working Tax Credit is discussed in Chapter 6, alongside other benefits for working claimants.

One Tax Credit award is made per family (made up of a claimant, or claimant couple, and any children for whom they are responsible; as with Child Benefit, Child Tax Credit may only be paid to one family on account of an individual child).[4] Unlike other benefits, a Tax Credit award is calculated on an annual basis, but payments are made more frequently (normally either weekly or four-weekly).

A Child Tax Credit award may be made up of a number of different 'elements' – a family element (paid once, at a rate of £545 per year, for each family receiving Child Tax Credit); a child element paid for each child in the family (worth £2,780 per year per child); and two disability elements. The family element is being phased out and the child element is gradually being limited to two children. This is explored further in Chapters 8 and 9.

Extra help is provided for disabled children through a disability element (and severe disability element). This is further discussed later, alongside other forms of support for people affected by ill health or disability.

One claim for Tax Credits is made per household, so a couple with children would put in a joint claim.

For example, Alison (35) and John (38) are a couple with two children. They claim JSA as a couple and receive £115. They also receive £34[5] in Child Benefit (for the two children) and Child Tax Credit of £117 per week (based on an annual entitlement of £6,105, from a family element plus two child elements).

This gives Alison and John's family an overall entitlement of £266 per week for their own needs and those of their children.

Both Child Benefit and Child Tax Credit can only be paid once per child. Normally it is pretty clear which household the child lives in, but where this isn't clear (for example, in cases of shared parenting), a decision needs to be made about which family should receive the money.

Help with housing costs

Housing Benefit

If the claimant rents their home they may be entitled to receive Housing Benefit to help with the costs of housing. The amount of support received is determined by a number of different factors; the calculation works very differently depending on whether they are renting in the private or social rented sector.

Local Housing Allowance

Local Housing Allowance (LHA) (introduced in 2008) determines the maximum amount of Housing Benefit paid to people renting from a private landlord. How much a claimant can get is determined by a number of different factors: their 'eligible' household size, where they live and their rent.

Their 'eligible' household size

Different household sizes need different sizes of accommodation to meet their needs. So (for example) a family with three children needs to rent a larger home than a single person living alone. The rules are that a claimant is allowed one bedroom for themselves (and for their partner if they have one), then extra bedrooms for children in the household on the basis that:

- two children under the age of 10 can share *and;*
- two children aged 10-15 years old can share if they are of the same gender.

This applies unless there are particular reasons why they can't share (for example, a severe disability). In addition, LHA is now limited to provide support for a maximum of four bedrooms. So, for example, a couple with two children (a girl aged 12, a boy aged 13), are eligible to a home with three bedrooms:

- one for the couple;
- one for the girl aged 12;
- one for the boy aged 13 (although if the 12-year-old girl and the 13-year-old boy had both been of the same sex they would have been expected to share).

There is an important difference to the normal calculation for single non-disabled people under the age of 35 who have no children – normally in these cases the so-called 'Shared Accommodation Rate' applies. This limits support to the cost of a room in shared accommodation (as opposed to a one-bedroom flat of their own). Until 2012, the Shared Accommodation Rate only applied to those up to the age of 25; new rules have extended this to 35.

Where they live

Help with housing costs is unusual within the benefits system in that the amount someone can get is directly affected by where they live in the country. This is because rents vary so much across the nation.

The UK is split into a wide range of Broad Rental Market Areas (BRMAs). A BRMA is an area 'where a person could reasonably be expected to live taking into account access to facilities and services.'[6] The idea is that by setting a single set of rates for each area of the country, people will look for a place with a reasonable rent within that area, but will not be forced to look further afield (where they might be able to find a cheaper rent) if this would make it impossible for them to access local jobs, health facilities, schools and so on.

In 2010, the maximum rate of LHA (for a given household size) was set at the median rent for the local area, meaning that if there were 100 two-bedroom private rental properties in the area, the maximum amount of support that someone entitled to rent a two-bedroom property could receive would be set at the cost of the 50th home. The intention was that Housing Benefit claimants renting in the private rental sector would be able to afford a 'normal' property for the local area.

Since 2010 a number of changes have been made which mean that this is no longer the case. These include:

- reducing the maximum LHA rate from the 50th percentile of local rents to the 30th percentile, meaning that a claimant would not be able to receive support to cover the rent of any of 50 out of 100 properties in the local area; instead, they would only be able to rent one of the cheapest 30;
- capping the maximum amounts that the LHA rates (for each size of home up to four bedrooms) could be, regardless of actual local rents.

The government also decided to make a number of changes to the way in which LHA rates rise over time as rents go up (including freezing LHA rates altogether in most parts of the country for several years). This issue is discussed in more detail in Chapter 7.

These rules set the maximum LHA rate for a given household size, and in a particular BRMA. Tables of maximum LHA rates for across the UK are regularly produced and updated.[7]

Their rent

In 2010, if a claimant's rent was lower than their maximum LHA rate, they could keep some of the difference (intended to encourage people to go for the best rental price, rather than whichever one was closest to the rent they were eligible for).

This has since changed, so that a claimant cannot now get more LHA than they actually pay in rent. So if someone's actual rent is £500 per month and their LHA rate is £550 per month, they will still receive no more than £500.

However, if they moved to a new place with a rent of £550 per month, they would still be eligible to get their rent covered in full – whereas if they moved from somewhere with a rent of £550 to somewhere with a rent of £600, they would not.

Eligible rent

For those receiving LHA, these three factors in combination – their household size, where they live and their actual rent – create what is known as their 'eligible rent'. Leaving aside issues of service charges and similar, this is basically the maximum amount of Housing Benefit they are actually eligible to receive; the amount they are likely to be entitled to if they have no earnings or other relevant income.

For example, Toni is a single parent aged 35, with two children (aged 7 and 9). She lives in a privately rented property for which she pays £170 per week. She is entitled to a two-bedroom property (one bedroom for her and one for her two children), and her maximum LHA rate is £150 per week.

In total, Toni receives JSA of £73 per week, Child Benefit of £34 and Child Tax Credit of £117 per week (based on an annual entitlement of £6,105, from a family element plus two child elements).

In addition, Toni receives £150 per week in Housing Benefit, which is not sufficient to cover her housing costs in full since her maximum LHA rate is £20 per week lower than her actual rental costs. She needs to find the additional £20 from other sources of income.

This gives Toni an overall entitlement of £374 per week, for her own needs, those of her children, and to pay for her housing costs.

Housing Benefit for households in the social rented sector

In 2010, working out eligible rent in the social rented sector was a little bit simpler than in the private rental sector.

Prior to the application of the 'Bedroom Tax' and other recent changes, the rent people actually paid for social housing would normally be equivalent to their 'eligible rent' (excluding any service charges). So they would not normally experience the kind of rent shortfall experienced by Toni (above).

The introduction of the Bedroom Tax in 2013 had a significant impact on support for many tenants in the social rented sector. The change (also known as the removal of the 'spare room subsidy' or as the 'under-occupancy charge' – with the term used very much dependant on one's attitude to the reform!) reduces a claimant's eligible rent by 14% if they are found to be 'under-occupying' their property by one bedroom, and 25% for two or more bedrooms.

The calculation for whether (and by how much) a claimant is under-occupying their property is largely[8] the same as for eligible household size in the private rented sector, which is explained above.

In addition, the government more recently decided to limit the Housing Benefit payable to tenants in the social rented sector to the relevant LHA rate for their area. While in most cases social rents are significantly lower than LHA rates (meaning tenants wouldn't be affected), this is not universally the case. Some groups, including young people who would have their LHA provision limited by the Shared Accommodation Rate, are particularly likely to be affected when this measure is introduced.

Support for Mortgage Interest

The benefits system will not pay off a mortgage, but in some circumstances it will provide support with mortgage interest payments so that homeowners can avoid eviction if they are struggling with their housing costs. Somewhat unimaginatively, this additional support is known as Support for Mortgage Interest or SMI.

SMI has a number of notable differences from Housing Benefit. Crucially, you can only get SMI if you receive an out-of-work benefit (such as income-based JSA, income-based ESA, Income Support or Pension Credit)[9] since it is paid as a supplement to these benefits (so, rather than getting JSA and Housing Benefit separately, the claimant just gets JSA with their SMI included within it). SMI is only usually paid after a waiting period of receiving a qualifying benefit – this is usually 39 weeks, although pensioners can get help immediately.

Interest on an eligible loan is calculated on the basis of a standard rate of interest (rather than on the basis of the actual interest paid). This can mean that SMI will not cover the full interest charges on an eligible loan.

Unlike Housing Benefit, in many cases SMI is time limited (normally you can only receive it for a period of two years if you are a JSA claimant, although there is no time limit for ESA, Income Support or Pension Credit claimants).

The government decided to change SMI payments from 2018, so that, where previously any money paid out did not need to be paid back if the claimant's circumstances changed, it is now provided as a loan to be repaid when the claimant sells their house.

For example, Janet and Joe are a couple with one child. They claim JSA as a couple with a personal allowance of £115.

They also have SMI included in their JSA claim. They have an outstanding loan of £100,000 on their property and the standard interest rate is 2.5%. This means they receive SMI in their JSA at a rate of £48 per week.

This gives them an overall JSA entitlement of £162 per week. In addition, they receive £21 Child Benefit, and Child Tax Credit of £64. Their overall entitlement is £247.

Council Tax Benefit

In 2010, those on a low income could receive help with any Council Tax they were liable for through Council Tax Benefit. For households with no other income or savings, Council Tax Benefit covered the full amount of their Council Tax.

From 2013 the national Council Tax Benefit scheme was 'localised', so that each council had to introduce its own Council Tax Reduction scheme. A reduction in funding available for these schemes means that they are now often (although not universally) less generous than Council Tax Benefit. In many cases this means that claimants with no income other than out-of-work benefits no longer receive support to cover their Council Tax bill in full. The impact of this is discussed later, in Chapter 18.

Extra help if you are off work due to illness, or have a disability

Additional assistance may also be provided to claimants who are affected by ill health or disability.

Employment and Support Allowance components

ESA is a benefit for people of working age who have limited capability for work as a result of illness or disability. It began to be introduced in 2008, replacing previous forms of support. For simplicity we will not discuss the predecessor system.

There are three main groups of ESA claimant. First, there are those who are awaiting an assessment of their condition (where the decision might be made that they are fit for work after all and would not be given ESA).

The second group is those who have been assessed and for whom it has been decided that they have 'limited capability for work', but who may still be required to do training or other work preparation activities. This group is sometimes known as the work-related activity group, or WRAG.

The third group is the 'support' group. This group has been assessed as having 'limited capability for work and work-related activities'; in other words, not only are they too ill to work, they are also too ill to be expected to do training and other work preparation activities.

The personal allowance for people in receipt of ESA is normally the same as for those receiving JSA or Income Support, although (as described above), if they have been assessed as being unfit for work, they are exempt from the lower young person's rate of personal allowance if they are single and under 25.

However, when the system was first introduced, in addition to the personal allowance, claimants who had been found to have either limited capability for work or limited capability for work and work-related activity could receive an additional amount in their ESA claim. Those in the work-related activity group received the work-related activity component worth £29, and those in the support group received a support component worth £37.

The government later decided to get rid of the work-related activity component for ESA for new claimants from 2017. This doesn't affect claimants in the support group. However, this reduces ESA entitlement by £29 per week for those in the work-related activity group. The impact of this is discussed further in Chapter 10.

Disability Premiums

In addition to these ESA components, claimants can also receive two additional disability 'components' as part of their ESA entitlement. (These can also be paid in addition to other benefits for those who are eligible for them but not claiming ESA.)

The *Severe Disability Premium* is paid to severely disabled adults (qualifying for higher levels of support with care needs through Disability Living Allowance [DLA], Personal Independence Payment [PIP], or Attendance Allowance – each of which is introduced below) who do not have a non-disabled person to provide care for them. This means that they live on their own, with another disabled adult or only with dependent children. The Severe Disability Premium is worth £62 per week.

The *Enhanced Disability Premium* is paid as an addition for ESA claimants in the support group for ESA, and those receiving the high rate care component of DLA, or the enhanced rate of the daily living component of the PIP. It is worth an extra £16.

> For example, Tom is 22 and has applied for ESA as a result of a serious illness. During the assessment phase he receives ESA of £58 (the young person's rate of personal allowance).

> Following the assessment, Tom has been found to be unfit for work-related activity and is placed in the support group. Since he is no longer in the assessment phase, his personal allowance increases from £58 to £73, and he also receives the support component of ESA, worth an additional £37, and an Enhanced Disability Premium of £16.

> Tom also receives the mid-rate care component of DLA (see below). Since he lives alone and doesn't have a carer looking after him, this means that he is entitled to receive a Severe Disability Premium worth £62 per week.

> This gives him an overall ESA entitlement of £188 per week.

Disability Living Allowance, the Personal Independence Payment and Attendance Allowance

Some people with an illness or disability may also claim DLA (either for disabled adults – those over the age of 16 – or for disabled children). DLA is intended to cover the costs associated with care and mobility needs as a result of a disability, so it is paid in addition to other benefits (like ESA, JSA or Income Support) that are paid to cover general living expenses.

DLA is intended to cover the *additional* costs of disability – it is about levelling the playing field for disabled people, enabling them not to have to eat into other income or savings in order to cover costs of living that an able-bodied claimant would not need to. For this reason, DLA is non-means-tested – the amount of the claimant's other income or savings does not make a difference to the amount of DLA that is paid.

DLA is paid in two parts: the mobility component and the care component.

The mobility component is paid to those who have difficulties when walking, and is provided at two different rates. The higher rate (worth £58 per week) is paid to those who are 'unable or virtually unable' to walk. The 'lower' mobility component (worth £22 per week) is paid to those who can walk, but who require guidance or supervision most of the time out of doors as a result of a physical or mental disability.

The care component of DLA is paid to people with attention or supervision needs as a result of their disability. It is paid at three rates: low, middle and high (varying greatly in value – from £22 to £83 per week at the time of writing in 2017).

Claimants who receive DLA may receive both a care and a mobility component.[10]

For example, John has Down's syndrome. He has great difficulty caring for himself during the day, and needs regular supervision, but he sleeps well at night. He can walk, but he needs help to get around outside of his home most of the time since his disability means he gets lost easily – particularly when he is trying to go to places he doesn't know well.

Since he sleeps well at night, but needs regular attention during the day, John receives the mid-rate care component of DLA. Since he can walk, but needs support and guidance outside his home most of the time, John also receives the low rate mobility component.

The Personal Independence Payment (PIP) has gradually replaced DLA for adults. PIP renames the care component of DLA the 'daily living component', though the name of the mobility component remains the same. More importantly, PIP changes the different levels of payment (effectively removing the low rate care component) as well as the approach to assessing entitlement. The impact of this is discussed in more detail in Chapter 15.

DLA for children and Attendance Allowance (the equivalent of DLA for those aged over 65) have not been replaced by PIP. In 2015 the possibility was raised that Attendance Allowance might be 'localised', with local authorities given responsibility for managing equivalent provision.[11] However, at the start of

2017, the government confirmed that they were no longer looking at this.[12]

DLA for children is only provided for children up to the age of 15; from 16 they transfer on to DLA/PIP for adults. Both DLA for children and Attendance Allowance have some significant differences from DLA/PIP for adults, but for simplicity we won't go into these further here.

Disabled child and severely disabled child elements of Child Tax Credit

In addition to DLA, families with disabled children can also receive some additional means-tested support for them through the Tax Credits system. These include the disabled child element and the severely disabled child element.[13]

The disabled child element of Child Tax Credit is worth £3,175 per year for those with no other income or savings, and the additional severely disabled child component is worth £1,290 (as mentioned previously, Tax Credit awards are paid based on an annual entitlement).

> For example, Alison is a single parent who cares for Imogen, her 12-year-old disabled child. They rent a two-bedroom flat in the private rented sector costing £120 per week, and pay Council Tax of £15 per week. Alison receives the low rate care component of DLA for Imogen.
>
> Alison receives £73 in JSA for her own needs.
>
> Alison's relevant LHA rate is £110 per week – so she receives £110 per week in Housing Benefit (£10 per week less than her rent). She also receives £15 per week support with Council Tax.
>
> Alison receives £21 in Child Benefit for Imogen. She also receives £22 per week in DLA for children (the value of the low rate care component).

Alison also receives a total of £125 per week in Child Tax Credit (based on an annual entitlement to a £545 family element, £2,780 child element and a £3,175 disabled child element).

This gives the family an overall benefit entitlement of £366 per week.

Support for carers

Additional support is provided through the benefits system for those providing care for someone who they look after. This is principally provided through (non-means-tested) Carer's Allowance, and through the Carer Premium (an additional component on means-tested benefits).

People can normally receive Carer's Allowance/the Carer Premium if they are providing 'regular and substantial care' (35 hours per week or more) for a 'severely disabled person' (defined as someone in receipt of the middle or higher rate of the care component of DLA or the daily living component of PIP), and are 16 or over and not in full-time education, or earning more than £116 per week.

Carers may receive *both* Carer's Allowance and the Carer Premium. However, the relevant amount for a person with no other income or savings (and not in receipt of contribution-based Benefits) is normally the value of the Carer Premium *not* the Carer's Allowance. This is because the Carer's Allowance is deducted pound for pound from other out-of-work benefits that the claimant receives.

For example, Lily (aged 35) lives alone and is not currently working. She receives JSA at a rate of £73 per week (in addition to Housing Benefit and Council Tax Reduction).

Lily starts caring for her disabled mother for 40 hours per week. This brings her into entitlement to Carer's Allowance. As a result of her care responsibilities (as explained towards the start of this chapter), she also moves from JSA to Income Support with a Carer's Premium.

Lily's maximum Income Support is now worth £108 (£73, plus a £35 Carer's Premium).

However, Lily's Carer's Allowance is deducted in full from her Income Support – giving her an actual income of £63 Carer's Allowance, plus £45 Income Support. This makes her overall income the same as her maximum Income Support entitlement. Her Housing Benefit and Council Tax Reduction continue to be paid in full.

The simultaneous payment of Carer's Allowance and a Carer's Premium (and then the deduction of the first from other entitlements) can seem convoluted. Broadly, Carer's Allowance exists to support those outside of the income-based benefits system who would not be entitled to receive the Carer's Premium, but for simplicity, we will not explore this further. More generally (as discussed in more detail in the following chapter), the 'layering' of one benefit over another in this way is not unusual, particularly (as we will see) as regards the layering of contribution-based benefits over income-based entitlements.

Universal Credit

A number of the key income-based benefits described above are being replaced by the introduction of Universal Credit.

The new system brings together entitlements to Income Support, income-based ESA, income-based JSA, Housing Benefit and Tax Credits. Instead of receiving these entitlements separately, in future, claimants receive them paid together as one lump sum (normally paid monthly, which will be a significant change for many claimants).

Contribution-based JSA, contribution-based ESA, Child Benefit, DLA and the PIP, and Council Tax Reduction (as well as a number of other benefits) are not incorporated into Universal Credit. Pension Credit will also not be merged with the new benefit, and (as discussed shortly) Universal Credit is not intended to be claimed by those over Pension Credit age.

Some of the terms used are different (for example, 'personal allowance' becomes 'standard allowance' and 'Housing Benefit' becomes the housing costs element of Universal Credit). However, in most cases, the level of support provided through Universal Credit (for those who have no other income or savings and without entitlement to contribution-based benefits) replicates support provided through the pre-existing benefits system (the cuts outlined are typically passed across as well). However, there are some extremely important exceptions.

The equivalent support to the disability element of Child Tax Credit is reduced to half its value under Universal Credit

This will cost of more than £30 per week for each disabled child. Disabled children will not be affected by this measure if they receive the high rate care component of DLA, or if they are registered blind.

Some claimants under 25 will receive lower rates of personal allowance

As mentioned above, rates of 'personal allowance' for Income Support or JSA may depend on the claimant's age. For example, the personal allowance for Income Support for a single person without children is currently £73 if they are 25 or over, but £58 if they are under 25. However, there is an exemption from this single young person's rate of personal allowance for those with a child, or those claiming ESA as a result of limited capability for work – meaning that a single parent, or single ESA claimant, aged from 18 to 24 receives the over-25s rate of personal allowance rate rather than the young person's rate.

However, under Universal Credit these exemptions will no longer exist. Instead, they will receive the same rate of allowance as an under 25-year-old without any children or limited capability for work. This means that out-of-work single parents, and young adults with limited capability for work, aged from 18 to 24, will receive £15 per week less than they would under the old system (a loss of £780 per year in total).

The Severe Disability Premium (worth £62) and the Enhanced Disability Premium (worth £16) are scrapped altogether

This leaves those who would be entitled to the Severe Disability Premium much worse off. However, the equivalent to the support component of ESA (pithily called the 'limited capability for work and work-related activity component') is increased in value (by around £37 per week, to be worth around £73, at the time of writing in 2017).

Notably, while the overall value of Universal Credit for a claimant in the equivalent to the support group is typically higher than ESA with the Enhanced Disability Premium, it is significantly lower if the claimant receives both the Severe Disability Premium and the Enhanced Disability Premium (typical of severely disabled people living alone and without a carer). The impact of the loss of the Severe Disability Premium under Universal Credit is discussed in more detail in Chapter 10.

Despite these important differences, the really big changes with Universal Credit are to do with how it interacts with work and earnings, which is discussed later, in Chapter 6.

Transitional protection

It is important to note that in developing Universal Credit, the government provided assurances that there would be no 'cash losers' in the transition across from the old to the new system. The inclusion of 'transitional protection' for claimants moving across to Universal Credit means that, for those who would otherwise lose out, Universal Credit payments will receive a cash 'top up' to the level of support they received prior to the move. While an important measure, this transitional protection has three key limitations:

- Only current benefit claimants will be protected. New claimants will receive no protection and could lose out substantially.
- The level of protection will not be uprated with inflation, meaning that the protection is eroded over time (effectively this means claimants have a permanent 'freeze' on their

Universal Credit entitlement until the amount of support they would have received without this protection catches up).

- Finally, where claimants' circumstances change, the transitional protection can be lost – such changes may include (for example) stopping work, or a partner joining or leaving the household. Such changes in circumstances leading to the loss of transitional protection can apply at the point of transition (so, for example, if a claimant moves across to Universal Credit as a result of needing to make a fresh claim for benefit on losing their job, they would receive no transitional protection, even if this leaves them significantly worse off as a result).

Universal Credit and older people

Not only is Pension Credit not to be merged with Universal Credit, but older people are intended to be kept out of the system altogether – with one of the basic qualifying conditions for Universal Credit being that the claimant 'has not reached the qualifying age for State Pension credit'.[14] In order to do this, the government has said that they will recreate the additions for children and housing costs as additional components of claimants' Pension Credit entitlement.[15]

However, there is one important caveat. At present (as discussed above), mixed age couples are able to claim Pension Credit so long as at least one of them is above the required age. Under Universal Credit this is no longer true – if one partner is above Pension Credit age and the other below, the couple may need to claim Universal Credit instead. This could have major implications for the entitlements of older people in mixed age couples, and is discussed further in Chapter 19.

The 'benefit cap'

In 2013 the government introduced the so-called 'benefit cap' – a limit on the maximum amount of benefit that could be received by an out-of-work household. Originally the cap was set at £500 per week for couples and families with children, and £350 per week for single people without children. The level of the cap was later reduced, and different rates were introduced for households in London and those in the rest of the country.

For example, Michael and Jen are a couple with four children and rent of £150 per week in receipt of Universal Credit. Without the benefit cap in place (and assuming they are not affected by the 'two-child limit'), their maximum benefit entitlement is £551 per week (£489 Universal Credit and £62 Child Benefit).

The couple live outside of London and have no reason for an exemption from the cap. As a result, their relevant 'cap' is £385 per week. Their Universal Credit entitlement is reduced to bring their overall benefit income in line with the cap – meaning their actual income is £385 per week, made up of £323 Universal Credit and £62 Child Benefit.

Working households are exempted from the cap – defined as households receiving Working Tax Credit (under the old system) or with earnings of more than £430 per month under Universal Credit. Households with someone in receipt of disability benefits (such as DLA, PIP, Attendance Allowance and those in the support group for ESA), as well as carers in receipt of Carer's Allowance, are also exempted from the cap.

One of Michael and Jen's children has a disability, and they receive the low rate care component of DLA for them. Their maximum benefit entitlement increases to £603 per week (£519 Universal Credit, £62 Child Benefit and £22 DLA). Since they now fall into one of the exempted groups, their benefit entitlement is not reduced as a result of the benefit cap.

While the benefit cap applies across the UK, the government in Northern Ireland decided to establish a system of 'supplementary payments' until 2020, to protect families affected by it.

Conclusion

This chapter has explored the way the benefits system works for those without other income or savings, and without any entitlement to contribution-based benefits. Before moving on to the role of contribution-based benefits alongside the means-tested system, it is worth reflecting on a few of the main concepts that have been explored.

First, differences in entitlement depend on differences in the circumstances of the claimant and their family. This can include how many people are in the household (how many are children and how many adults), their age and that of their partner, if they have one, what their housing costs are, whether anyone in the household is sick or disabled, whether anyone is providing care for another person, and even where they live in the country.

Second, in order to respond to this range of different circumstances, claimants' overall entitlements are typically constructed from a number of different benefits (and components within those benefits).

Third, even without factoring in more complicated circumstances, benefits already interact with each other – meaning that overall entitlement cannot be calculated simply by adding together different components to which a claimant is entitled. This is shown in the case of the interaction between Carer's Allowance and Income Support.

Finally, Universal Credit significantly changes provision for some claimants with no income, savings or entitlement to contribution-based benefits. However, the main changes resulting from its introduction relate to the interaction of entitlements with earnings and other income, as well as changes to the way in which benefits are delivered – both of which are discussed in more detail in later chapters.

5

Contribution-based benefit entitlements for people with no other income or savings

Chapter 4 looked at financial support for those who have no income or savings and who are not entitled to receive so-called 'contribution-based benefits' – those paid on account of having made sufficient National Insurance Contributions. The picture we have built up so far is made slightly more complicated once these are taken into account. There are a number of contributory benefits, but we focus on three of the most important here – contribution-based Jobseeker's Allowance, contribution-based Employment and Support Allowance, and the State Pension.

One key difference between contribution-based and means-tested benefits is that they are individual – as opposed to household – entitlements. This has two key consequences. First, you can receive more than one payment per household – so, if two partners in a household are both entitled to contribution-based JSA they can each receive it (whereas income-based JSA is paid at a couple rate, as explained in Chapter 4). This is made more complicated if one partner is entitled to a contribution-based benefit and the other isn't, as outlined below. Second, it changes the way in which household earnings and savings affect entitlements (the difference is explored in detail in Chapter 6).

A second point to keep in mind about the contribution-based benefits system is that it is 'layered' over equivalent entitlements in the means-tested benefits system. By this I mean that contribution-based entitlements are calculated first, but if this entitlement is insufficient to meet a household's basic needs, means-tested benefits provide an underlying 'safety net' to fall back on – frequently topping up incomes to a minimum level. The consequence of this is that many households receive both contribution-based benefits and income-based benefits simultaneously, with the latter being reduced to take account of any contribution-based support received. Examples given in the course of this chapter show how this operates in practice.

Note that throughout this book we distinguish between contribution-based JSA and ESA, and income-based JSA and ESA, by identifying them as JSA(C)/ESA(C) and JSA(IB)/ESA(IB) respectively.

Contribution-based Jobseeker's Allowance and Employment and Support Allowance

We won't go into the details of what National Insurance Contributions a claimant needs to make before they are entitled to receive JSA(C) and ESA(C). On the assumption that the claimant has made sufficient contributions to receive support, the value of contributory benefits is (normally) equivalent to the relevant personal allowance for a single claimant in JSA(IB) or ESA(IB), plus the value of any work-related activity component or support component to which an ESA claimant is entitled.

> For example, Amy is claiming ESA(C) and has been placed in the support group. She is entitled to £73 personal allowance, plus a support component of £37. This gives her an overall ESA(C) entitlement of £110 per week.

However, additional components discussed in Chapter 4 (such as the Enhanced Disability Premium, Severe Disability Premium or Support for Mortgage Interest) are not provided through ESA(C) or JSA(C). As a result, claimants may have their contribution-based ESA entitlement 'topped up' through the means-tested system. This happens where the income-based benefit entitlement is higher than the equivalent contributory benefit entitlement. For example, to continue with Amy's case:

Since Amy is in the support group for ESA, she is entitled to receive the Enhanced Disability Premium within her ESA(IB) entitlement. As a result, her ESA(IB) entitlement is £16 per week higher than her ESA(C) entitlement.

As a result, Amy receives a £16 income-based 'top up' to her contribution-based entitlement. Her total ESA entitlement is £126 – made up of £110 ESA(C) and £16 ESA(IB).

Technically, what happens is that the contribution-based benefit entitlement is deducted in full from the equivalent income-based entitlement, so, if the claimant is entitled to £110 ESA(C) and a £110 ESA(IB) entitlement, they receive £110 ESA(C) and no ESA(IB). If they have an ESA(C) entitlement of £110 and an ESA(IB) entitlement of £126, they receive £110 ESA(C) and £16 ESA(IB). This process of deducting one from the other results in the 'layering' of contribution-based benefits over income-based equivalents.

As explained above, JSA(C) and ESA(C) are individual entitlements, meaning that claimants receive them in their own right (and there is no 'couple' rate of these benefits). So, for example, if two partners in a couple both lost their job and claimed JSA(C) at the same time, they would each be entitled to receive it independently, which would give them a payment at a higher rate than making a joint claim for JSA(IB).

For example, Joan and Elaine are a couple who have just lost their jobs. They each receive JSA(C) at a rate of £73 – giving them an overall JSA entitlement of £146 – £31 per week more than they would receive through a joint claim to JSA(IB). Therefore they receive £146 JSA(C) and no JSA(IB).

It should be noted that this additional income may affect the amount of Housing Benefit the couple receive; however, while this may reduce the gain, it does not eliminate it altogether.

If one partner is entitled to receive a contribution-based benefit and the other isn't, the rules are a little more complicated. In this case, the partner entitled to contribution-based benefit receives their entitlement, but (if they have no other income or savings) their joint entitlement to income-based benefit as a couple is likely to be higher than the value of the contribution-based entitlement received by one partner. As a result, they are likely to be entitled to an income-based top up to their contribution-based benefit.

> For example, Simon and Meg are both looking for work. Simon recently lost his job and receives JSA(C) of £73. Meg is not entitled to receive JSA(C). Simon and Meg's joint entitlement of JSA(IB) is £115. Since this is higher than the £73 Simon receives, they are entitled to receive the difference; as a result, they receive £73 JSA(C) and a top up of £42 JSA(IB). Altogether, their overall rate of payment as a couple is no higher as a result of Simon's JSA(C) entitlement than it would be without this entitlement.

JSA(C) is time limited to six months of entitlement. After this period the claimant would have to move across to JSA(IB) (if they are entitled to it), or would no longer be entitled to continue to receive JSA of either type. In the past ESA(C) was not time limited; this changed in 2012, since when claimants in the work-related activity group (WRAG) have been limited to one year of entitlement. The impact of this change is discussed later, in Chapter 10.[1]

The 'old' State Pension

In 2010, the State Pension age for women was 60 and for men it was 65. Those who had reached that age were entitled to receive the State Pension if they had made sufficient National Insurance Contributions. For those entitled, the amount of State Pension received also depends on the amount of contributions made.

Since 2010, the State Pension age for women has been gradually rising in order to align it with that of men (a process that will be complete by 2018). From the end of 2018, the State Pension age of both men and women will rise to reach 66 by October 2020. From 2026 the State Pension age will rise again, to reach 67 by 2028.

In addition, the State Pension paid to those making a claim from 2010 is being phased out from 2016 – we refer to this as the 'old' State Pension, and the incoming system as the 'new' State Pension.

The old State Pension[2] is formed of three main categories: a pension paid to people on account of their own National Insurance Contributions record ('category A'), a pension paid on account of their partner's National Insurance Contributions record ('category B') and a pension for the over-80s, paid regardless of National Insurance Contributions ('category D'[3]).

The category A State Pension, often known as the Basic State Pension, was worth up to £122 per week in 2017-18. Claimants qualify to receive the pension in full if they have met the required National Insurance Contributions conditions for 30 years.

If the claimant meets the National Insurance conditions for some proportion of 30 years, but not all of them, they are able to receive a partial entitlement – so, for example, if they made National Insurance Contributions for 10 years, they may be entitled to receive a third of the category A Basic State Pension.

The category B State Pension (worth £73 per week) has similar contribution conditions, but these are met by the claimant's partner rather than by the claimant themselves. If a claimant is entitled to some level of category A pension *or* category B pension entitlement, they may be entitled to receive the higher of the two.

For example, Anthony and Rose are a married couple, both of whom are 67. They both started receiving the State Pension in 2015. Anthony worked for 40 years as a teacher before retirement and paid National Insurance Contributions throughout. Rose worked for 10 years as a school assistant, but hasn't been in paid work for the rest of her working life, and has not got any record of National Insurance Contributions for other periods.

Anthony receives a Basic State Pension of £122 per week since he has paid sufficient National Insurance Contributions for more than 30 years. Having paid National Insurance Contributions for 10 years, Rose would be entitled to receive a third of her category A maximum entitlement (about £41 per week). However, as a result of a category B entitlement, she actually receives a Basic State Pension of around £73 per week.

The category D pension, paid to those aged over 80 without sufficient National Insurance Contributions to receive either of the other categories of pension, is worth £73 per week.

Claimants for category A and B State Pensions can claim from the point at which they reached State Pension age. They can 'defer' claiming, but we won't go into the details of how deferrals operate. Claimants in category D may claim from the age of 80.

In addition to these entitlements, under some circumstances, claimants might receive an Additional State Pension (sometimes known as the State Second Pension). This may be worth up to around £160 per week. The Additional State Pension is normally based on additional National Insurance Contributions paid above the minimum level required for the old State Pension, but may also be provided to people who have been carers or had received certain benefits as a result of illness or disability.

The 'new' State Pension

The new State Pension was introduced for people reaching State Pension age after April 2016 (those who reached State Pension age before this point would still claim under the old system, even if they deferred receiving their pension entitlement). Announcing the introduction of the measure in 2016, the Chancellor called it 'the most significant (reform to the State Pension) since its inception'.[4]

The new State Pension is paid at a rate of up to £160 per week (£38 per week higher than the maximum rate of the old Basic State Pension). The full entitlement is received by those who have 35 years or more of National Insurance Contributions record.

Although the maximum basic rate is higher, unlike the old system, the new State Pension will not have an additional top up through the Additional State Pension (although older people who have already built up an Additional State Pension entitlement prior to the introduction of the new State Pension may still get support through protected payments).[5]

As with ESA(C) and JSA(C), low-income claimants in receipt of State Pension (whether old or new) may receive a top up of an income-based benefit; for pensioners this would normally be

Pension Credit. The State Pension is deducted pound for pound from any Pension Credit entitlement.

> For example, Ron is a single pensioner aged 68; he owns his home outright, and pays Council Tax of £17 per week. He receives a State Pension (under the 'old' system) of £122 per week, but no Additional State Pension. Ron's Pension Credit entitlement is £159.

> As a result, Ron receives a top up to his State Pension of around £37 per week in Pension Credit. In addition, he also receives £17 per week in support with his Council Tax.

Contribution-based benefits and Universal Credit

Contribution-based JSA and ESA, as well as the State Pension, are all being kept separate from Universal Credit (as highlighted in Chapter 4, unless they are in a mixed age couple, pensioners will not normally claim Universal Credit at all).

Working-age claimants will normally be able to claim both their contribution-based benefit entitlement *and* Universal Credit. However (as is often the case in the benefits system), the two cannot simply be added together. In a similar way to the old system, contribution-based benefits are 'layered over' Universal Credit – and for each £1 of contribution-based benefit the household receives, their Universal Credit entitlement is reduced accordingly.

> For example, Glen is a 45-year-old man who lives on his own, with private rental costs of £120 per week and Council Tax of £15 per week. He has recently claimed ESA, and (based on his contributions record) is entitled to ESA(C). Glen has been assessed and placed in the work-related activity group. His ESA(C) entitlement is worth £102 per week.

> Glen also claims Universal Credit, which includes a standard allowance of around £73, a limited capability for work component of £29,[6] and a housing costs component (his LHA rate is £110, so his housing costs component is limited to this, despite his actual rent being slightly higher). In total this gives him a maximum Universal Credit

entitlement of £212. However, his ESA(C) is deducted in full from this, so Glen's actual entitlement is £102 ESA(C) and £110 Universal Credit. Glen also receives £15 per week in Council Tax Reduction.

Glen would have received exactly the same entitlement had he not been entitled to ESA(C), but would have received £212 per week of Universal Credit instead.

However, there is a significant difference between the treatment of contribution-based benefits in Universal Credit compared to the old system. Under the old system contribution-based benefits are deducted in full from *equivalent* benefits (for example, JSA[C] from JSA[IB], or ESA[C] from ESA[IB]), but, while they may affect other benefits (such as Housing Benefit or Tax Credits), they will not be deducted from them pound for pound. Under Universal Credit, they can be deducted in full from *any benefit forming part of the household's Universal Credit entitlement*. Effectively this means that deductions are made pound for pound not just from out-of-work income-based benefits, but also from in-work benefits like the Universal Credit equivalents of Housing Benefit or Tax Credits.

The impact of this is that Universal Credit claimants in receipt of contribution-based benefits will rarely be better off as a result of receiving contribution-based entitlements rather than income-based ones – including those in households where someone is in work. The explanation for this, and the impact of it, is discussed in more detail in Chapter 14.

Treatment of contribution-based benefits as taxable income

Unlike most income-based benefits, some contribution-based benefits (including ESA[C] and the State Pension) are treated as taxable income for the purposes of Income Tax, so that where an individual has a high enough overall income over the course of a year, they may pay Income Tax on them at a rate of 20%.

We won't further discuss the (truly bizarre) implications of this here, but it is addressed in considerably more detail in Chapter 14.

Conclusion

This chapter intended to give an introduction to how contribution-based benefits affect the overall entitlements of claimants without any independent income or savings.

While contribution-based benefits can provide significant extra support for some people, others – particularly those who would otherwise receive equivalent means-tested provision – receive no additional income as a result of them. As we will see in later chapters, many claimants can even be left worse off as a result of their contribution-based benefit entitlements. Worryingly, many of the problems with contribution-based benefits are likely to become considerably more common following the introduction of Universal Credit.

However, whether with or without contribution-based entitlements, working out the amount of benefit a claimant might receive if they have no other income or savings is often only the first part of calculating their actual entitlement. The next chapter looks at how support is affected by the income and savings of a claimant and their partner – and in particular, how it is affected by someone making the move into work.

6

How support changes on moving into work

If earnings did not affect benefit entitlements, millionaires would receive as much in benefits as those without any income or savings to rely on. The system would, as a result, would be many times more expensive than it is at present.

However, at the same time, if everyone lost their full entitlement to support at the point at which they moved into work, many people would be much worse off in work than staying out of work and remaining 'on benefits'.

The balance between the two is struck by gradually (or, as we will see, not so gradually) reducing entitlement as a claimant earns more money. The process of assessing entitlements against income is known as a 'means test', and the rate at which benefits are reduced as earnings increase is known as the 'taper' rate.

This chapter is separated into two parts: means testing of so-called out-of-work benefit entitlements (including Jobseeker's Allowance, Employment and Support Allowance and Income Support), and means testing of in-work benefit entitlements (including Housing Benefit, Council Tax Reduction and Tax Credits).

The chapter also explains how the introduction of Universal Credit gets rid of much of the division between in-work and out-of-work benefits, replacing them with a single means test (with a number of important caveats).

'Out-of-work' benefits

JSA, ESA and Income Support are out-of-work benefits. This means that they can only be received by a claimant who is not in full-time paid work (normally this means that a claimant is not working 16 or more hours per week if they are single, or 24 hours in some cases for members of couples). However, this doesn't always mean that claimants can't earn *anything* while receiving these benefits. Different rules apply to how these benefits are affected by earnings, depending on which of them is received.

Jobseeker's Allowance and Income Support

When a claimant receiving income-based JSA or Income Support takes on a few hours of work, the first £20 per week of their earnings are ignored if the claimant is a lone parent (and in certain limited other cases), or £10 if the claim is for a couple, and £5 in other cases. After that, all earnings are deducted in full from the benefit entitlement. Earn an extra £1 and you lose an extra £1, earn an extra £20 and you lose an extra £20.[1]

This continues until *either* the claimant has no entitlement to benefit left to be deducted, *or* the claimant is working 16 hours per week (if single) or in some cases 24 hours per week (if the claim is for a couple).

> For example, Brian claims JSA(IB) and earns £30 per week on an occasional job as a window cleaner. His maximum entitlement to JSA is £73. He has a social rent of £60 per week.
>
> £5 of his earnings is ignored, and the other £25 per week is deducted from his JSA entitlement, giving him an actual JSA entitlement of £48. His Housing Benefit entitlement is unaffected by his work.
>
> £30 earnings, plus £48 JSA, plus £60 Housing Benefit, give him an overall entitlement of £138. This is only £5 higher than his out-of-work entitlement.

For JSA(IB) and Income Support, both the earnings of the claimant and of their partner are taken into account in calculating how much is deducted from their claim. This can mean that someone who is out of work and has no income or savings themselves can't receive any support because of their partner's work. Household savings can also affect the claimant's entitlement (discussed further in Chapter 13).

As described in Chapter 5, contribution-based JSA is an individual entitlement, which means that the partner's earnings are ignored (although the claimant's own earnings are taken into account in a similar way[2] as for JSA[IB]). Savings of either the claimant or their partner are also ignored.

For example, Lucy (26) and Jim (23) are a couple where Lucy is in full-time work and earns £200 per week after tax. Jim recently lost his job and is claiming JSA(C); however, he still does £20 per week of paid work.

Jim's maximum JSA(C) entitlement is £58 per week (the young person's rate since he is under 25). However, while Lucy's earnings are ignored, £15 per week of Jim's own earnings (all of them except for £5 disregarded earnings) are deducted from his entitlement, giving him an actual JSA(C) entitlement of £43.

Employment and Support Allowance

The means test works slightly differently for ESA than for JSA or Income Support. Claimants in receipt of ESA can normally work up to 16 hours per week, where earnings do not exceed £120 per week, without this affecting their ESA entitlement (known as 'permitted work'). However, claimants are not able to do any work over this limit.

Until April 2017, a time limit of a year often applied to the £120 limit on permitted work, and a separate set of rules applied for ESA claimants working over this time limit. However, from this point the time limit was removed.

For example, Toby is in the assessment phase for ESA and has a maximum ESA entitlement of £73. He also does 7 hours of 'permitted work' each week and earns £60. Toby keeps both his earnings of £60 per week, and his £73 ESA entitlement in full.

Although the ESA claimant cannot work except for doing permitted work, their partner, if they have one, might be undertaking some work. For income-based ESA, £20 of the claimant's partner's income is ignored, and the rest of their income is deducted pound for pound from the couple's ESA(IB) entitlement. If the partner works 24 hours per week or more, the couple are not entitled to receive ESA(IB).

For example, June lives with her partner Alex and receives ESA(IB). She doesn't do any permitted work. Alex works 12 hours per week and earns £95.

June's maximum ESA(IB) entitlement is the couple rate of £115 per week.[3] £20 of Alex's earnings are ignored, but the remaining £75 is deducted in full from June's entitlement. This gives June an actual ESA(IB) entitlement of £40 per week.

As with contribution-based JSA, if the claimant is receiving ESA(C), their partner's earnings are ignored. Similarly, as with JSA, household savings may affect entitlement to ESA(IB) but not ESA(C).

Means testing for people not receiving out-of-work benefits

Once a claimant earns too much, or works too many hours, to be entitled to out-of-work benefits,[4] the system changes.

While up to that point, earnings are typically deducted pound for pound from their out-of-work benefit entitlement, after this point, other benefits may start to be affected instead. However, at the same time, claimants may become entitled to additional in-work support – particularly through the Tax Credits system.

Means testing at this point becomes rather more complicated than for people working small numbers of hours, as a result of a number of different benefits being simultaneously 'tapered' (or reduced as earnings increase).

Benefits frequently received by working claimants include Tax Credits (both Working and Child Tax Credit), Housing Benefit and Council Tax Reduction. The way in which each of these are means tested is discussed below. Additionally, claimants may continue to receive benefits not affected by earnings such as the Personal Independence Payment (PIP) or Disability Living Allowance (DLA), and Child Benefit (which is only affected by income if someone in the household earns more than £50,000 per year).

Tax Credits

When a household moves into 'full-time paid work', they may begin to be entitled to Working Tax Credit. This is an additional benefit that is paid in order to support the move into employment. Confusingly, what counts as 'full-time paid work' for Tax Credit purposes varies to reflect the individual circumstances for the claimant household.

It is worth emphasising that Working Tax Credit can be a large amount of money for low-income working families – often several thousand pounds per year. Gaining Working Tax Credit normally ensures that families are better off when they make the move into work.

Disabled people, and single parents with children, can claim Working Tax Credit if they work 16 hours or more per week. In 2010 this was also true of couples with children, but the rules have since been changed to require this group to work 24 hours per week (with one partner working at least 16 hours) before they are able to receive this support.

People without children or a disability can only claim Working Tax Credit if they are 25 or over (which can make a big difference in income for young people on low pay). If they meet this condition, they need to work 30 hours or more per week to be considered in 'full-time paid work'.

Maximum Working Tax Credit entitlement is added to the household's maximum Child Tax Credit entitlement (if they have one), to give an overall maximum amount of Tax Credit support. A proportion of any annual household earnings over £6,420 (before tax) is then deducted from the household's entitlement.

In 2010, 39p was deducted for each extra £1 of earnings; this has since increased to 41p.

> For example, Linda and Jack are a couple with two children who claim Tax Credits. Linda works 16 hours per week and earns £7,000 per year (before tax); Jack works 13 hours per week and earns £5,000.
>
> Linda and Jack's maximum entitlement is £10,075 per year (made up of one £545 family element of Child Tax Credit, two £2,780 child elements of Child Tax Credit and £3,970 in Working Tax Credit).
>
> Their £12,000 earnings before tax is £5,580 over the £6,420 of earnings that are ignored for Tax Credit purposes; 41% of this is deducted from their maximum Tax Credit entitlement (£2,288). As a result, their actual Tax Credit entitlement is £7,787.

As with JSA(IB), ESA(IB), Income Support and Housing Benefit, household savings may also affect Tax Credit entitlements, although, as discussed in Chapter 13, the impact on Tax Credits is considerably less.

An additional top up of support of £810 per year[5] is also added to a claimant's maximum Working Tax Credit entitlement when the claimants in the household work 30 hours or more per week (making it very worth Linda or Jack's while to work an extra hour per week).

Families who are entitled to Working Tax Credit can also receive help with their childcare costs through the benefit, although support with childcare costs through the Tax Credit system has faced some turmoil in recent years. In 2010, the Tax Credits system provided help with up to 80% of childcare costs of up to £175 per week for one child or £300 for two or more children. This was later reduced to 70%.

As we shall see in Chapter 12, this change has less of an impact on some of the lowest-income working families than is often imagined, because of the interaction with other benefits.

> Linda and Jack require £100 per week of childcare costs (on average over the course of the year) to enable them to work; 70% of these costs can be covered through the Tax Credits system. This means that

their maximum Tax Credit entitlement is £70 per week higher (£3,650 per year). As a result, their actual Tax Credit entitlement is £11,437 rather than £7,787.

Additional help with childcare costs is also provided through Housing Benefit and Council Tax Reduction schemes (see below).

In 2010, deductions made at a rate of 39p for each extra £1 of earnings continued until just the family element of Child Tax Credit remained. This was a £545 element in Child Tax Credit that continued to be paid in full until household earnings reached £50,000 per year. After this point it tapered away slowly (at a rate of just under 7p for each extra £1 of earnings). However, since 2010 the separate rules for tapering of the family element have been removed, so it is reduced in just the same way as the rest of Tax Credits, and as described in previous chapters, the family element is now gradually being removed altogether.

A confession...

I'm afraid this is actually a rather simplified version of means testing in the Tax Credits system.

In the examples above (unlike previous examples) you may have noticed that annual entitlement figures and incomes are given. This is because (unlike other benefits) Tax Credits are an annual entitlement, and means testing is calculated on the basis of on annual household income. However, they are typically paid weekly or four-weekly (because people can't normally afford to wait until the end of the year in order to get the support that they are entitled to).

This means that during the course of the year, claimants need to estimate what their overall earnings for the year will be. For this reason, there can be a mismatch between the estimated household earnings that are used for calculating the claimant's weekly or monthly payments, and the household's actual earnings – calculated at the end of the year.

In the early years of Tax Credits, this led to high levels of overpayments – where people were paid on the basis of their estimate of household earnings for the year, which turned out to be substantially lower than their actual annual income (for example, as a result of someone in the household getting a job during the course of the year).

For this reason, in the mid-2000s, a rule was introduced which meant that if the claimant household's earnings were higher in the current tax year than in the previous year, up to £25,000 of this 'additional' income could be ignored for Tax Credit purposes. This is called an 'income disregard'.

This means that if the claimant's actual earnings turn out to be higher than they predicted, they are much less likely to be 'overpaid' and have to return the money.

For example, let's follow Linda and Jack's case through to the following financial year, and assume that while their earnings start out at £12,000 (meaning their estimated annual award and payments are based on this), Linda gets a promotion and household earnings for the year increase by £5,000, to £17,000.

Without the income disregard – their £17,000 earnings before tax are £10,580 over the £6,420 of earnings that are ignored for Tax Credit purposes; 41% of this is deducted from their maximum Tax Credit entitlement (£4,338). Since their entitlement is significantly affected by the increase in earnings, they may well find that they have been overpaid.

With a £25,000 income disregard – their £17,000 earnings before tax are £5,000 higher than in the previous financial year. This falls within the £25,000 limit, and so this £5,000 of earnings are disregarded. The remainder (£12,000) is £5,580 over the £6,420 of earnings that are ignored for Tax Credit purposes; 41% of this is deducted from their maximum Tax Credit entitlement (£2,288). Their entitlement is not affected by the earnings increase, and they are not overpaid.

Since 2010, the government has significantly reduced the level of this income disregard, and from 2016 it has been reduced to £2,500. In addition, the government also introduced a disregard of £2,500 for *falls* in earnings – meaning that if household earnings fell by £2,500 between two years, their Tax Credits would see no resulting increase in the second year.

The impact of these changes on error in the Tax Credit system is discussed in more detail in Chapter 16.

Income Tax and National Insurance

Clearly Income Tax and National Insurance are not benefits themselves. However, they equally obviously have an important effect on overall incomes for working households, and as a result are important to consider in any discussion on means testing.

Income Tax and National Insurance also have an important interaction with those parts of the benefit system where means testing is undertaken on net rather than gross household income. This is the case with Housing Benefit and Council Tax Reduction schemes and, crucially, Universal Credit entitlements.

As previously mentioned, some benefits (principally contribution-based) are also themselves counted as income for the purposes of Income Tax. This has some perverse consequences, and will be explored further in Chapter 14.

Unlike Tax Credits, Income Tax and National Insurance costs are calculated on the basis of individual rather than household earnings. Income Tax is charged at a rate of 20p for each £1 of taxable income over the individual's Income Tax personal allowance – in 2017/18 this allowance was £11,500.[6] Earnings over £11,500 per year are typically liable for Income Tax at a rate of 20p for each additional £1 of earnings. Earnings over £45,000 are liable for the 'higher rate' tax of 40%.

National Insurance liabilities are calculated on the basis of weekly (rather than annual) earnings. In 2017/18, earnings over £157 per week[7] were liable for National Insurance at a rate of 12p in the £1. Unlike Income Tax (which is paid at a higher rate for higher levels of earnings), higher levels of earnings face a lower National Insurance rate, with earnings over £866 per week facing National Insurance Contributions of 2p for each additional £1 earned over this threshold.

National Insurance is calculated differently for self-employed people, but for simplicity we will not discuss this here.

For example, John earns £21,500 per year (£412 per week). £21,500 is £10,000 over John's Income Tax personal allowance, so he pays

£2,000 of Income Tax. £412 is £255 over John's National Insurance allowance, so he pays around £31 per week (£1,596 per year) in National Insurance.

This makes John's overall tax liability £3,596 for the year, and as a result, his net earnings are £17,904.

Overall, for each extra £1 earned by someone paying the basic rate of Income Tax and National Insurance, they pay an extra 20p in Income Tax and 12p in National Insurance – a total of 32p. So, if John earned an extra £100 per year, he would pay an additional £20 in Income Tax and £12 in National Insurance.

These tax deductions from earnings can be made at the same time as Tax Credits are tapered.

For example, Sarah and Andrew are a couple with two children. Sarah works 24 hours per week and earns £21,000 per year; Andrew works 12 hours and earns £10,000 per year.

£21,000 is £9,500 over Sarah's Income Tax personal allowance, so she pays £1,900 of Income Tax. £403 is £246 over Sarah's National Insurance allowance, so she pays around £30 per week (£1,539 per year) in National Insurance.

£10,000 is under Andrew's Income Tax personal allowance, so he doesn't pay any Income Tax on this. However, the weekly equivalent (£192) is £35 per week (£1,814 per year) over his National Insurance threshold. As a result, Andrew pays £218 per year in National Insurance.

This means that overall their net household income is £27,343.

Overall Sarah and Andrew's maximum Tax Credit entitlement is £10,885 per year (made up of one £545 family element of Child Tax Credit,[8] two £2,780 child elements of Child Tax Credit, the £1,960 basic element of Working Tax Credit, the £2,010 couple element of Working Tax Credit and the £810 30-hour element of Working Tax Credit).

Their gross household earnings of £31,000 are £24,580 in excess of the £6,420 that are ignored for Tax Credit purposes; 41% of this is £10,078 – this amount is deducted from their maximum Tax Credit entitlement, meaning that their actual Tax Credit entitlement is £807.

Their net household income, plus Tax Credit entitlement, is £28,150.

If Sarah was paid £22,000 rather than £21,000, she would pay an additional £200 per year in Income Tax, and £120 in National Insurance Contributions. In addition, the extra £1,000 of earnings would be added to the household's income for Tax Credit purposes, meaning that a further £410 was deducted from the household's Tax Credit entitlement.

In total, once these deductions of £200, £120 and £410 are factored in, the household's income is £28,420 – only £270 more than it was with £1,000 less household income; 73% of Sarah's additional earnings are lost in deductions.

However, some in-work benefit claimants do not just receive Tax Credits and pay Income Tax and National Insurance. We also need to look at the deductions that are made from Housing Benefit and Council Tax Reduction.

Housing Benefit

Chapter 5 discussed how a claimant's maximum Housing Benefit entitlement is calculated. However, we now need to discuss how maximum Housing Benefit entitlements are reduced for those who are earning money in work.

There are four key steps to calculating how much of your maximum eligible rent you actually get to keep in Housing Benefit. This operates in the same way for someone renting privately as for someone living in social rented housing. (Different rules apply for people who own their own home, but we will come on to that later.)

Passporting to full entitlement

The first step is to check if the claimant is eligible to be 'passported' to full Housing Benefit ('passporting' is when receipt of one benefit or Tax Credit leads to eligibility for another). Broadly, claimants will be passported to full Housing Benefit entitlement if they receive a means-tested out-of-work benefit – including income-based JSA, income-based ESA or Income Support.

The 'income-based' bit is crucial here – contribution-based JSA and ESA do not passport to full Housing Benefit – the household has to go through the full means test (outlined below). This can create confusion (and result in people who have paid their National Insurance Contributions ending up worse off than if they hadn't paid in at all).

If not passported

If a claimant isn't passported to full Housing Benefit, their maximum Housing Benefit entitlement is means tested to check how much of it they actually get to keep.

The first stage is to calculate their 'applicable amount': the amount of income (including income from other benefits) that is ignored for living expenses before the remainder is means tested. This is similar to the rate of out-of-work benefit entitlement paid if the household has no other income or savings (so, for example, similar to the amount of support that a family might receive through a combination of JSA, Child Benefit and Tax Credits, and any disability premiums). This ensures that if a claimant is living on benefit income alone, and has no other earnings or savings, they still get their maximum entitlement to Housing Benefit as well.

The second stage is to calculate their income for the purposes of Housing Benefit. This works on the basis of income after tax, but including income from most benefits or Tax Credits received. There is often a small amount of income that is also disregarded: £25 per week for a lone parent, £20 for disabled people and carers (as well as a range of other groups), and £5 or £10 for single people and couples respectively, who do not fall into these other groups. In addition, earnings from permitted work for ESA claimants are also ignored.

To calculate a claimant's actual Housing Benefit entitlement, take their income for Housing Benefit purposes, and deduct their 'applicable amount', and any earnings disregard from this. Then deduct 65% of the remainder (their 'excess' income) from their maximum Housing Benefit entitlement (as calculated in the way described in Chapter 4), to get their actual Housing Benefit entitlement.

As with other income-based benefits, savings may also affect Housing Benefit entitlement (see Chapter 13).

For example, John privately rents a flat. His maximum Housing Benefit entitlement is £100 per week, and he works 20 hours a week and earns £195 after tax.

His applicable amount for living expenses is £73; he also has £5 of earnings disregarded.

This gives an 'excess' income of £117 (= £195-£73-£5); 65% of this (£76) is deducted from his maximum Housing Benefit.

This gives him an actual Housing Benefit entitlement of £24 per week (= £100-£76).

If income for Housing Benefit purposes increases (say, by an extra £10 per week), Housing Benefit entitlement correspondingly falls (by £6.50 per week).

Deducting nearly two-thirds of income from Housing Benefit entitlement may sound like a lot. It is, and even more so when you take taxes and deductions from other benefits into account at the same time. While most benefit claimants are significantly better off in work than out of work – because of the additional support provided by Working Tax Credit – deductions from benefits like Housing Benefit create enormous problems in making sure that taking on *additional* work pays.

Deductions from maximum entitlements on account of earnings work in exactly the same way in the private and social rented sectors – in both cases, the applicable amounts are the same, and the rate of withdrawal remains at 65%. The key difference is that social rents are likely to be much lower than private sector rents – for example, analysis from the Valuation Office Agency shows that in 2016 (across England) the average rent for a property in the private rental sector was £820 per month;[9] the average rental price for a property in the social rented sector at a similar point was £394 per month.[10] Since the lower the claimant's level of maximum entitlement, the lower the household income at which entitlement disappears, claimants in social rented housing typically 'escape' the Housing Benefit system at a considerable lower level of earnings than those in the private rental sector.

For a couple with two children renting with an average social rented sector rent, Housing Benefit entitlement ends when (with one partner working) earnings reach around £410 per week (around £21,400 per year).

Were a family of the same type eligible for a maximum Housing Benefit entitlement equivalent to the average private sector rent (£820 per month), they would continue to be entitled to Housing Benefit until their earnings reached around £767 per week (around £40,000 per year).

Support for Mortgage Interest

As highlighted in Chapter 4, unlike Housing Benefit, Support for Mortgage Interest (SMI) is paid as part of a claimant's income-based out-of-work benefit entitlement. This means that where Housing Benefit can be paid to those in full-time paid work, SMI is not, although people may be able to do small amounts of paid work and continue to receive this assistance.

Council Tax Benefit

In 2010, claimants could receive Council Tax Benefit to provide support with Council Tax costs. Passporting to full Council Tax Benefit, and means testing for other claimants, happened alongside and in the same way as means testing for Housing Benefit. The deduction rate for Council Tax Benefit was 20%, meaning that for each extra £1 of income for Housing Benefit and Council Tax Benefit purposes, 85% was deducted from these benefits (65p from Housing Benefit and 20p from Council Tax Benefit).

From 2013, responsibility for providing Council Tax Benefit was passed across to local authorities, with each setting up their own Council Tax Reduction scheme. The impact of this is discussed in Chapter 18. For simplicity, in the examples used in the following sections, it is assumed that the claimant's local Council Tax Reduction scheme follows the same rules as Council Tax Benefit.

Help with childcare costs through Housing Benefit and Council Tax Reduction

Both Housing Benefit and Council Tax Reduction may provide help with claimants' childcare costs. This is because an amount of earnings equivalent to the claimant's childcare costs is ignored for the purposes of calculating a claimant's Housing Benefit and Council Tax Reduction entitlement.[11]

So, for example, if a claimant has £100 per week of childcare costs, £100 per week is deducted from their earnings for the purposes of calculating their Housing Benefit and Council Tax Reduction entitlement. Given that this income could otherwise be deducted from their Housing Benefit/Council Tax Reduction entitlement at a combined rate of 85%, this effectively provides substantial additional support with childcare costs through the benefits system.

The mechanics of how this works in tandem with help with childcare costs through the Tax Credits system are complicated – but essentially, for working claimants receiving Housing Benefit, Council Tax Reduction and Tax Credits, the combination of support means that they may receive up to around 96% of their childcare costs paid through the benefits system – the other 4% the claimant needs to find from their earnings.

Combination of tapers

Tax Credits, Housing Benefit and Council Tax Benefit can all be means tested in parallel, against the same earnings. For those earning enough, the withdrawal of these benefits also happens alongside paying Income Tax and National Insurance.

This can mean that in some cases, for each extra £1 earned by a working claimant, they may get to keep very little in increases to their overall income. This rate of deductions, which they incur on earning an additional £1, is sometimes known as their 'effective marginal tax rate' (EMTR).

More specifically, the mechanics of in-work tax and benefit deductions are as follows when withdrawals are at their maximum rate[12] (that is, when Housing Benefit, Council Tax Benefit and Tax Credits are all being withdrawn, and the claimant is paying both Income Tax and National Insurance – the 'peak' EMTR for working claimants). At this point, for £1 additional earnings:

- the claimant pays an additional 20p Income Tax and 12p National Insurance;
- 41p is deducted from Tax Credit income (a withdrawal of 41% based on gross income);
- this leaves 27p; 17.6p of this is deducted from Housing Benefit (65% withdrawal rate net of tax), and 5.4p is deducted from Council Tax Benefit (20% withdrawal rate);
- this leaves **4p** that the claimant retains.

There are a large number of different combinations of benefits, Tax Credits and tax deductions that may be deducted from a claimant's additional earnings. EMTRs for different combinations of benefits and Tax Credits are as follows (see Figure 6.1).

Figure 6.1: Effective marginal tax rates for different combinations of benefits, Tax Credits and tax liabilities (old system)

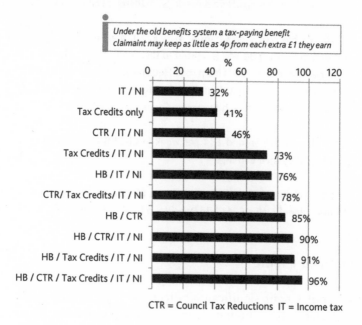

Under the old benefits system a tax-paying benefit claimaint may keep as little as 4p from each extra £1 they earn

CTR = Council Tax Reductions   IT = Income tax

Calculating an overall entitlement for a working household

We can see how the combination of in-work benefits and Tax Credits provide an overall entitlement by considering an example case.

> For example, John and James are a couple with two children. They rent their home privately, and have a rent of £170 per week. They are liable for Council Tax of £20 per week. John works 30 hours per week and earns £300 per week (and his earnings have been consistent in both the current and previous financial year).

> Their maximum Tax Credit entitlement (a combination of Child Tax Credit and Working Tax Credit) is £10,885. Their earnings are in excess of £6,420, which means that their actual Tax Credit award is less than their maximum award. Their actual Tax Credit entitlement is around £136 per week.

John pays around £16 per week in Income Tax and £17 in National Insurance Contributions. His net earnings are therefore £267 per week.

Their eligible rent (see Chapter 4) is £150, meaning that their maximum Housing Benefit is limited to this amount. They also face earnings-based deductions from their Housing Benefit of around £72 per week. Their actual entitlement is therefore around £78 per week. Their earnings are too high to receive Council Tax Reduction.

They also receive around £34 per week in Child Benefit, which is unaffected by their earnings.

In total their income is £267 (earnings), plus £136 Tax Credits, plus £78 Housing Benefit, plus £34 Child Benefit – a total of £516 per week.

Universal Credit

Universal Credit significantly affects the way that in-work entitlements are means tested for working-age claimants. There are three main differences – a reduction in the distinction between 'out-of-work' and 'in-work' benefits, the application of a single 'work allowance', and of a single 'taper'.

The distinction between 'out-of-work' and 'in-work' benefits is reduced

As explained in Chapter 4, Universal Credit brings together six key benefits – income-based JSA, income-based ESA, Income Support, Working Tax Credit, Child Tax Credit and Housing Benefit – into a single benefit.

This reduces[13] the distinction that exists in the old system between 'out-of-work' and 'in-work' benefit entitlements. As we have seen, under the old system, once working a certain number of hours or earning over a given amount, a claimant would lose their entitlement to their out-of-work benefit entitlement (JSA, ESA or Income Support), and may receive some new benefit (particularly through Working Tax Credit). Under Universal Credit the 'extra support' for working claimants is provided through retaining Universal Credit in work (with the level reduced as earnings increase).

> *On the old system* – Stuart, for example, is an out-of-work single parent, and receives income-based JSA, Housing Benefit, Child Tax Credit, Council Tax Reduction and Child Benefit. After moving into work, Stuart receives Housing Benefit, Child Tax Credit, Working Tax Credit, Council Tax Reduction and Child Benefit.
>
> *Under Universal Credit* – Stuart is an out-of-work single parent, and receives Universal Credit, Council Tax Reduction and Child Benefit. After moving into work, Stuart continues to receive the same benefits (although the Universal Credit and Council Tax Reduction are likely to be paid at a lower rate).

One important consequence of this is that reductions in support that under the old system would only affect out-of-work benefit entitlements, under the new system, *provision is affected both in and out of work.* For example, the removal of the work–related activity component of ESA (and equivalent in Universal Credit) would only affect out-of-work claimants under the old system, but under Universal Credit will also affect in-work entitlements for low-income workers affected by illness or disability. This issue is discussed further in Chapter 10.

SMI can be paid as part of a claimant's Universal Credit. However, a new rule has been introduced which means that this cannot be paid if the household has any earnings at all – no matter how little they are. This 'zero earnings' rule has consequences for work incentives, which are discussed in Chapter 13.

It is important to note that contribution-based JSA and ESA will remain outside of the Universal Credit system. Those in receipt of these benefits will continue to receive them separately, and the same rules apply as under the old system. This group may also receive Universal Credit as a 'top up' to this support (as described in Chapter 5).

A single 'work allowance' is applied

Under the old system, different benefits have different applicable amounts and income 'disregards'. As has been seen, these vary a great deal – for some out-of-work benefits, claimants may keep as little as £5 per week before additional earnings reduce their benefit entitlements. For Tax Credits the allowances are considerably higher – with families typically able to keep their full Tax Credit entitlement until their earnings reach £6,420 per year (around £123 per week).

Universal Credit introduces a single rate of 'work allowance', an amount of earnings that claimants can keep before additional income affects their entitlement. The level of the work allowance applied depends on the composition of the household and whether or not the claimant receives help with housing costs as part of their claim.

The rates of work allowance in Universal Credit were significantly reduced in 2016. The implications of this for work incentives are discussed in Chapter 13.

A 'single' combined taper rate is applied to earnings in excess of the work allowance

Earnings below this work allowance do not affect the claimant's entitlement to Universal Credit, but deductions will be made for earnings above this threshold. This replaces deductions made from a claimant's Tax Credits and Housing Benefit under the old system (as well as income-based ESA, JSA and Income Support for claimants not in full-time paid work).

The rate at which these deductions are made (the 'taper rate') has been set at 63% of net earnings. This means that for every £1 of earnings above their work allowance (calculated after tax and National Insurance Contributions), the claimant loses 63p from their Universal Credit entitlement.

It is important to note that since Council Tax Reduction is retained separately to Universal Credit, its taper (typically 20%) may be applied on earnings left after deductions from Tax/ National Insurance and Universal Credit have been made.

As shown below, this results in an overall EMTR of 75% for Universal Credit claimants who are also taxpayers (or typically around 80% for those receiving Council Tax Reduction). At this point, on earning an additional £1:

- the claimant pays an additional 20p Income Tax and 12p National Insurance
- this leaves 68p; 43p of this is deducted from Universal Credit (63% withdrawal rate)
- this leaves 25p.
- *(then, for Council Tax Reduction recipients)* 5p of this is deducted from Council Tax Reduction (20% withdrawal rate)
- this leaves **20p** that the claimant keeps.

For some claimants this leads to a substantially reduced taper rate – with a 'peak' EMTR of 80% rather than 96%.

The gain for current unemployed benefit claimants doing small amounts of work is particularly notable – as described previously, these people may currently face pound-for-pound withdrawal from their earnings. For this group, additional earnings will either not affect their Universal Credit entitlement at all (because their earnings are below the level of their work allowance) or have a 63% taper rate, rather than 100%.

However, other groups will face higher taper rates under Universal Credit than the old system. For example (as shown above), those receiving Tax Credits only and paying Tax/National Insurance currently face a taper rate of 73% – this increases slightly to 75%. Those facing a Tax Credits taper but not paying Tax/National Insurance may see their taper rate increase from 41% to 63% – this is particularly likely to affect low-income second earners in a household.

Figure 6.2: Effective marginal tax rates for different combinations of benefit entitlements and tax and National Insurance liabilities (under Universal Credit)

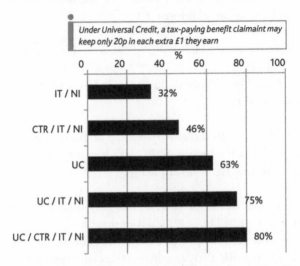

CTR = Council Tax Reductions IT = Income tax HB = Housing Benefit
NI = National Insurance UC = Universal Credit

Looking in more detail at Stuart's case:

Let's suppose that Stuart (aged 30) has one child and a social rent of £700 per month. Stuart works and earns £1,200 per month.

Stuart pays around £111 per month in Income Tax and National Insurance Contributions – leaving him with net earnings of around £1,089 per month.

Stuart's maximum Universal Credit includes a £318 per month standard allowance (since he is over 25), £277 in child elements[14] and a £700 housing costs component – a total of £1,295.

Stuart's work allowance for Universal Credit is £192 – his earnings above this (£897) result in reductions in his Universal Credit entitlement. Since these reductions are applied at a rate of 63%, this results in a deduction of £565. After deductions, Stuart's Universal Credit entitlement is £730 per month.

Stuart's overall monthly income is comprised of £1,089 net earnings, £730 Universal Credit and £90 Child Benefit: a total of £1,909.

If Stuart earned an extra £100 per month, he would pay £20 more in Income Tax, £12 more in National Insurance and 63% of the remaining £68 (£43) would be deducted from his Universal Credit entitlement. After deductions his overall income would increase by £25 per month (to £1,934).

It is important to note that this approach only explains the treatment of earned income on Universal Credit entitlements. Some forms of so-called 'unearned income' including occupational pensions and (as described in Chapter 5) contribution-based benefits are deducted pound for pound from a claimant's Universal Credit entitlement. This has important consequences, as discussed in detail in Chapter 14.

A Minimum Income Floor is applied for self-employed claimants

It is also important to note that, under Universal Credit, low income self-employed workers may be affected by a 'Minimum Income Floor' (MIF). This sets a minimum amount that self-employed workers will be treated as earning – even if their actual earnings are less than this. In most cases this amount will be set at 35 hours at the claimant's relevant level of minimum wage after tax (at the time of writing in 2017 this would be the equivalent of around £1,050 per month for a worker aged over 25).[15]

For the first 12 months of setting up a new business, self-employed claimants are exempted from the minimum income floor, in recognition that it can take a while for a business to become profitable.

Savings rules are the same as for JSA(IB), ESA(IB), Income Support and Housing Benefit, and different to Tax Credits

As with other means-tested benefits, household savings can affect entitlement to Universal Credit. The rules for the treatment of savings are similar to JSA(IB), ESA(IB), Income Support and Housing Benefit – and rather harsher than for Tax Credits. The impact of this on working households with significant levels of savings is discussed in Chapter 13.

Universal benefits

Some benefits are not affected by any of the claimant household's earnings or National Insurance Contributions. These are often known as 'universal benefits' (not to be confused with Universal Credit!). Universal benefits include some disability payments including Disability Living Allowance (DLA), Attendance Allowance and the Personal Independence Payment (PIP) (these benefits were introduced in Chapter 4, and are discussed further in Chapter 15).

Child Benefit used to be entirely non-means-tested. This has now changed and it is what we might describe as 'semi-universal'. Families can receive Child Benefit in full if no one in the family earns over £50,000 per year. If someone earns in excess of this threshold, the value of their Child Benefit is reduced[16] by 1% for each additional £100 (so that it is removed entirely by the time their earnings reach £60,000).

For those entitled to them, universal benefits are paid in addition to the means-tested benefit entitlement, as is shown in Stuart's case above (regarding Child Benefit).

Conclusion

This chapter has introduced how the benefits system operates for a working claimant. A few summary principles are worth reiterating.

What counts as an 'in-work' benefit is a grey area. Some claimants receiving 'out-of-work' benefits under the old system (JSA, ESA or Income Support) may be undertaking small amounts of paid work – although, in many cases, they see very little financial gain from doing so. This changes with the introduction of Universal Credit, where the gains from undertaking a small number of hours of work may be significantly greater.

Over a certain threshold (of hours and/or income), claimants can no longer receive 'out-of-work' benefits. Instead, working claimants may receive certain benefits (such as Child Tax Credit, Housing Benefit and Council Tax Reduction) that may be paid both in and out of work, and they may also receive support *only* paid to working claimants through Working Tax Credit. Like out-of-work claimants, working claimants can receive a number of different benefits and Tax Credits simultaneously. This distinction between 'out-of-work' and 'in-work' benefits is reduced (although not eliminated) under Universal Credit since the new benefit replaces a number of out-of-work benefits but is paid both in and out of work.

A benefit claimant's maximum entitlement is *not necessarily the same* as their actual entitlement – deductions are made from the maximum entitlement on account of other income. These deductions can be very high in some cases, and are different under the old system to under Universal Credit.

Under the old system, additional incentive to move into (low-paid) work was provided through Working Tax Credit, an additional payment *only* made to those in work. Under Universal Credit these additional payments in work no longer exist. Instead, work incentives are promoted through retaining Universal Credit entitlement in work.

In addition to their 'means-tested' and 'contribution-based' benefits, both working and non-working claimants may also receive 'universal benefits' – these are benefits like Child Benefit and DLA, and are typically paid on top of a claimant's other entitlements.

Taken together, these last three chapters have given an introductory account of the structure of benefit entitlements – both in terms of calculating maximum entitlements for those with no other income or savings, and showing how entitlements reduce as earnings increase.

This provides a framework for understanding the reformation of the system since 2010. Exploration of some of the radical changes introduced – and what the benefits system may look like by 2020 – is the focus of the next two parts of the book.

Part III
A thousand cuts

The 2010s have seen reform to the benefits system on an astonishing scale. New limits on entitlements and changes to how they increase as prices rise; new approaches to assessing sickness and disability; and changes to the age at which claimants can receive retirement benefits – these have all affected people's experiences. As if these weren't enough, they are set against the backdrop of the introduction of Universal Credit, the biggest shake-up of the means-tested benefits system since the time of Beveridge.

The following two parts of this book explore key changes to the benefits system in recent years, and what they mean for claimants. This part looks at the *value* of different benefit entitlements. Areas explored include (in Chapters 7 and 8) 'hidden' cuts to provision when benefits fail to rise in line with prices, as well as the introduction of new 'limits' on entitlements, such as the 'two-child' limit in Child Tax Credit and Universal Credit.

This part also looks at some of the groups most affected by benefit cuts. Chapters 9 and 10 raise concerns that some of the most vulnerable people – such as children and sick and disabled people – are seeing support reduced the most. In contrast, Chapter 11 shows how benefits for some groups of older people have been treated rather differently in recent years, including through the introduction of the Basic State Pension 'triple lock'.

One of the common justifications for introducing cuts to benefits for families is to increase the 'fairness' of the benefits system, and above all, fairness to working families. However, as Chapter 12 shows, lower-income working families have by no means been protected from the impact of benefit cuts. Furthermore, we will see how the government's approach to increasing the incomes of working households in recent years (particularly through tax cuts) actually gives little help to many of the lowest-income working families who most need additional support.

The introduction of Universal Credit has sought to address some of the reasons why the benefits system often provides inadequate support for low-income working families. However, in Chapter 13, we will see that inadequate investment in the new system has meant that it has failed to achieve many of the things it was intended to, whilst introducing a number of new problems of its own.

Finally, Chapter 14 raises concerns over the value of contribution-based entitlements for claimants who have paid National Insurance Contributions – with many receiving no additional support as a result of their contributions, and some actually left *worse off*.

Understanding the ways in which changes to the benefits system are affecting different entitlements for different groups will help both with assessing the fairness of the system as a whole, and in considering options for the future direction of welfare reform.

7

A freeze is as good as a cut

A £1 is a £1, right? Well, yes and no. Depending on inflation, what you can actually do with your £1 changes over time. Put simply, a £1 remains a £1, but the world around it changes. As a result of price inflation, in order to buy the same amount of 'stuff' in 2020 as you could with £1 in 2010, you would need to have around £1.35.[1] Sometimes it seems that the government (perhaps somewhat conveniently) forgets this.

One of the most hidden cuts to the benefits system in recent years has been repeated reductions in support relative to rising costs of living, either through below-inflationary increases or through absolute freezes – and most recently with the decision to freeze benefits and Tax Credits for four years.

Such cuts to support are hidden because they don't result in a reduction to the amount of cash people have in their pocket. There is no point at which a claimant experiences a sudden drop in income levels. Instead, the impact is felt through the gradual drip, drip, drip of an extra few pence on a loaf of bread or packet of cereal, a slight increase in the mobile phone bill, or having to put an extra £1 on the meter in order to get the same amount of electricity that they used to. Politicians can pretend that they aren't cutting support even when they are.

Below-inflationary uprating, 2010–20

When benefits are increased to compensate for inflation, this is called 'uprating'. Until 2010, many benefits were uprated in line with the Retail Prices Index (RPI).[2] The RPI, which measures the change in prices of a representative set of goods and services, is one of the principal measures of inflation used in the UK. Based on the RPI, and as shown below (see Figure 7.1), prices are expected to rise by more than a third over the course of the 2010s.

However, as a result of years of below–inflationary benefit uprating, followed by a four-year benefit freeze, some benefits will have risen much more slowly. By 2020, the value of personal allowances for Jobseeker's Allowance (JSA) may have risen by less than 12%. Child Benefit – which David Cameron called 'one of the most important benefits there is' – has particularly suffered. Based on policy at the start of 2017, it will have risen by just 2% over the course of the decade – one-seventeenth of the increases in prices.

The rest of this chapter considers the impact that below-inflationary uprating has had in three key areas – children's benefits, support with housing costs, and support for sick and disabled people.

Figure 7.1: Compound inflation (RPI), 2010-20

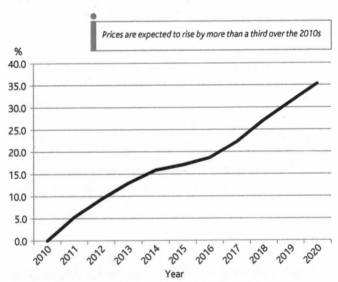

Source: Based on RPI forecasts from OBR (Office for Budget Responsibility) (2017) March 2017 economic and fiscal outlook, http://cdn.budgetresponsibility.org.uk/ March-2017-EFO-charts-and-tables-economy-1.xlsx

Freezes to children's benefits

Both Child Benefit and Child Tax Credit remain popular. In the run-up to the 2015 election, during the television debates, the then Prime Minister David Cameron was put on the spot about the government's plans, and promised that Child Benefit and Child Tax Credit would not be cut.

> *Audience member:* 'Will you put to bed rumours that you plan to cut Child Tax Credit and restrict Child Benefit to two children?'
>
> *David Cameron:* 'No I don't want to do that – this report that was out today is something I rejected at the time as Prime Minister and I reject it again today.'
>
> *[Later ...] David Dimbleby:* 'You said you didn't want to put to bed rumours that you were going to cut Child Tax Credits – you meant you did want to put to bed the rumours?'
>
> *David Cameron:* 'Yes – we have increased Child Tax Credits.'[3]

The post-election reality, when David Cameron was faced with delivering a manifesto promise of £12 billion of benefit cuts, was rather different.

In particular, promises that Child Tax Credit and Child Benefit wouldn't fall certainly don't appear to have taken any account of rises in costs of living. From 2016, both Child Benefit and Child Tax Credit rates were frozen for four years. Around 7.5 million children across the UK are living in families that will be affected by this freeze.[4] This freeze comes after years of below-inflationary increases, particularly affecting Child Benefit rates.

At the start of 2010, benefit income for an out-of-work single parent with two children (excluding housing costs) was around £198 per week. In order to keep up with rises in costs of living, by 2020 this would have to rise to around £267 per week. The family's actual 2020 income is expected to be £214.

The real loss of £53 per week leaves this parent worse off by nearly £2,800 per year.

Cuts in support relative to prices (along with the many cash cuts to support, outlined in the following chapters) can mean that families have to cut back on many of the essentials that they used to purchase. One poll of parents in 2015 found that one in five families – the equivalent of 1.5 million across the UK, with 2.5 million children – said that they had cut back on food, and a similar proportion had cut back on heating their home as a result of benefits being increased below inflation.[5]

Children's benefits aren't the only area of people's lives where real-term cuts have had a severe impact.

Freezing help with housing costs

As explained in Chapter 4, until recently, Local Housing Allowance (LHA), which determines entitlement to Housing Benefit for people renting in the private rental sector, was based on average rents and increased in line with rises in local rental prices. This ensured that as local rents rose, people were still able to afford to live and work in their own community.

As well as reducing LHA rates from the 50th percentile of local rents to the 30th – and imposing caps on maximum rates – since 2010 the government has also made changes to the way in which LHA rates rise over time as rents go up. Instead of increasing LHA rates with local rents, from 2013 the government decided to restrict increases in LHA rates in line with the Consumer Prices Index (CPI) measure of inflation. This was then followed by a decision to further restrict LHA rises to no more than 1% for two years (with exceptions for the fastest rising rents through a Targeted Affordability Fund).

As a result of this (and other changes), LHA rates no longer bear any relationship to typical local rents. Where LHA tenants' rents have risen between 2010 and 2015 in line with average rental price inflation (a total rise of 11.7% over the five-year period), a family renting a typical two-bedroom property in 2015 would face a shortfall of £83 per month on their maximum Housing Benefit entitlement compared to their actual rent.

Particularly concerning is what may happen to Housing Benefit as rents continue to rise in the second half of the decade. In 2015, the Conservative government decided to freeze LHA rates, from 2016 through to 2020. If actual rents rose by another 11.7% during the second half of the decade, families in a typical two-bedroom property could see the shortfall increase by £72 per month – creating a total shortfall of around £155 per month by 2020.

Again, some money will be made available to support those areas where rental prices rise the fastest, through continuation of the Targeted Affordability Fund. The intention is to spend 30% of the savings generated from freezing LHA rates (compared to the cost of increasing them in line with inflation). However, the amount of money made available for this fund is linked to inflation measured by the CPI.[6] While private rents rose by 2.8% between 2014 and 2015, the CPI rate was –0.1%.[7] As a result, despite rental costs going up, no money was made available in 2016 for helping those with the fastest increases in rents.

Even if the increase in the average shortfall between 2015 and 2020 was reduced by 30% as a result of the Targeted Affordability Fund, this would still leave an LHA tenant in a typical two-bedroom property with an expected shortfall of £133 per month by 2020. In contrast, their maximum Housing Benefit would have covered their full rent in 2010.

Based on rental price rises between 2010 and 2020, forecast shortfalls on Housing Benefit compared to local rents for rooms in shared accommodation and one-, two- and three-bedroom properties are shown in Figure 7.2.

The government's own evaluation[8] of LHA reforms found that, faced with the prospect of tenants experiencing these kind of shortfalls, some landlords said they were attempting to stop renting to Housing Benefit claimants. In other cases, concerns about the increased risk of arrears had led many landlords to tighten up vetting procedures for applicants.

Figure 7.2: Estimated monthly shortfall between average LHA rates and local average rents (including 30% reduction as a result of the Targeted Affordability Fund), 2010-20[a]

LHA tenant in a typical two-bed home could face an expected Housing Benefit shortfall of £133 per month by 2020

Room in shared accommodation ▬▬ **One-bed home** ▬▬ **Three-bed home** ▬▬ **Two-bed home**

Note: [a] For 2010 to 2015, this shortfall is calculated as the difference between actual average LHA rates across all English Broad Rental Market Areas (BRMAs) and 2010 average LHA rate uprated in line with rental price inflation; 2015-20 rates are calculated in the same way, and on the basis of rental price inflation 2015-20 being equivalent to 2010-15, and average LHA rates increased by 30% of inflation (to take account of the Targeted Affordability Fund

Most worryingly, nearly half of landlords renting to people receiving LHA said they had seen an increase in rent arrears, and one in five said they have taken action to evict, not renew or end tenancies, specifically because of the impact of the LHA reforms. In some cases landlords would now rather leave homes empty than rent to people on Housing Benefit. One landlord interviewed in the research said:

'We've managed to get rid of a lot of the people who are on DSS[9]... the tenants don't have a job and therefore they can't meet the shortfall ... they can't pay and eventually a court proceeding takes place to get rid of them, so I'd rather leave my property empty than give it to these people and then try and get them out, it's bad practice. I'd rather not do that, so I just leave it empty.'

Moving home is a difficult and costly thing to do – it may not only make it harder to find work, but it can uproot children from their schools, costing a great deal in fees and charges associated with the move itself. Many people affected by these cuts will do whatever they can to stay put and take the loss through reductions in disposable income. While much of the rhetoric around the reforms may be around moving home to a place within your means, even the government itself appears to recognise that this is not an option for many of those affected by cuts like these. It is notable that, when they initially decided to link LHA with inflation rather than local rents, the government did not expect this cut to lead people to move home:

No behavioural impact is assumed over the forecast period as differences in rents will be small in the early years compared to the transaction costs of moving. The current estimate of the anticipated reduction in benefit expenditure is in the order of £400m in 2014/15 (real terms, 2012/13 prices).[10]

Benefit rises below inflation and 'protection' for the sick and disabled

When, in 2013, the government introduced measures to limit increases in benefits for three years (a policy that was later followed up with the further four-year freeze discussed previously), they promised that disabled people would be protected. The then Pensions Minister Steve Webb announced the measure, saying:

> In difficult economic times we've protected the incomes of pensioners and disabled people who have little means to increase their income. We have also committed to helping people who rely on working age benefits and Tax Credits and will increase that support by 1%.[11]

The detail of the measure revealed that the disability elements of Tax Credits, Disability Living Allowance (DLA) and the support component of Employment and Support Allowance (ESA) (and equivalents paid through Universal Credit and the Personal Independence Payment [PIP]) would continue to be uprated in line with inflation. The same benefits would continue to be protected from the four-year benefits freeze from 2016.

However, to say that disabled people were protected is somewhat disingenuous. First, those in the work-related activity group (WRAG) for ESA did not receive any protection at all (although since the government later decided to substantially cut support for this group, as discussed in Chapter 10, this perhaps shouldn't be a surprise).

Second, and most important, while a proportion of the overall benefit entitlement received by many disabled people is exempted from below-inflationary uprating, *all the other support that they receive is included*. This means, for example, that they are still affected by freezes to Housing Benefit entitlements and non-disability-related Tax Credit entitlements. It is even the case that personal allowances for ESA were not exempted (while the support component was; the difference between the two parts of the benefit was described in Chapter 4).

This does not amount to real protection at all. In order to receive any one of the benefits mentioned that was protected (other than DLA), the disabled claimant would have to receive at least one benefit that was not protected.[12]

As a result, the government's own impact assessment found that disabled people were *more likely* than other groups to be affected by below-inflationary increases in benefit entitlements – with around a third of households with someone describing themselves as disabled being affected, compared to around a quarter of all households.[13]

This inconsistency between rhetoric and reality shows the importance of considering the overall impact of changes to the benefits system *as a whole* on claimants, as well as changes to individual benefits. We consider these combined impacts of welfare reform later, in Part V.

Conclusion

Freezing benefits may not reduce the amount of cash in people's pockets, but cash isn't what matters – what matters is what people are able to afford to buy with it.

It is understandable why the government seeks to uprate benefits below inflation – it doesn't, on the face of it, look like a cut, and because it affects a large number of people, it saves a lot of money. The four-year benefit freeze alone is expected to save £4 billion per year (in 2020 prices) by the end of the decade.[14] However, hiding a cut doesn't stop it having a real impact on people's lives. The gradual erosion of benefits means a deterioration in living standards for those who most rely on this support.

Despite government promises, disabled claimants will be in no way protected from this. Most of the benefits disabled people receive will still be frozen until 2020, despite a small number of particular forms of support being exempted. As we have seen, disabled claimants are more likely than average to be affected by the change. Families with children – who are more likely to rely on benefits than those without children – are also likely to suffer significant losses.

However, not all benefits have been cut in this way. Most notably (and as we discuss in Chapter 11), some benefits targeted at pensioners (including, most importantly, the Basic State Pension) have risen more rapidly. Just as benefit freezes save a lot of money, the State Pension 'triple lock' costs a great deal. We discuss just how much, and the impact that this has on the overall cost of social security, later, in Chapter 20.

8

'Unlimited' welfare

In making the case for reform of the benefits system, former Chancellor George Osborne argued that 'the worst thing you can do for families is to have unlimited welfare'.[1] As a result of this, some of the key changes made to the benefits system since 2010 have been to 'limit' maximum entitlements. This chapter looks at the application of these limits, and the consequences – both intended and unforeseen.

What is 'unlimited' welfare?

It is worth clarifying what is and is not meant by 'unlimited' welfare. What it does not mean is that people put in a request for cash and get as much as they want. Rather, it means that the system has no fixed limits to how it responds to the level of household need – as needs grow, support through the benefits system grows in proportion to this. The largest benefit payments are made to those with multiple needs – larger numbers of children in the household, disabled people in the household, and/or high housing costs as a result of renting in a high cost area of the country (and being unable to access lower cost social housing).

In a 'limited' welfare system, there is a point at which even if household 'needs' increase (for example, as the result of an additional child, or rents being hiked), no additional support is paid. For example, as mentioned in Chapter 2, a 'wage stop' used to be applied to national assistance rates to prevent them from being higher than the amount a household might earn in work (in order to retain a financial incentive to move into employment). Many households had minimum needs that were higher than the level of the 'wage stop', resulting in them being trapped on a level of provision below that required for basic subsistence. This was scrapped in the 1970s. Since then more sophisticated approaches have been employed to retain work incentives without 'limiting' provision – in particular, through the 'tapering' of support for in-work claimants.

Since 2010, the government has done a great deal to reintroduce limits on the extent to which the benefits system responds to household need. This includes three key measures: the two-child limit for Child Tax Credit, the introduction of a 'benefit cap' (somewhat reminiscent of the old 'wage stop'), and the introduction of caps on Local Housing Allowance (LHA) rates.[2]

The 'two-child limit' for Child Tax Credit and the child element of Universal Credit

In the first budget after the 2015 General Election, the Conservative government announced that they would limit the child element of Child Tax Credit to the first two children in the family. That year, the then Work and Pensions Secretary Iain Duncan Smith claimed at the Conservative Party Conference that this measure would teach parents that 'children cost money'[3] (apparently, prior to this, parents were blissfully unaware of the fact).

The child element of Child Tax Credit (and the equivalent within Universal Credit) is worth around £2,800 per child per year – so a family with three children loses up to £2,800 from this, and a family with four up to £5,600.

The change will be introduced gradually, so some parents with more than two children born before April 2017 will continue to receive additional provision. In a small number of cases, children will be excluded from the limit – including some born as a result of a multiple birth, adopted children and those in non-parental caring arrangements, and those born as a result of non-consensual sex (the latter being the much criticised 'rape clause', which requires women to provide evidence that their child was born as a result of rape before they can receive additional support[4]).

This change is part of a wider set of reforms designed to limit the maximum amount of support that families can receive through the benefits system.

The 'benefit cap'

The intention of the 'benefit cap' (introduced under the coalition government) was to restrict benefit entitlements for families who were not in work, so that there was a limit to the maximum amount of support that they might receive. Full-time working families[5] are exempt, meaning that support for this group remains 'unlimited' in this sense. Families with someone in receipt of Disability Living Allowance (DLA) or the Personal Independence Payment (PIP), or with someone in the support group for Employment and Support Allowance (ESA) are also exempted.

The level of the benefit cap was introduced at £26,000 per year for families with children. (There is a lower rate for single people without children, but despite this, only a very small proportion of those affected are in this group.) When it was introduced, the then Chancellor George Osborne suggested that the new policy would mean that a family couldn't receive more on benefits than the average working family received from work, saying:

> ... for the first time we will introduce a limit on the total amount of benefits any one family can receive. And the limit will be set according to this very simple principle: Unless they have disabilities to cope with, no family should get more from living on benefits than the average family gets from going out to work.[6]

This apparent 'equal' treatment was misleading. The level of the cap for families with children was not set in line with average *income*, as government pronouncements on the cap seemed to imply, but rather with average *earnings* – a lower, sometimes much lower, figure, since in-work benefit entitlements were ignored. No similar rationale about earnings for the average family was presented when the level of the benefit cap was later reduced to £23,000 in London and £20,000 in the rest of the country.

The Local Housing Allowance cap

As explained in Chapter 4, LHA is a way of calculating Housing Benefit for tenants in the private rental sector. Maximum rates are broadly in line with the 30th percentile of local private rents for an appropriate household size (although, as shown in the previous chapter, LHA rates are falling increasingly far behind this).[7] The coalition government decided to cap the maximum amounts that the LHA rates could be, regardless of actual local rents – as of March 2016, the rental caps were as outlined in Table 8.1 below.

In some areas (especially in inner London) LHA rates would be considerably higher if there were no caps. For example, in 2015 in Inner North London (the area of the country with the highest level of rent), the 30th percentile of local rents was £30 per week higher than the cap for a one-bedroom property, rising to £158 higher for a four-bedroom property (see below). The shortfall makes this area (along with increasing numbers of other areas) effectively unaffordable for those unable to make up the price difference.

Table 8.1: LHA cap, 2015, compared to 30th percentile of local rents in Inner North London, and the expected shortfall for someone renting there

Property	Weekly LHA cap	30th % of local rents in inner North London[8]	Shortfall between 30th % and LHA cap
One bedroom	Up to £260.64	£290	£30
Two bedrooms	Up to £302.33	£350	£48
Three bedrooms	Up to £354.46	£460	£106
Four or more bedrooms	Up to £417.02	£575	£158

Is it right to cap benefit entitlements?

There are two key questions to ask about this policy of a 'limited' benefits system – does it encourage claimants to make the right choices, and does it improve the fairness of the system?

Can limiting benefits encourage claimants to make the 'right' choices?

If benefit claimants are able to make the 'right' choices in order to limit their reliance on the benefits system, it might be considered reasonable to restrict entitlements to encourage people to make those choices. So, for example, the government believes that the two-child limit will ensure that people consider whether they can afford to have a third child before they decide to have one – teaching parents that 'children cost money'.

Whether we want a society in which only the wealthy can afford a third child is a question that goes somewhat beyond the scope of this book. But even if this was a reasonable position, the extent to which people can practically plan their lifetime reliance on the benefits and Tax Credits system is extremely questionable.

For example, a couple with three children may have very carefully planned and budgeted before deciding to have a third child. They may have decided that this was affordable without significant reliance on benefits and Tax Credits. But if one of the parents dies after the birth of their third child (particularly if that partner was the main earner in the household), it is likely to make it much more difficult for the household to manage. Many bereaved parents become considerably more reliant on the benefits system after the death of a loved one. Many will struggle financially regardless, but the government's decision not to exclude widowed parents from the two-child limit will make their situation much, much harder.

Similarly, the out-of-work benefit cap is designed to discourage families from choosing to remain out of the labour market. However, for most of those parents who are out of work,[9] this is not a choice but a circumstance forced on them. Furthermore, for many families, the result of the benefit cap (as well as the LHA caps) is that they have to move out of areas with high rents (since these push up benefit entitlements and result in people being affected by the cap). Where families do move home, they are likely to need to move away from those areas where rents are rising the fastest. Unfortunately, as analysis by Shelter shows, this is likely to require them to move away from key job-creating cities like London, Cambridge and Manchester,[10] which may not only risk working families' jobs but also make it harder for those looking for work to find it.

Despite George Osborne's claim in 2010 that the benefit cap would limit benefit entitlements 'for the first time', this was not, of course, an entirely new policy. The 'wage stop' that was abolished in the 1970s had a similar role. It could, perhaps, be argued that in the absence of significant in-work benefit provision in the early days of the welfare state, it was necessary to preserve some incentive to move into employment. The provision of in-work benefits now provides an alternative (and more progressive) way of promoting work incentives. As we will see later, in Chapters 12 and 13, if the government seeks to promote work incentives, it would be much better to address the decline in in-work provision than seek to reduce entitlements for out-of-work claimants.

In other cases, policies designed to make sure that families make the 'right' choices are likely to result in exactly the opposite. For example, families fleeing domestic violence have not been exempted from the two-child limit. It is frequently the case that leaving a violent partner can be a difficult decision, not least because of the financial consequences of escaping the relationship. The decision not to exempt this group from the two-child limit may make it more likely that some parents decide to stay with a violent partner – exactly the wrong decision for the safety of themselves and their children. In other cases (as discussed in the following chapter), policies such as the benefit cap can introduce a severe couple penalty that pushes loving relationships apart.

While there may be some circumstances in which the benefits system may be used successfully as a tool for encouraging people to make the 'right' choices (requirements to seek work as a condition of receiving unemployment benefits, for example), it is questionable whether this can work in cases such as those outlined above. In some cases, it is likely to be actively counterproductive.

Does limiting entitlements promote 'fairness' in the benefits system?

The second argument for limiting benefits is that it promotes 'fairness' in the benefits system – principally between working families and those 'on benefits'. Certainly (as previously noted) this was the intention of the benefit cap. Similarly, Grant Shapps, Housing Minister at the time the LHA caps were introduced, commented that:

> 'Just because you are on Housing Benefit, that shouldn't give you the ability to live somewhere, where *if you are working and not on benefit you can't.* We'd all love to live in different areas, but I can't afford to live on x street in y location. The Housing Benefit system has almost created an expectation that you could almost live anywhere, and that's what has to stop.' (emphasis added) [11]

This is somewhat disingenuous, since, while the benefit cap was targeted at non-working households (although some claimants working small numbers of hours are affected), the LHA caps were not. As has been repeatedly highlighted over the course of this book, Housing Benefit is not an out-of-work benefit. Indeed, because of the high rates of maximum entitlements, some working households with high levels of earnings may still be entitled to receive support.

For example, a family with four children and a maximum LHA entitlement of £417 per week (the weekly cap for a household eligible for four or more bedrooms) could earn up to around £1,600 per week, or nearly £84,000 per year, before their Housing Benefit entitlement is withdrawn in entirety.

Given that many of those affected are in work, in some cases, the application of LHA caps could put people's jobs at risk – by imposing limits on entitlements that mean that they have to move away from where their job is based. At the same time, reductions to in-work support (discussed in Chapters 12 and 13) have since made a nonsense of the idea that the process of welfare reform is promoting fairness between working and non-working households.

However, there is a further key concern about policies that introduce blunt limits on entitlements, and this is the impact that this has on *children*. In November 2015, around 21,000 households across Britain had their benefits capped. Of the 106,000 people in those households, 79,000 are children, meaning that they represent around three-quarters of those affected.[12]

Once you take into account that there are a lot more adults in the country than children, the difference becomes much more stark. The figures make children more than eight times more likely than adults to be affected.[13] Benefits included within the scope of the benefit cap include all key children's benefits (including Child Benefit and Child Tax Credit).

It must be somewhat questionable whether it is appropriate to increase fairness between working and non-working *adults* by cutting support for *children*. The assumption that it is right for children's benefits to be limited to encourage the right choices from parents implies that either (1) the money is fundamentally the parents' money, or (2) it is appropriate to withhold money that is principally the child's – somewhat like robbing their piggy bank to make mum and dad do the right thing.

Children's benefit entitlements are paid to meet their needs and to ensure that they have a decent childhood. They are paid to parents because they are responsible for the household bills and for meeting the child's needs – they are the stewards for the child.

No child ever shirked work in order to live a life on benefits, yet it is their support that is threatened. If parents are making the wrong choices, cutting children's benefits means that children are being punished for this. Perhaps the response to this is that it is the parents' fault for failing to take responsibility for their children. But is this ever a legitimate excuse for society to neglect to protect children?

If parents are making the wrong choices, if they (unwisely) decide to have children simply to get bigger handouts from the state, and if they are spending benefits paid for their children on their own needs, a more substantial intervention than simply capping their benefits is needed. We need to make sure these children are protected, and that payments are going towards improving their wellbeing. As a first step we could look at paying additional benefits for larger families more as 'benefits in kind', such as direct rental payments or help with fuel bills. Simply limiting payments for children is a blunt tool that won't help. On the other hand, if parents are making the 'right' and 'responsible' choices about supporting their children, limiting children's benefits punishes children for factors beyond anyone's control. The truth is that the vast majority of families in receipt of benefits fall into this latter group – struggling to make ends meet, and trying to do the very best they can for their children.

Conclusion

Limiting benefit entitlements doesn't encourage the right choices. Indeed, it can result in people being forced to make the wrong choices – from staying with a violent partner through to keeping apart a loving relationship.

Nor does limiting entitlements do anything to promote 'fairness' in the benefit system between working and non-working households; indeed, it often leads to benefits being cut for those working families who need support in order to stay in their home, and retain their job.

Perhaps most importantly, limiting entitlements affects no group more than children. It is children who pay for bad decisions made by either their parents or by the government. Children can make an easy target for cuts. They don't vote, some of them don't even talk, and in the end, it can always be suggested that the cuts aren't aimed at them but at their 'good-for-nothing' parents. It may even be suggested that cuts are being introduced for their own good, as the government put it in the astounding ending to the impact assessment for the two-child limit on Child Tax Credits:

> The proposed changes enhance the life chances of children as they ensure that households make choices based on their circumstances rather than on taxpayer subsidies. This will increase financial resilience and

support improved life chances for children in the
longer term.[14]

Seven-and-a-half million children across the UK rely on the
benefits system[15] (and this is leaving out the ones getting just
Child Benefit). It may sound less cruel than taking away their
pocket money, but placing blunt limits on support for children
is far worse, for it puts their food, their warmth and their homes
at risk.

9

Welfare reform and the 'family test'

The Conservatives have always claimed to be proud to be the 'party of the family'. As far back as 2008, David Cameron, then leader of the Opposition, said:

> My ambition is to make Britain more family-friendly. To make our country a better place to bring up children. Not just because it's the right thing to do; not just because my family is the most important thing in my life; but because families should be the most important thing in our country's life.[1]

After entering government this commitment was reaffirmed through the introduction of the 'family test' – a check to ensure that government policy is fair to the family. The 'test' comprised a set of questions that all policy across government needed to address before it could be agreed by ministers.[2] David Cameron maintained that the introduction of the test would ensure that government policy supported family life.[3]

As we explore in this chapter, however, the impacts of welfare reform on family incomes; particular impacts of reforms on new parents; and the creation of substantial new 'couple penalties' in the benefits system all deeply undermine this promise.

Poverty and the 'family test'

The 'family test' does not directly address the impact of government policies on family incomes. However, it recognises the pressures created by income reductions, emphasising that factors contributing to family stress and breakdown include 'family members with poor physical and/or mental health, those facing financial problems, poverty or unemployment'.[4]

Despite the government appearing to accept that poverty presents a major challenge to family life, this problem is not going to go away in coming years. The Institute for Fiscal Studies (IFS) estimate that by 2020 an extra 1 million children will be living in poverty compared to 2015 (in contrast to an expectation of no change in the number of working age non-parents living in poverty).[5]

A number of factors contribute to this. First, low-income families with children are likely to be more reliant on benefit entitlements than equivalent working-age families without children, because of higher levels of need in the household. This means that benefit cuts that are not specifically targeted at families with children (such as benefit freezes, cuts to Local Housing Allowance [LHA], the introduction of the benefit cap and so forth) are nevertheless likely to have a disproportionate impact on this group.

Second, many of the cuts that have been introduced in recent years have placed a particular emphasis on children's benefits. These include the loss of the family element of Child Tax Credit, the two-child limit for the child element of Child Tax Credit and Universal Credit, and the reduction in disability support for many families in receipt of Universal Credit.

Cuts to Child Tax Credit

In Chapter 7 we discussed below-inflationary increases in Child Benefit in some detail. However, the government has also made a number of changes to Child Tax Credit since 2010.

The child element of Child Tax Credit rose *above* inflation in 2011, with the government stating that it was using some of the savings from restrictions on Child Benefit for higher-income families to fund this.[6] Announcing the increase, the then Chancellor George Osborne said, 'we will provide additional support to families in poverty. These are among the most vulnerable people in our society and they need our help'.[7]

However, a further planned increase in 2012 was cancelled,[8] and since then, considerable cuts have been made. This includes several years of below-inflationary uprating (discussed in Chapter 7), as well as cuts to the cash value of provision.

In 2010, the elements that made up Child Tax Credit included, first, a family element (worth £545 and paid once per family, effectively providing a supplement for the first child – recognising the additional costs of having children, regardless of family size). The family element also included a 'baby addition', worth an extra £545, to help families with the additional costs of a new child.

Second, entitlement included a 'child element' paid for each child in the family. Finally, Child Tax Credit included an additional 'disability element' (and a 'severe disability element'), to help with the additional needs of disabled children.

Since then, cuts have included the removal of the baby addition and then the family element of Child Tax Credit, three years of below-inflationary uprating, followed by a four-year freeze, and the introduction of a two-child limit on the child element. The transition to Universal Credit also included cuts to the value of the child disability element (discussed further below).

> For example, Sally is a single parent with two children, neither of whom is disabled. In 2010, her maximum Child Tax Credit entitlement (the amount she would receive if her entitlement was not affected by other income or savings) was £5145 – made up of £545 for the family element and £2,300 for each child element.
>
> Allowing for inflation, the equivalent of this value in 2020 would be £6,946. However, the actual expected maximum entitlement for a family like Sally's making a new claim in 2020 is £5,560 – a reduction of nearly £1,400 in real terms. (See Table 9.1 for a detailed breakdown.)

For someone affected by the two-child limit, or by reductions in disability support (as described below), the cuts would be much larger.

Table 9.1: Family with 2 non-disabled children – maximum Child Tax Credit entitlement for new claims in 2010 and 2020

	Entitlement in 2010	Value of 2010 entitlement (in 2020 prices)	Expected entitlement in 2020 (following cuts)
Family element	£545	£736	£0
Child element	£2,300	£3,105	£2,780
Child element	£2,300	£3,105	£2,780
Total	£5,145	£6,946	£5,560

This only describes changes to maximum entitlements. Further changes have also been made to the rate at which all Tax Credits (including Child Tax Credit) are withdrawn from working families as earnings increase (discussed further in Chapter 12).

Disabled child additions within Universal Credit

In the longer term, Child Tax Credit will no longer exist. This is because (as explained in Chapter 4) Universal Credit replaces Tax Credits, and Child Tax Credit will be replaced by child additions within Universal Credit.

In some respects there is little change with regard to child additions in Universal Credit compared to those in Child Tax Credit – the amounts are largely similar. Cuts such as the introduction of the two-child limit, the four-year benefit freeze and the removal of the family element apply for both Tax Credits and Universal Credit. The key change will be how the new benefit is means tested, which (as discussed in more detail in Chapter 13) is very different.

There is an important exception to this. Buried away in the regulations around the introduction of Universal Credit was a provision that cuts the value of the disabled child element in half. In 2016, the disabled child element in Child Tax Credit was worth £262 per month. Following the introduction of Universal Credit, it will be worth £126 per month. It has been estimated that by the time Universal Credit is fully introduced, around 100,000 disabled children could lose out as a result of this cut in support.[9]

Furthermore, it is worth noting that the reduction in the value of the disability element was intended to bring support for disabled children into line with support for sick and disabled adults.[10] Given that equivalent support (through the work-related activity component of ESA) was later removed for disabled adults (as discussed in Chapter 10), a question remains as to whether the disabled child addition could follow.

In some circumstances, when families claim Universal Credit, this may also act as the *trigger* to cuts in support for their children, which are being introduced for new claimants in both Tax Credits and Universal Credit.

Additional support for disabled children is also provided through Disability Living Allowance (DLA) for children – this is not affected by reductions in disability support paid through Universal Credit.

Cuts to support for young single parents under Universal Credit

As discussed in Chapter 4, under Universal Credit, single parents under the age of 25 will no longer be entitled to receive the higher over-25s rate of personal allowance (known as the 'standard allowance' in Universal Credit). This means that out-of-work single parents between the ages of 18 and 24 will receive £15 per week less than they would under the old system.

Under the old system, an out-of-work 23-year-old single parent with one child would be entitled to around £158 per week if they have no other income or savings. Under Universal Credit, this would reduce to around £143 per week – a loss of around 10% of their overall income after housing costs.[11]

There are currently nearly 100,000 non-working single parents under the age of 25[12] who are likely to be affected by this measure. However, this will also affect working single parents as, under Universal Credit (as shown in Chapter 6), these personal allowances continue to form part of a household benefit entitlement in work. There are currently around 63,000 working single parents aged 18-24 in receipt of Tax Credits.[13]

Assuming these families would all be affected by this measure, a total of around 173,000 single-parent families will be affected by this change to the amounts awarded to under-25s with children. The government has itself acknowledged that changes to personal allowances for under-25s in Universal Credit will push 100,000 more people into poverty[14] than would otherwise have been the case.

New families

It is well understood that at the point of having a new child, family incomes are likely to be particularly stretched, and that additional support is needed to give families assistance through this exciting – but very costly – time. In the UK, families with children aged 0-4 are at the highest risk of poverty, with more than a third of children in a family with a very young child living below the poverty line (see Figure 9.1). [15]

This can be a financially difficult period from, as it were, both ends. Expenditure is pushed up because of buying all the extra essentials needed for a baby – from nappies to furniture (as the Money Saving Expert website puts it, 'babies are as costly as they

Figure 9.1: Percentage of children living in poverty (below 60% of median household income after housing costs) by age of youngest child in household

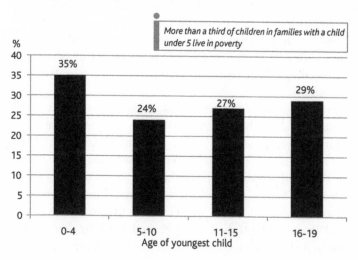

are cute'[16]). At the same time, incomes are squeezed because of parental leave, and reduced hours when parents return to work.

This is, of course, just one of the many pressures facing families with new children, pressures that should make this group a priority for the 'family test'. Indeed, one of the questions for the family test is:

> What kind of impact will the policy have on families going through key transitions such as becoming parents, getting married, fostering or adopting, bereavement, redundancy, new caring responsibilities or the onset of a long-term health condition?[17]

Given this, it is unsurprising that in recent years there has been some extra support in the benefits system for families with new children. This has included things such as the Sure Start Maternity Grant (a one-off grant of £500 to help with the costs of a new child), a Health in Pregnancy Grant (of £190) to help expectant mothers to eat healthily during pregnancy, and the baby element of Child Tax Credit (£545), which provided additional support through the Tax Credits system for the first year of a child's life. The last Labour government had also planned to introduce a 'toddler element' from 2012 (of £209) to provide some extra help for children aged 1 and 2.

Such extra support also included the Child Trust Fund, which provided a £500 savings voucher for children in low-income families (with additional payments for children with disabilities). This provided a small nest egg for children, so that when they grew up they would have some savings with which to start their adult life.

However, extra support like this made an easy target when it came to cutting benefits. By 2015, the Sure Start Maternity Grant had been restricted to the first child (although, at the time of writing in 2017, the Scottish Government plan to use new devolved powers to replace the Sure Start Maternity Grant with a 'Best Start Grant', which will make payments to second and subsequent children[18]). The Health in Pregnancy Grant and Child Trust Fund had also been abolished, the baby element had gone, and plans for a toddler element had been reversed. In total this could amount to cuts in maternity benefits of £1,735 over pregnancy and the first year of a child's life alone.

In addition, families with new children are among the most likely to be affected by changes to the levels of income disregard in the Tax Credits system (discussed in Chapter 16), since periods of parental leave result in fluctuating incomes. Parents can suffer once when they take parental leave and their incomes fall (as a result of the new disregard of any fall in annual income up to £2,500). These families may then be affected a second time when their incomes rise again on returning to work, because of the reduced disregard for rises in income. Where previously they could have seen an increase of up to £25,000 ignored for Tax Credit purposes, this is now just £2,500. This change alone could cost new parents returning to work after parental leave up to as much as £9,225.[19]

The 'family test' and the 'couple penalty'

When the Department for Work and Pensions (DWP) led on developing the 'family test', they emphasised the importance of checking the impact of policies on 'family formation'. One of the questions in the test is:

> What kinds of impact might the policy have on family formation? Couple relationships are the starting point for most families, and committed couple relationships bring significant benefits for the individuals themselves and children in those families. The formation of couple relationships is a private matter for individuals, but *government policy can act to support, for example though law on marriage and civil partnerships, or inadvertently undermine commitment including for example through the structure of the benefit system.* Policy makers need to think carefully about how they are supporting or constraining couples in making the right choices for them and their families. (emphasis added)[20]

One of the concerns that led to the introduction of the 'family test' was that there was a 'penalty' in the benefits system for being part of a couple. The problem exists because households living apart may receive more support than equivalent households living together – so, for example, two single parents (with one young child each) who aren't currently working, and who each privately rent a two-bedroom flat costing £100 per week are each entitled to receive the following support:

- Income Support: £73
- Tax Credits: £64
- Housing Benefit: £100[21]
- Child Benefit: £21
- Total: £258

So between them, they receive an overall entitlement of £516 per week.

Now suppose these single parents are in a relationship and decide to move in together. In this case their Income Support is paid at the couple rate, but this is not even close to double the single person rate (it's about £40 per week higher). In addition, the Housing Benefit rules specify that not only can the partners share a bedroom, but since the children are young, so can the children – so they still do not qualify for any additional bedrooms that might lead to more help with rental costs.

- Income Support: £115
- Tax Credits: £117
- Housing Benefit: £100
- Child Benefit: £34
- Total: £366

Effectively, they see their overall income fall by £150 per week (£7,800 per year). Now a lot of this fall is justified because living costs are lower for a couple with two children than for two single parents living separately, each with one child – you only need one TV licence, food costs tend to be lower when cooking meals as a family, you only need to heat one home, and so on. In addition, parents in a couple with children may be more likely to be able to move into work, or be more flexible in their employment requirements – it is certainly worth noting that lone-parent households are considerably more likely to be living in poverty than couple families.

However, is it really the case that the family's overall financial needs fall by nearly 30%? Certainly in a case like this, the family may find finances rather more squeezed living together as one household.

A 'couple penalty' may also be said to exist when a partner in receipt of benefits moves in with a partner with an income too high to receive any entitlement. This is because while tax liability is calculated on an individual earnings basis, benefit entitlements are normally based on household income (although, as discussed in Chapter 5, contribution-based benefits are an important exception to this).

Given the focus of the 'family test', you might expect recent welfare reforms to aim firmly at eliminating the 'couple penalty'. In fact, they have done the opposite. For example, the two-child limit applies to the number of children for which each family may receive the child element of Child Tax Credit. This means that two single-parent families can each have two children and receive support for all four, but when living together as a couple, they would receive support for only two of the children. This measure could cost two single-parent families, with two children, each nearly £6,000 in Tax Credit entitlement if they decided to move in together.

A coalition of faith leaders went so far as to call the reform 'fundamentally anti-family', going on to say that 'It would, in our view, fail on all six of the DWP's "family test Questions"'.[22] A similar problem occurs with the benefit cap, which (as discussed in more detail in Chapter 8) places a maximum 'cap' on benefit entitlements for out-of-work families. As with the two-child limit, this introduces a fixed threshold of benefit income that a single household can receive. Should they live together as two separate households (resulting in each having a lower benefit income) they may avoid the impact of the cap.

The benefit cap limits benefit entitlement for most out-of-work families to around £441 per week if they live in London. A single parent with three children and with rent of £150 per week would have an overall entitlement of around £442 per week – putting them at pretty much exactly the level of the cap.

If they moved in with a partner with two children, forming a large family with five children, and they saw a modest increase in their rent for a slightly larger property (£200 rather than £150), their benefit income would increase (without the cap) to £668 per week. *This means that they would see a loss of £226 per week as a result of the cap.* Neither household living separately would be affected by the cap, but simply by living together they lose nearly £12,000 per year as a result.

Should they choose to continue to live separately (pretty likely, given the circumstances), their overall benefit payments would be £884 per week.[23] Keeping the couple living apart costs the Exchequer an additional £216 per week over their uncapped income living together.

Given this, it is unsurprising that the Liberal Democrat peer Baroness Tyler warned that:

> ... it has been suggested by experts in the field that the cap will introduce one of the most substantial couple penalties ever seen in the benefits system, so it could have the perverse consequence of breaking up families as well as deterring people from entering new relationships and forming new households.[24]

Both of these policies mean that some families will face a clear financial incentive against couple formation (or even incentivise separation, given how large some of the losses may be). But in addition, where families do make the decision not to form couples as a result of this, it will – absurdly – mean higher payments through the benefits system than there would have been in the absence of the policy altogether (since, as described above, higher benefit payments are typically made for households living apart than for one larger household living together). Through these policies, the government has effectively decided to pay families to live apart – in some cases, to the tune of many thousands of pounds each year.

Conclusion

The government introduced the 'family test' in order to ensure that all policies across government departments support family life. However, welfare reform to date not only fails to contribute to this goal; it actively undermines it. It is still the case that:

- families with children are among the groups most likely to live in poverty – with the proportion of children living in poverty expected to rise substantially by the end of the decade;
- families with new children face particular financial pressures – and reductions in support for this group just make those pressures all the more severe;
- in some cases, the government is paying families to live apart – and they have now introduced some of the largest couple penalties the benefits system has seen;
- there aren't sufficient incentives in the benefits system to help families move into sustainable work. As we shall see in Chapters 12 and 13, attempts to create a system that is fair to working families have been undermined by cuts to in-work provision.

These are the real challenges of fixing social security. The profound failure to address these problems is why reform of the benefits system has failed the 'family test'.

10

Cuts to Employment and Support Allowance and the 'limited capability for work' component of Universal Credit

There are perhaps few more concrete signs of how civilised a society is than how it treats those within it who are sick or disabled. Over recent years the government has repeatedly said that they have protected the most vulnerable people in society, including disabled people.

This chapter looks at how welfare reform has cut support for disabled people through changes to support for those receiving Employment and Support Allowance (ESA) (and equivalent entitlements through Universal Credit), through disability premiums such as the Severe Disability Premium, and for children through the disability element of Child Tax Credit.

It is important to note that this chapter addresses reductions to the amount of support that eligible claimants receive, but this is only one of two important kinds of change to support for those affected by sickness or disability. The second is changes to the application and claims process. While there is significant overlap with the issues discussed here (since many of the changes to the application and claims process have been designed in order to reduce claimant numbers), we discuss this separately in Chapter 15.

About Employment and Support Allowance and 'limited capability for work' in Universal Credit

When ESA was initially introduced, three different groups of claimants received three different levels of support. The assessment group received a rate equivalent to what the claimant would receive on Jobseeker's Allowance (JSA) without any additional disability-related enhancements.

Following the assessment, different levels of additional support were made depending on whether they were placed in the work-related activity group (WRAG) or the support group. The details of this decision-making process are discussed later, in Chapter 15, but the principle was that those found to have 'limited capability for work' (their disablement being such that it would not be reasonable to require them to move into work immediately, but who would be able to undertake some training or other work-related activities) were placed in the WRAG. Those who have both 'limited capability for work *and* work-related activity' (who it would not be reasonable to require either to work or to undertake work-related activities) were placed in the support group.

If the claimant was placed in the WRAG, then, on top of their 'personal allowance', they received an additional top up worth around £29 per week (in 2015/16), known as the 'work-related activity component'. If they were placed in the support group, the addition (the 'support component') was higher – around £36 per week in 2015. However, in addition, claimants in the support group could also receive what is known as the Enhanced Disability Premium – a top up on their means-tested entitlement worth £16 per week – taking their overall addition over JSA rates to around £52 per week.[1]

Significantly, the personal allowance for under-25s found to have limited capability for work or for work-related activity was paid at the older person's rate (£73 rather than the £58 paid to most under-25s).

The structure of ESA was intended to be reflected in Universal Credit, where claimants may receive a standard allowance with or without a 'limited capability for work' element (equivalent to the 'work-related activity component' or a 'limited capability for work-related activity' element, equivalent to the support component). However, and as discussed later in this chapter, it was decided that under Universal Credit, young claimants with limited capability for work would no longer be exempt from the young person's rate of personal allowance.

Changes to Employment and Support Allowance entitlements – removal of the 'work-related activity' component

In 2016, despite strong opposition from the House of Lords, the Welfare Reform Act removed the work-related activity component (and Universal Credit equivalent) for future claimants. The reasoning given was that this would help 'remove financial incentives that could otherwise discourage claimants from taking steps back to work'.[2]

This change cuts support both for ESA claimants in the WRAG and Universal Credit claimants with 'limited capability for work'. In the future, this group will receive no additional support compared to those in receipt of JSA.

It is increasingly becoming the case that claimants with limited capability for work in the WRAG aren't seen as 'properly' sick or disabled at all. Not only do this group face significant work requirements, and have increasingly faced sanctions for not fulfilling them, but in addition, they may no longer receive any additional financial support on account of their condition.

Just two days before replacing Iain Duncan Smith as Work and Pensions Secretary, Stephen Crabb posted the following on his Facebook page, justifying his support for removal of the ESA work-related activity component:

> Any disabled person who is unable to work due to ill health or disability is in the support group of ESA. They are wholly unaffected by the change, as only those who are fit to work and actively seeking work are included in the work-related activity group.[3]

Although the comment was later corrected, this myth, that people in the WRAG are 'fit to work', has been heavily perpetuated in the media.

This has been a gradual creep – bit by bit, the distinction between the WRAG of ESA and the support group has been made larger, and the difference from those in receipt of JSA made smaller and smaller.

The impact of removing the work–related activity component on in–work support in Universal Credit

As mentioned, the removal of the ESA 'work-related activity component' is carried through into Universal Credit by removing the 'limited capability for work' element of the new benefit. There is a significant difference between removal of the two. In the old system, additional support for disabled people who are in work of 16 hours or more is not provided through ESA (which, as discussed in Chapter 6, is not paid to full-time working claimants) but through *an extra element in their Working Tax Credit* – the 'disabled worker' element, worth nearly £60 a week. This is in recognition that a disabled person who is working is likely to face additional extra costs of work that non-disabled colleagues will not.

However, under Universal Credit, because of the removal of the distinction between in- and out-of-work benefits, the 'limited capability for work' element can continue to be paid as a claimant moves into work – so long as they continue to be found to have 'limited capability for work' under a work capability assessment. This helps replace the disabled worker element of Working Tax Credit, by providing crucial additional in-work support for disabled people.

The result therefore of cutting the 'limited capability for work' element in Universal Credit is to reduce by about £30 a week the entitlement of disabled people who would qualify for the 'limited capability for work' group *both in and out of work*. The Department for Work and Pensions (DWP) itself doesn't appear to understand the impact of this measure – suggesting in the impact assessment of this change that removal of the Universal Credit 'limited capability for work' element would increase the difference between out-of-work support provision and that provided in work.[4]

The removal of this element of Universal Credit is a cut in sickness and disability support levels for working claimants – but with an underlying rationale that this will help to boost employment rates among exactly this group! It will not be a surprise if future statistics indicate this has not succeeded in meeting this goal. In-work disability support under Universal Credit is further discussed in Chapter 13.

While there has been some limited increase in the proportion of disabled people in employment in recent years, the proportion of non-disabled people in employment has also increased. The success of disability employment policy might be considered by looking at changes over time in the difference between disabled and non-disabled people in employment – the 'disability employment gap'. While the government has a stated ambition of halving the disability employment gap,[5] a recent review of this gap found that following a gradual decline from 2000 to 2010, there has been limited change since then.[6]

The reality is that the government's agenda to close the disability employment gap is being undermined by cuts to welfare provision for in-work claimants – particularly those introduced as Universal Credit is rolled out. Rather than properly supporting disabled workers, the government has sought to rely on a combination of poorly targeted cuts to entitlement, along with punitive sanctions, in order to get sick and disabled people back into work. (The use of these sanctions on sickness benefit claimants is further discussed in Chapter 17.)

Time limiting of contribution-based Employment and Support Allowance

A further example of the increasing distinction between ESA claimants in the WRAG and the support group is the decision to time limit contribution-based ESA to one year, for claimants in the WRAG.

Prior to 2012, those who had paid their National Insurance Contributions were entitled to continue to receive contribution-based sickness benefits indefinitely. It was a genuine form of insurance – an assumption that having paid in, when claimants needed support, they would get this back for as long as was needed. As noted in Chapter 2, William Beveridge himself had said it would be wrong to time limit insurance-based entitlements.

This change meant that after a year of entitlement, claimants would either be moved onto income-based ESA, or if their partner's work or household savings meant that they did not meet the stringent means test for this, lose entitlement to support altogether. Those in the support group for ESA were excluded from this change. The government estimated that around 700,000 claimants would be affected by this change up to 2015-16, with around 40% of them losing their ESA entitlement altogether.[7]

In February 2012, there were 2.41 million claimants of out-of-work sickness benefits[8] – by February 2013 this had fallen to 2.29 million, a fall of 120,000 across the course of the year. This fall in claimants cannot be entirely attributed to the loss of contribution-based ESA – the ESA reassessments (discussed in Chapter 15) were happening at the same time – but a very significant proportion of this is down to this change.[9]

The loss of the 'work-related activity component', and the time limiting of contribution-based ESA, are not the only cuts in support that the government delivered for ESA claimants. In particular, a number of hidden changes were made in the transition across to Universal Credit. One (already mentioned) is the reduction in personal allowances for young sick or disabled people. Another absolutely critical change is the removal of the Severe Disability Premium.

Cuts to support for sick and disabled young people under Universal Credit

In the last chapter we saw how under the old benefits system young parents receive the higher over-25s rate of personal allowance for out-of-work benefits such as JSA – meaning that they typically receive about £15 per week more for their personal needs than equivalent young people without children. We saw how following the move onto Universal Credit they will lose this higher rate – costing them the equivalent of around £780 per year. Similarly, young ESA claimants also receive the higher rate of personal allowance. As with young parents, a rather hidden cut means that under Universal Credit this reduces by £15 per week until they reach the age of 25.

Severe Disability Premium

The Severe Disability Premium is an additional amount added to a claimant's ESA entitlement where they, first, receive at least the mid-rate care component of Disability Living Allowance (DLA) (or equivalent within the Personal Independence Payment [PIP]), and second, don't have a non-disabled carer to look after them.[10] Universal Credit scraps the Severe Disability Premium outright. This is not a small amount of money – it is worth nearly £62 per week, or more than £3,200 per year.

The removal of this Premium is one of the most unfair and under-recognised benefit cuts introduced in recent years. It is paid to some of the most socially excluded sick and disabled people in society. Many use the SDP to pay for additional private care they couldn't otherwise afford – for example, for help with getting to the shops once a week, or for additional help with cleaning their home. Since it is only paid to those without carers, for many claimants it is a lifeline, enabling them to stay in social contact, and to afford a decent standard of care.

When the government introduced this change, it was justified on the basis that these costs should be covered through social care services, despite social care provision already being inadequate to meet the additional needs of many people affected by disabilities. Of respondents to one survey who would be eligible for the Premium, only 13% were receiving two hours or more of support each week from an outside agency.[11]

When the SDP was scrapped, no additional funding was made available to local authorities to pick up the pieces. At a time when local authority budgets are under severe pressure, there is no evidence whatsoever that they are likely to be able to deal with the additional demand caused by loss of this provision.

Research by Citizens Advice and The Children's Society[12] asked claimants who would be entitled to receive the Severe Disability Premium what the likely impact of a £50 reduction in benefit entitlement would be on their lives. The responses were extreme, but perhaps not surprising. For those eligible, 83% said a reduction in benefit levels of this amount would mean they would have to cut back on food, and 80% said they would have to cut the amount they spent on heating. One claimant said:

> 'I'd probably be out on the streets homeless! I already eat the most basic of diets and am very frugal with heating and electricity. I struggle to keep warm in winter and have to wrap up in extra clothes and blankets or stay in bed to keep warm. I either eat a meal or have some heating on. I can't afford both.'

Others said that a change like this would cut them off from all social engagement, or even mean that they had to move into residential care. Several comments reflected the level of desperation experienced by many:

> 'I've thought about suicide as my quality of life has been so much reduced already (I've lost my job, friends and colleagues, exercise, social activities, holidays, life's little luxuries, I'm in pain every day etc etc). There has to be a point beyond which it's just not worth trying to stay alive – I can't imagine how someone in my situation would cope with less.'

Overall impact of Employment and Support Allowance and Universal Credit 'limited capability for work' changes

The overall impact of changes to support for sick and disabled claimants under Universal Credit could be truly tremendous.

For example, Luke is a young ESA claimant. He is 23 years old and as a result of severe fatigue and vision problems caused by Multiple Sclerosis, is found to have 'limited capability for work'. He also receives the daily living component of the PIP, as he needs help with his care needs on a regular basis, including help with cooking and cleaning, which he struggles to manage on his own.

Since he doesn't have a carer, under the old system, Luke receives the Severe Disability Premium on his ESA entitlement.

In total, Luke's ESA entitlement is comprised of a work allowance of £73 per week, a work-related activity component of £29 per week, and a Severe Disability Premium of £62.

A new claimant for Universal Credit, in the same position, would receive a lower personal allowance of £58 (the young person's rate), no work–related activity component (since this does not exist for new claimants) and no Severe Disability Premium. In total, their Universal Credit equivalent to their ESA entitlement is cut by *nearly two-thirds* – down from £164, to just £58 per week (see Table 10.1).

Table 10.1: Employment and Support Allowance/ Universal Credit comparison, for under-25-year-old with limited capability for work, and receiving the SDP on their ESA entitlement (2017 rates, weekly entitlements)

	Employment and Support Allowance	Universal Credit	Reason for change
Personal allowance	£73	£58	Removal of exemption from young person's rate of personal allowance for Universal Credit claimants with limited capability for work
Work-related activity/limited capability for work component	£29	£0	Removal of the limited capability for work component of Universal Credit
Severe Disability Premium	£62	£0	Scrapping of the Severe Disability Premium
Total	**£164**	**£58**	

Conclusion

Despite promises that they have *no reason to be fearful*,[13] sick and disabled claimants have been among the hardest hit by reform of the welfare system.

Many of the changes described in this chapter particularly apply to those considered to have limited capability for work, but who are found to have some capacity to undertake training and other activities to prepare for moving back into the workplace (and to children with a similar level of disability).

Increasingly, support for this group has become little different to that for JSA claimants (and indeed, more rigorous work-related requirements, and a more active sanctions regime focused on this group – as described in Chapter 17 – have exemplified a move in that direction too). They are seen as 'kind of' sick, but pretty much ready to move back into work.

Despite the focus on getting this group back into work, cuts under Universal Credit have also significantly reduced the amount of support provided to help them *when they are working*. Encouragement to get this group working appears to have moved from carrot to stick – from providing extra help in work, to providing less help out of work, and a more punitive regime to move them into employment – we look at what a fairer, alternative, settlement for this group might look like in later chapters.

However, as mentioned at the start of this chapter, reductions in support for those claiming these sickness benefits only tell half the story. Changes to application and assessment processes have made it harder for many sick and disabled people to receive support in the first place. We address this crucial issue later, in Chapter 15.

11

Triple locked?
Benefits for pensioners

Unlike many other benefits, the State Pension and Pension Credit have not been affected by the three-year 1% cap on increases in benefit rates, nor the four-year freeze on entitlements that has followed. In fact, the reverse is true, with increases in the Basic State Pension. Instead of making the uprating rules less generous, the decision was made to make them significantly more so – through the introduction of a so-called 'triple lock'.

Prior to 2010, the Basic State Pension was increased in line with the higher of increases in prices or 2.5%, although in 2007, the Labour government made a legislative commitment to restore the earnings link that had last been in place in the 1970s.[1] By the 2010 election, the Conservatives had announced that they would seek to increase the State Pension if they gained power. The Liberal Democrats went one step further by suggesting a 'triple lock' that would increase the State Pension with increases in earnings, prices or by 2.5% – whichever was the highest.[2]

The coalition agreement confirmed that the government would put in place this triple lock, and it was announced in the emergency budget after the election, in June 2010. At the same time as making major cuts to provision for working-age claimants, the then Chancellor George Osborne said: 'With this coalition government pensioners will have the income to live with dignity in retirement.'[3]

Pension Credit (support for low-income pensioners) has not been subject to the triple lock. Typically, the main part of the benefit has been increased in line with earnings, but notably for 2011 (and for most years since then), it has been increased in line with the cash increase in the Basic State Pension. As the former Chancellor put it in 2010:

> ... To ensure the lowest income pensioners benefit from the triple guarantee, the standard minimum income guarantee in Pension Credit will increase in April 2011 by the cash rise in a full Basic State Pension.[4]

This is slightly disingenuous – while the cash increases did mean that low-income pensioners kept the cash rise in the State Pension, the higher value of Pension Credit means that (as shown below) the percentage rise is significantly below that of the triple lock. Pension Credit has, however, still gone up significantly faster than most other benefits and Tax Credits.

Over time Pension Credit is likely to become less significant as a benefit as a result of changes brought in with the 'new' State Pension' (described in Chapter 5). Under the 'old' State Pension, levels of entitlement are significantly lower than Pension Credit rates. As a result, a pensioner living on a State Pension with no other income would receive a 'top up' of Pension Credit to take their entitlement to the Pension Credit rate. (It is worth noting that this means that for many of the lowest-income single pensioners, incomes have never been 'triple locked', because the relevant rate of entitlement was Pension Credit, even if they also received the Basic State Pension.)

For example, Jim is a 67-year-old single pensioner entitled to the Basic State Pension at the full rate of £122, but has no additional pension or other income. Since Pension Credit guarantees his minimum entitlement to be £159, he receives a Pension Credit 'top up' of £37 per week.

This is not the case with the 'new' State Pension – for those eligible, the maximum level of entitlement (in 2017) is the same as the Pension Credit rate. This means that a single pensioner in receipt of the new State Pension at the maximum rate would receive no additional Pension Credit top up.

Of course, there will still be older people for whom Pension Credit will remain an important entitlement (single people not entitled to receive the State Pension in full, or couples where only one partner is entitled to a full State Pension), but over time, Pension Credit numbers are likely to decline. However, this process will be slow, since only those reaching pension age after April 2016 will receive the new State Pension – existing pensioners will remain on the old system.

Figure 11.1 shows the relative increases in the values of different benefits between 2010 and 2016. As can be seen, the Basic State Pension has risen substantially faster than other benefits over the last six years – rising by nearly a quarter over its 2010 amount. It also increased faster than costs of living,[5] which have risen by around 19% over the same period.

The value of personal allowances for Jobseeker's Allowance (JSA) has fallen in value at a similar rate to the rise in the value of the State Pension, rising by less than 12% in a period when prices have risen around one-and-a-half times as fast.

Child Benefit languishes at the bottom, having risen by just 2% in the last six years, including several years of being frozen altogether. It has risen at less than one-eleventh of the rate at which the Basic State Pension has risen.

Yet despite this, while in 2015 the Conservative government committed to a further four-year freeze on most benefits and Tax Credits, it was decided that the State Pension would continue to be 'triple locked' up to the end of the decade, since 'pensioners have paid into the system throughout their working lives, and are the group least able to increase their income in response to welfare reform.'[6] In their 2017 election manifesto, the Conservatives pledged to end the triple lock from 2020 – instead promising a 'double lock', which removes the commitment to uprate pensions by 2.5%, if this is exceeded by neither earnings nor inflation.[7] Writing in 2017, the future of the triple lock from 2020 still appears uncertain – but it seems likely that it will continue until at least the end of the decade.

The growth in pensioner entitlements compared to those for working-age households has been a trend for some time. Analysis from the Institute for Fiscal Studies (IFS) shows that at the end of the 1980s, once household composition is accounted for, average

Figure 11.1: Percentage increase in the cash value of the Basic State Pension, Pension Credit guarantee, Jobseeker's Allowance and Child Benefit, 2010-16

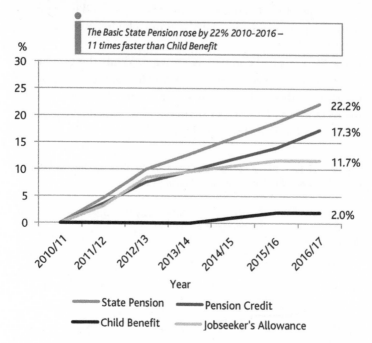

pensioner incomes were barely more than two-thirds the rate of average non-pensioner incomes. By the new millennium, this had increased to 85% of average non-pensioner incomes, and has now *overtaken* average working-age incomes. The head of the IFS, Paul Johnson, noted that

> There's been an amazing 30 years or so where pensioner incomes have risen relative to non-pensioner incomes.... In many ways it has been a triumph.[8]

It *has* been a triumph. Unsurprisingly, when the average pensioner was living on only two-thirds of what non-pensioners were, pensioner poverty was astonishingly high. It was right to create and to invest in Pension Credit through the 2000s in order to alleviate this.

As official statistics show, in 1994 27% of pensioners lived in poverty. While this was still less than the proportion of children living in poverty, it was more than the average, and much more than the proportion of adults without children who lived in poverty.

By 2013 this had completely changed. While the proportion of children in poverty had gradually fallen, and the proportion of adults without children living in poverty had slowly risen, the proportion of pensioners living in poverty had fallen rapidly – down to less than 15% (see Figure 11.2).

Figure 11.2: Percentage of individuals in poverty (living on less than 60% of median household income) after housing costs

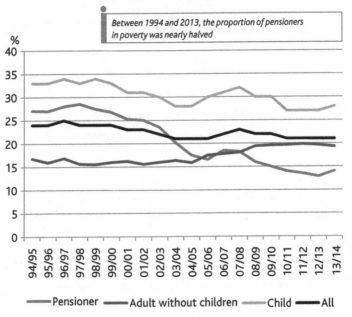

This is a great achievement, but the IFS has been equally right to call for the triple lock to be reconsidered.[9] There are three main reasons for this. First, at a time when pensioner incomes are rising faster than costs of living, but support for families with children is falling rapidly, the measure appears inequitable. As we will see later, in Chapter 19, it is also the case that many low-income older people also miss out on support through the triple lock by being redefined as working-age claimants.

Second, since many low-income pensioners do not benefit from the value of the State Pension rather than Pension Credit, the triple lock of the State Pension is not a good (and certainly not cost-effective) mechanism for alleviating pensioner poverty. In fact, analysis from the IFS indicates that pensioner poverty rates will increase by around half a million between 2010 and 2020 (from 1.4 million pensioners living in poverty in 2010 to 1.9 million in 2020).[10]

Third, the triple lock is also a very expensive policy. The original 2010 budget forecast its cost to be £450 million per year by 2014-15. (It is worth noting that the line in the 2010 budget announcing the triple guarantee on pensions was immediately preceded by savings from a three-year freeze on Child Benefit.) By 2015, it had become clear that this was an enormous miscalculation. The Office for Budget Responsibility (OBR) found that by that year, it was expected to cost £2.9 billion[11] – over five times more than it was originally expected to.

The OBR expected these costs to continue to grow in the following years, both in 2015-16 and in 2016-17. It is reasonable to expect the costs to grow considerably further by the end of the decade.

At the end of 2015, the Government Actuary's Department produced a paper on the current and ongoing costs of the triple lock that was accidentally put online and was then taken down very shortly afterwards – with the Treasury saying it had been an internal discussion paper only, and had been published by mistake by the IT department. Happily, 'Money Box' presenter Paul Lewis published a copy of the paper on his blog site, so it remains in the public domain.[12] It indicates that the cost of the triple lock over increasing the State Pension in line with earnings was £6 billion per year in 2015/16.

This is a significant factor contributing to overall rises in the cost of the benefits system. While real spending on benefits for people of working age and children is expected to fall by around £7 billion per year by 2020 compared to 2010, these savings are expected to be almost completely offset by increased spending on pensioners rising by around £11 billion.

This means that overall, where in 2010 pensioner benefits accounted for 50% of overall benefits spending, by 2020 this is expected to increase to 56%. While in previous years some of this increased expenditure may have been the result of an increasing number of pensioners, this doesn't appear to be the case in coming years, with the total number of people receiving a State Pension expected to fall by more than 300,000 between 2015 and 2020 (we will come on to why this is the case later, in Chapter 19).

Protections to other benefits for pensioners

Pensioners have also been protected from a number of welfare reforms affecting working-age claimants.

Pensioners living in social rented accommodation have been protected from the Bedroom Tax (so won't see a reduction in their maximum Housing Benefit entitlement if they have 'spare bedrooms' in their home). It has been estimated that this exemption costs in the region of £400 million per year;[13] however, in future, some mixed age couples (where one is a pensioner but the other is not) may not be exempt. The issue of mixed age couples and Universal Credit is further discussed in Chapter 19.

Second, when Council Tax Benefit was localised, councils were instructed that, despite having to find overall 10% savings from the Council Tax Benefit bill, pensioners would need to be protected. The IFS found that after providing this protection for pensioners, the actual cut to funding for Council Tax Benefit for working-age claimants was around 19% – although this varied depending on the local pensioner population. One in ten councils saw funding for Council Tax Benefit for people of working age cut by more than a quarter.[14]

Also, unlike Disability Living Allowance (DLA), Attendance Allowance (a disability benefit for older people) wasn't reformed with the intention of reducing the number of claimants.

However, low-income pensioners are not protected from every cut in support. For example, pensioners living in private rented accommodation may still face reductions in Local Housing Allowance (LHA) rates (as discussed earlier, in Chapters 7 and

8). In addition, pensioners looking after children are likely to receive Child Benefit and Child Tax Credit – in both cases, cuts to support will still be passed on to pensioner households.

Finally, it is worth mentioning that one of the main 'protections' provided by Pension Credit is not financial – it is the exclusion from the labour market requirements placed on working-age benefit claimants. As these requirements become more stringent, and the application of sanctions more punitive, the exemption from them becomes all the more important to protect the health and wellbeing of older people. We discuss the issue of older people facing labour market requirements later, in Chapter 19.

Conclusion

Financial support for pensioners through the benefits system tends to be significantly more generous than support for equivalent households of working age. It is right that people are guaranteed a decent standard of living in retirement if they don't have other income to rely on. It is also right that even if people do have an independent income that they can draw on, if they paid their contributions, they are able to benefit from this through the State Pension.

However, the differences can seem stark at times. For example, a single man in his early sixties, having worked all his adult life, may have become too sick to continue. Until he reaches Pension Credit age, he may expect to claim Employment and Support Allowance (ESA) – and if placed in the work-related activity group (WRAG), receive benefit at a rate of £73 per week (plus support with his rent through Housing Benefit) – no higher than he would on JSA.[15] He will be expected to undertake work-related activity, and may face sanctions if he doesn't comply.

As soon as he reaches Pension Credit age, he can expect to receive a minimum income of £159, in addition to help through Housing Benefit (including, as previously noted, exclusion from the Bedroom Tax if he is living in social rented housing). Perhaps even more important than the money, he will be allowed to retire and no longer face labour market requirements.

It hasn't always been this way; as we have seen, as recently as the mid-1990s, poverty rates among pensioners were well above average (although notably still lower than for children). This is no longer the case – the focus on improving pensioner incomes has been a huge success.

In addition, although the amount of support provided to pensioners is generous (compared to benefits for those of working age) and is increasing, the group of people entitled to receive it is becoming ever more restricted. In particular, low-income older people are seeing their effective retirement age increase rapidly as a result of changes to the age of entitlement for Pension Credit. We consider this issue in more detail in Chapter 19.

In the context of significantly reduced pensioner poverty, considerably higher entitlements for pensioners than for those of working age and rapidly falling support for those of working age and children (and with people on a low income spending an increasing proportion of their lives in this 'working age' group) it is right to question whether to continue a policy like the triple lock.

And yet, turning back from the triple lock has real risks as well. As former Pensions Minister Steve Webb rightly pointed out in an article in *The Telegraph* in 2015 defending the policy, 'We have the chance to make sure that old age is no longer synonymous with poverty. We must resist the siren voices who would have us turn back just as we are starting to win that battle.'[16]

However, the triple lock is having little success in tackling pensioner poverty, with poverty among the elderly expected to *rise* between 2010 and 2020.

In Part VI we return to how we can build a benefits policy for older people that is both fairer than the current direction of travel, and doesn't risk a return to the soaring pensioner poverty rates we saw not so long ago.

12

Welfare that works?
The 'old' system

If there is one image that sums up contemporary attitudes to welfare more than any other, it is surely that of the layabout slob, sprawling on the sofa, can of beer in hand and vacant eyes fixed on daytime TV – living a 'life on benefits'.

In fact, so compelling do some find this image, that following the decision to cap annual increases in benefits and Tax Credits to just 1%, the Conservative Party decided to launch an online campaign. It asked the viewer who they thought the government should be giving more support to: 'hard working families' or 'people who won't work' – alongside a picture of our iconic layabout, complete with sofa (although admittedly in this instance without a beer can).[1]

In this vision, the 'slob' is taking it easy, sleeping while the hard working schmuck gets up early, with only their sense of 'doing the right thing' to warm them as they head to work. The scene may seem clichéd, but it is built on a story that goes to the heart of public understanding of the benefits system – that those 'on benefits' are (by definition) out of work. It is frankly a myth, and one so pervasive that even those receiving state welfare often don't see themselves as 'on benefits'.

This chapter and the next explore how the benefits system works for the millions of low- to middle-income working families who receive support through it. This chapter looks at in-work benefits support under the 'old' (pre-Universal Credit) system. Chapter 13 then considers how Universal Credit changes provision for this group.

Working families living 'on benefits'

A while ago I spoke to one working mum, whose view of people 'on benefits' was, perhaps, pretty representative of a large number of people in the UK. She said that she felt that too much was paid in benefits, and more needed to be done to get those on benefits out to work. However, she also told me that she received Child Benefit and Child Tax Credit (most mums, and certainly those on low to middle incomes, do so). She was also getting Housing Benefit and (what was at that point) Council Tax Benefit.

So she received some benefits and Tax Credits, but didn't view herself as 'on benefits' – does this matter? Such expressions could be considered an insignificant semantic tic, a distinction between being 'on' out-of-work benefits and 'receiving' in-work benefits.

But this nicety has found itself at the heart of key current social policy debates. When the government talk about benefits and Tax Credits, they often talk, like this mum, as if they mean out-of-work benefits – unemployment benefits like Jobseeker's Allowance (JSA) and sickness benefits like Employment and Support Allowance (ESA). But when they *cut* benefits, they cut them for all recipients – which means working as well as non-working households.

Take what former Chancellor George Osborne said about the Welfare Benefits Uprating Act 2013 that limited increases in benefit and Tax Credit payments to 1% for three years. He said this was about:

> ... being fair to the person who leaves home every morning to go out to work and sees their neighbour still asleep, living a life on benefits ... we have to have a welfare system that is fair to the working people who pay for it.[2]

The Conservative Party even produced a poster about the Labour Party's opposition to the Bill, which screamed 'Today Labour are voting to increase benefits by more than workers' wages'.[3]

Certainly the Act (as well as the four-year benefit freeze that followed) cut support for out-of-work benefits, but it also cut uprating on Housing Benefit, Child Benefit and Tax Credits, all of which are received by working people such as this mum. It even cut uprating on Working Tax Credit, which is *only* received by working households.

And it is not only minimum wage workers who are affected by this: around 40,000 soldiers, 150,000 primary school teachers and 300,000 nurses have been estimated to be affected by the change.[4]

Far from the Benefits Uprating Act providing fairness for working families facing sluggish earnings growth, it compounded the impact by hitting them with below-inflation increases in benefit payments.

The benefits system provides crucial support for working as well as non-working families, and cuts to support frequently harm those in work as much as (in some cases more than) those who are out of work. Below-inflationary benefit uprating has not been the only example of this – 21 cuts affecting working families were introduced in the 2010 emergency budget and Comprehensive Spending Review alone.[5] Since then there have been many more – including the aborted attempt to cut Tax Credit entitlements for working families in 2015 (which we will come back to in a moment).

Benefits and Tax Credits are crucial to supporting low-paid workers to have a not-too-far-off-decent standard of living and provide an incentive to work.

For example, Emma is a single parent, currently not working in order to look after her son. To make things simple, let's assume she has no other income or savings. She rents a two-bedroom flat privately, which costs £130 per week, and has a Council Tax bill of £20 per week.

Her current income, before she pays her rent and Council Tax, is £308 per week in benefits. Now suppose Emma finds a part-time job at her local supermarket. She works 16 hours per week and earns £120 (the minimum wage at the time of writing in 2017). She now has a total income of £379 per week. This is made up of her earnings, plus a combination of benefits and Tax Credits.

Notably, Emma is £71 per week better off in work than out of work, but this is only because she still receives much more in benefits and Tax Credits than she earns (£120 of earnings and £259 of benefits).

Her earnings on their own would be £188 per week (or nearly £10,000 per year) less than she receives through out-of-work benefits. They would not even be enough to cover her very modest rent.

Emma's benefits and Tax Credits are crucial to ensuring she is able to move into work and maintain a decent standard of living. This is not a life of luxury – her family is living on around £19,000 per year – but it is enough to just about get by.

However, the benefits of work as illustrated here aren't enormous – £71 per week in this case – and that's before we take into account the costs of taking on work. These costs, like childcare, work clothes and travel, can easily eat up much of that additional gain.

But the incentives to 'progress' in work can be even more hopeless. This is because, as discussed in Chapter 6, for each extra £1 that is earned, the worker may not only pay tax, but also see reductions in their benefit and Tax Credit entitlements.

In fact, for a worker in receipt of Tax Credits and Housing Benefit, each additional £1 they earn may incur deductions from tax and benefit reductions of up to 96p. This means that on working an additional hour at the new National Living Wage (currently £7.50 per hour) they may keep only 30p.

These sharp reductions in benefit payments are made in order to keep down the welfare bill, and to ensure that higher earning households aren't still receiving significant amounts of benefit payments. But rather than providing a fair welfare system that encourages people to move into work, this undermines work incentives.

In 2015, the government decided to make these reductions even sharper, by increasing the rate at which Tax Credits are withdrawn as earnings increase. In addition, the government also proposed reducing the level of earnings at which additional pay would start to affect Tax Credit entitlements.

It was these two proposals together that first started to reveal major cracks in the government's plans to cut benefits. For five years there had been some success in pretending that benefit cuts had been about delivering fairness for working families, but these measures could not be presented in this way.

Following pressure from the House of Lords and from Conservative backbench MPs,[6] the government backed down on these changes. In the 2015 Autumn Statement, the Chancellor agreed that, in the shorter term, the proposals in part would not go ahead as planned – although we will come on to how this was a postponement rather than withdrawal of the cut.

Despite this, it remains the case that many workers retain a meagre 4p in each additional £1 that they earn. To put this in context, the government decided to reduce the top rate of tax from 50p in the £1 to 45p, on the basis that a higher rate of tax was uncompetitive and would discourage the most talented people from doing business in the UK. It is not the purpose of this book to discuss whether a higher top rate of tax is uncompetitive, but this does raise questions about the effectiveness of taking 96p in each extra £1 earned from working benefit claimants.

The National Living Wage and Income Tax cuts

For the reasons outlined above, the problem of inadequate work incentives cannot be entirely solved by better pay.

The government announced the introduction of the National Living Wage with much fanfare in the Summer Budget 2015 (notably the same point at which major reductions in in-work support through the Tax Credit system were proposed). The proposal was that pay for over-25s would be set at a minimum of £7.20 per hour in April 2016, rising to £9 per hour by 2020. Endorsing the new proposals, former Prime Minister David Cameron said:

> By the end of the decade, it will reach at least £9 an hour. Combine that with an increase in the personal allowance to £12,500, and you can see the power of the modern Conservative Party's One Nation message. We back work. We promote well-paid work. We want you to keep more of your own money. That's

why we can say: we are the true party of working
people in Britain today.[7]

All good so far. The proposals were widely endorsed by left and
right alike. Indeed, for those working households not in receipt
of benefits or Tax Credits, the changes undoubtedly make a
real difference. Typically these are either working-age people
without children (where lower benefit entitlements may mean
they are not caught within the benefits system), and those on
the minimum wage who are living with a partner on a higher
rate of earnings, which take them out of the benefits system.

However, for the reasons discussed above, many of the working
families most in need of an income boost are likely to see the
least gain as a result of this pay rise. Sticking with our working
mum above, let's suppose Emma's employer decides to fast track
the National Living Wage rise promised by 2020 and pay Emma
£9 per hour. This would take her earnings up to £144 per week
– about £30 per week more than at present. However, not just
some, not even the majority, but *almost all* of Emma's additional
earnings are lost through deductions to her benefit entitlement.
Despite her employer deciding to pay Emma around £1.50 per
hour more than legally required, her actual income increases by
a little more than £2 per week.

This means that employers choosing to increase the earnings of
their lowest-paid workers are, in great part, providing subsidies
to the Exchequer, through savings from increased taxes and
reduced benefits.

Despite the increase in pay and reduction in benefits, Emma
still receives nearly £230 per week in benefits and Tax Credits.
This means that not only does she still receive some level of
benefit top up to her income, but she also receives approaching
twice as much in benefits as she does in wages.

A similar problem is true of increases in Income Tax personal
allowances (which set the amount that a worker can earn before
they start to pay tax). While Tax Credits are calculated on the
basis of income before tax (gross income) rather than income
after tax (net income), Housing Benefit and Council Tax
Reductions are not.

This means that any income gains from increases in personal allowances for Income Tax (as well as National Insurance) are treated as increases in income for the purposes of Housing Benefit and Council Tax Benefit.

Prior to the 2015 election, the Conservative Party made a manifesto commitment to raise the Income Tax personal allowance from £10,600 to £12,500 – an increase of £1,900 over five years.

The gains from this for a working person earning £12,500 per year *should be* relatively easy to calculate. By increasing the threshold, you take £1,900 of earnings out of the basic Income Tax band – basic Income Tax is charged at a rate of 20% of income that falls within the band, so the gain should be 20% of £1,900, or £380.

However, for those in receipt of Housing Benefit and Council Tax Reduction, the gain is not so simple. This £380 gain is treated as additional income for the purposes of Housing Benefit/Council Tax Reduction. Extra income for these benefits is deducted at a rate of 85%, leaving the claimant with 15% of their £380 – just £57 per year.

Increasing the Income Tax personal allowance threshold is extraordinarily costly; the £500 increase in the tax threshold introduced in 2017 alone (along with an increase in the higher rate tax threshold) is forecast to cost £9.5 billion over a four-year period.[8] The benefits of this for low–income working families are minimal.

The real gains go to those households with incomes too high to be in receipt of Housing Benefit and Council Tax Benefit. While many of these people are on relatively low levels of income (particularly where they are living in social housing, with lower levels of rent that take them out of Housing Benefit receipt at a lower income level), many earn considerably more. In fact, because of the way Income Tax bandings work, unless the higher rate tax threshold is reduced in order to claw back the savings, the full £380 gain is even kept by most higher rate taxpayers. In the 2016 budget, when increasing the Income Tax threshold, the Chancellor decided to *increase* rather than reduce the higher rate tax threshold. This means that gains that would not be seen by working families on the lowest incomes would be the greatest for those on some of the highest.

This problem becomes more widespread under Universal Credit, as discussed in the following chapter.

There is a simple solution to this problem, ensuring that any gains from cuts in Income Tax payments are passed on to those low-income earners who need them the most – increase the amount people can earn before additional pay starts to affect their benefit, in line with any increases in personal allowances for taxation. This measure would mean that any gains from reduced Income Tax liabilities are ignored for the purposes of benefits and Tax Credits.

However, this is not the approach this government has taken; in fact, it has gone in exactly the opposite direction, deciding to cut work allowances while increasing Income Tax thresholds. It was only pressure from the government's own backbenches that prevented this going ahead within the Tax Credits system, and, as we will see in the following chapter, cuts to work allowances are still being pursued within Universal Credit.

However, there is a second reason why increasing pay, or reducing Income Tax liabilities, is not sufficient to abolish the need for in-work benefits – neither of these reflects family size. For a single person with no dependents, £144 per week – as Emma would earn working 16 hours per week on £9 per hour – may be enough to just about scrape by on. For a couple with three children, including one with a disability, it is a million miles away from being sufficient. Unless you introduced a pay regime that reflected household size in pay (a radical change, which would surely be impossible to implement in practice), then, as discussed in Chapter 3, pay increases can never really reflect variations in household need.

Making work pay and childcare costs

Given the high costs many families with young children face for childcare, it is unsurprising that childcare costs are often seen as a major barrier to 'making work pay'.

For many families, the costs of childcare can be a real barrier to moving into, and progressing in, work. However, as we saw in Chapter 6, for some working families on the lowest levels of incomes, up to 96% of childcare costs can be covered through the benefits and Tax Credits system – with 70% covered through Tax Credits and the other 26% through childcare costs being disregarded for Housing Benefit and Council Tax Reduction. Overall this means that for a family facing childcare costs of £100 per week, up to £96 of this may be covered through additional payments of benefits and Tax Credits.

This is not to say that parents necessarily *know* that this is the amount of support available. Many will believe that they can get 70% of their childcare costs covered through Working Tax Credit, but be unaware of the additional support they may receive through Housing Benefit and Council Tax Reduction. Even many experts are unaware of the additional support with childcare costs offered through the childcare cost disregard in Housing Benefit.

For many such families, it may be that a *lack of information* about the level of support with childcare costs available presents more of a disincentive to move into and progress in work than the actual childcare costs.

Working people living in poverty

Given how difficult it can be to increase the incomes of the lowest-income working families, it is perhaps unsurprising that in-work poverty has presented a deeply intractable problem. Back in 1997, just under four in ten people living in poverty were in working households. The latest statistics (for 2015) show this has now risen to well over half of all people in poverty. This rise is particularly stark when you consider that those in non-working households include not only unemployed people, but also pensioners and those who are not working as a result of sickness or disability.

This represents a total of more than 7 million people in poverty living in working families – 2 million more than 15 years ago.[9] And this is probably a significant underestimate, since calculations of whether a household lives above or below the poverty line do not take into account additional costs of working mentioned previously, such as childcare and travel costs. For too many low-income households a move into work does not result in a move out of poverty.

Conclusion

With a rising proportion of those in poverty living in working households, while millions of low-income working families receive next to nothing for endless hours of work, serious change is needed.

It is right that we encourage employers to pay more to the very worst-off families, but it is not right that so little of this extra pay ends up in the pockets of their workers. There are approaches that could be taken to address this – for example, increasing work allowances for benefits in line with increases in the National Living Wage (and with any increases in personal allowances for Income Tax). This, and other changes that could help to make sure work pays, are discussed in more detail in Part VI.

However, it isn't just policy change that is needed. We need to stop talking about benefits and Tax Credits as if only those out of work receive them. In fact, at the moment this may be downright dangerous. If we are to have a reasonable conversation about the rights and wrongs of the benefits system, we need to understand who the claimants are. This doesn't mean that we should never cut benefits or Tax Credits regardless of circumstances, but that they should not be cut without recognising the impact on *all* those affected.

The government has not entirely ignored the problems of work incentives for the lowest-income working families. A key intention of the new Universal Credit being gradually introduced across the UK is to make work pay for lower-income families. How it attempts to do so, and how well it is succeeding, are the subjects of the next chapter.

13

Welfare that works?
Universal Credit

Recent governments have not been entirely blind to the problems of making work pay; indeed, the new Universal Credit system was born out of a desire to deal with this problem.

Shortly after the election of the coalition government in 2010, the *Universal Credit: Welfare that works* White Paper was published. In his Foreword, the then newly appointed Secretary of State for Work and Pensions, Iain Duncan Smith, wrote:

> Universal Credit will mean that people will be consistently and transparently better off for each hour they work and every pound they earn. It will cut through the complexity of the existing benefit system to make it easier for people to get the help they need, when they need it.... Our reforms put work, whether full time, part time or just a few hours per week, at the centre of our welfare system. As such it extends a ladder of opportunity to those who have previously been excluded or marginalised from the world of work.[1]

The White Paper went on to (rightly) highlight that:

> Currently, when combined with tax and National Insurance payments, the withdrawal of Tax Credits, Housing Benefit and Council Tax Benefit can lead to Marginal Deduction Rates which are nearly 96 per cent, much higher than the highest rate of Income

Tax. The current system incentivises many people to work no more or less than the minimum hours required to qualify for Working Tax Credit. This fails to reflect the flexible working pattern that modern employers and individuals need.

There is no question that what the White Paper says is absolutely right. The system provides such poor work incentives that – while there is normally some level of gain on first moving into employment – some working people effectively see no incentive at all to work longer and earn more. The new system fundamentally reforms the way that benefits respond to people as they move into work – a necessary and overdue measure.

The question is, does Universal Credit really represent 'welfare that works?'

How does Universal Credit work for working claimants?

As outlined in Chapter 6, in the old system there is a fundamental separation of out-of-work benefits (such as Jobseeker's Allowance [JSA] and Employment and Support Allowance [ESA]) and in-work support.

Once a claimant works (normally) 16 hours per week, the household loses their entitlement to out-of-work support. Instead, support is received through benefits that apply both in and out of work (such as Housing Benefit and Child Tax Credit), with additional support provided through Working Tax Credit. Under Universal Credit, this separation is reduced. For many claimants, instead of additional payments of in-work support being made at 16 hours per week, *all payments will be made both in and out of work, and reduced gradually as earnings increase.*

In order to do so, Universal Credit will subsume a number of current benefits and Tax Credits into one payment. These include Child Tax Credit and Working Tax Credit, Housing Benefit, income-based ESA, income-based JSA and Income Support.

An individual household will have a maximum entitlement to support. Deductions from this maximum entitlement will be made on account of any household earnings in excess of the household's 'work allowance'. The level of the work allowance will depend on the composition of the household, and whether or not their claim includes support with housing costs.

In terms of promoting work incentives, Universal Credit does a number of good things:

First, the rate at which Universal Credit will be withdrawn is set at 63% of net earnings. This sounds like a lot, and it is – it means that (above the relevant level of the earnings disregard) nearly two-thirds of any income after tax is deducted from the claimant's Universal Credit entitlement. Once you factor in Income Tax and National Insurance (for those earning enough to pay them) this goes up to 75% – three-quarters of any additional earnings.

However, when compared to the old rate of deductions highlighted in the last chapter, it can seem relatively generous.[2] And as will be seen, this is threatened by the way Council Tax Benefit is treated and because of the potential interaction with passported benefits such as free school meals.

Second, people working small numbers of hours per week no longer face pound for pound deductions of their earnings from their out-of-work benefit entitlement. This is a key improvement under Universal Credit. Instead, claimants undertaking small amounts of paid work either keep the entirety of their Universal Credit entitlement (below the level of their work allowance), or they see it reduce at a rate of 63p in the £1.

In addition, help with childcare costs can be claimed by parents working less than 16 hours per week. This is a significant change from the old system, where help with childcare costs through the benefits and Tax Credits system is only provided to single parents working 16 hours or more per week (or couples where both partners are working at least 16 hours).

Third, the income 'bump' caused by undertaking sufficient work to gain entitlement to Working Tax Credit no longer exists. Under the old system (as we have seen), for many claimants there is very little benefit in doing small amounts of paid work because earnings are lost almost in entirety through reduced benefit entitlement. Once they move into 'full-time paid work' (the definition of which, as set out in Chapter 6, varies depending on the household's circumstances), claimants will stop receiving any out-of-work benefit entitlement, but many will start to receive Working Tax Credit, which provides a big income boost. However, working *more* hours than required to gain Working Tax Credit entitlement may provide little additional income (as we have seen, in some cases the combination of different deductions from additional earnings for this group may mean that they keep as little as 4p from each extra £1 they earn). For this reason, for many claimants there is a strong incentive to work *exactly* enough hours to gain entitlement to Working Tax Credit.

This is a mixed blessing. While the Working Tax Credit threshold creates 'inflexibility' in the labour market, receiving an income boost can have work incentive benefits, since it provides a point at which passported benefits can be withdrawn without causing claimants a significant loss of income on earning more (we come on to this issue in more detail in a moment).

Finally, for all its faults, Universal Credit is a simpler system in some respects. Claimants have to claim fewer benefits, so, for example, rather than making separate claims for Tax Credits, Housing Benefit and income-based JSA, only one claim is needed for Universal Credit. Claimants also do not change between benefits when they move to working over 16 hours per week; instead, their Universal Credit claim is amended (although, as we have discussed in previous chapters, the interaction with contribution-based benefits that remain outside of the Universal Credit system can create considerable additional complexity).

The government believes that a simpler system will lead to higher benefit take-up under Universal Credit. Modelling estimates for Universal Credit assume that of those taking up some but not all of their current benefit entitlement, 100% will take up their full entitlement to Universal Credit, and that of those taking up none of their current benefit entitlement under the old system, 50% will take up their entitlement to Universal Credit.[3] This is a big claim, and sadly, is probably rather over-optimistic, since the advantages of a simpler benefits system have been undermined by problems with delivery.

Although it does have notable advantages, Universal Credit is far, far from being a perfect system from the perspective of supporting working claimants.

'Taper rates' under Universal Credit

Universal Credit does succeed in significantly reducing rates of benefit withdrawal for those facing the highest, most punitive, rates (the 96%-ers). However, those claimants who only receive Tax Credits (typically those who own their own home, or whose income is too high to receive Housing Benefit) are likely to face a *higher* withdrawal rate under the new system.

At 63% of net income, the Universal Credit taper rate is rather higher than many had recommended. Much of the original thinking behind the introduction of Universal Credit was set out in the Centre for Social Justice's paper *Dynamic benefits*,[4] where it was suggested that a taper rate of 55% (net of tax) would be the most 'efficient' withdrawal rate, since it reduces disincentives to work, while avoiding increasing the rate at which benefit is withdrawn for higher earners in the benefits system.

A higher taper rate is particularly significant for second earners, since work allowances are only applied once per household. This means that low-income second earners will typically have a full 63% of their pay deducted from their Universal Credit entitlement (rather than having some of it ignored). In contrast, in the old system, the same second earner would only see 41% of their earnings deducted from their Tax Credit entitlement.

Like Housing Benefit and Council Tax Benefit (but unlike Tax Credits), the means test for Universal Credit is also applied to net rather than gross earnings. This has some advantages – in particular, it means that incentives to work longer and earn more are more consistent before and after the Income Tax personal allowance threshold. However, this also creates the same problem as occurs with Housing Benefit and Council Tax Reduction in the old system (highlighted in the previous chapter), meaning that when personal allowances for Income Tax (or National Insurance) are increased, claimants lose most of any gain they would have accrued as a result of consequent deductions from their benefit entitlement. The numbers of claimants affected under Universal Credit will be much larger – resulting in a much higher proportion of working households keeping only a small amount of any additional income resulting from reductions in tax bills.

As a result, as Universal Credit is introduced, the benefits of reduced tax burdens (the government's preferred method of increasing the incomes of working households) will increasingly be passed on to better-off households earning too much to receive Universal Credit.

Council Tax Reduction and Universal Credit

As discussed in Chapter 4, responsibility for providing support with Council Tax bills was handed over to local authorities in 2013. This localisation of provision has meant that Council Tax Benefit hasn't been integrated into Universal Credit.

This decision undermines the taper rates offered within the Universal Credit system, since as earnings increase, deductions are made not only from Universal Credit entitlement, but also from any Council Tax Reduction received as well. This is often forgotten or ignored in discussions about the work incentive effect of Universal Credit – which assume that the maximum deduction from earnings for those in receipt of Universal Credit is 76% (through a combination of Universal Credit deductions and tax payments).

Under the national system of Council Tax Benefit (pre-localisation), support was reduced at a rate of 20p for each extra £1 earned net of tax and Tax Credits. Many councils have retained the same taper rate post-localisation. On this basis, a tax-paying worker, facing a reduction of 75p for each extra £1 they earn through a combination of tax, National Insurance and Universal Credit, would then lose a further 20% of their remaining 25p in deductions from any Council Tax Reduction they receive – this leaves them with an overall marginal deduction rate of 80p in the £1, rather than 75p.

Work incentives may still be better for this group than under the old system, where they can lose the aforementioned 96p in the £1 if they receive a combination of Housing Benefit, Council Tax Benefit and Tax Credits. However, discrepancies like this between rhetoric and reality regarding work incentives under Universal Credit mean the system doesn't deliver nearly as much as it promises.

In-work disability support and Universal Credit

Universal Credit has a real problem of lack of additional support for working people with disabilities – particularly for those with children. Working Tax Credit includes a 'disability element' paid to disabled working people – 121,000 families receive this, worth £58 a week in 2017. This extra support helps disabled people with the extra costs they face in work that either can't be, or aren't, covered by other help with working for disabled people.[5]

Research has also found[6] that the extra money helps with higher costs around the home as a result of being in employment – for example, many disabled people report feeling more exhausted by their work than their non-disabled colleagues, as a result of their impairment. This means that they may need to pay for help with housework, or with additional childcare, in order to make staying in the workplace sustainable. One disabled person told researchers:

> '… holiday childcare costs are higher because I need to pay for my son to have care even when I'm NOT at work so that I can rest and therefore be able to work.'

Another said:

> 'I have a cleaner because I am so tired I cannot cope with cleaning my home after work, she comes two hours each week.'

Under Universal Credit, Working Tax Credit no longer exists. Instead, when Universal Credit was initially designed it included two forms of additional support to help working people with the cost of a disability.

The first form of support (discussed in Chapter 10) was that many of those with 'limited capability for work' (equivalent to the work-related activity group [WRAG] for ESA under the old system) would be entitled to keep this additional support as they moved into work. However, this support was removed when the government decided to scrap the work-related activity component of ESA and the equivalent limited capability for work element within Universal Credit.

The second form of support Universal Credit provided for disabled working claimants to help them with the additional costs they face in employment is through a higher work allowance (so that they can earn more money when they move into work before this starts to affect their benefit entitlement). However – and with no real rationale at all – this will only be provided to those without children. This is because you can get a higher rate of work allowance on account of a disability, *or* you can get a higher rate of work allowance because you are a parent – but you can't get both.

This means that working disabled parents receive no additional support to help them with the additional costs of work that they face on account of their disability *at all* – typically costing them around £58 per week.

The government wants to ensure that disabled people are able to make the move into work. As Iain Duncan Smith put it in a speech in 2015:[7]

> 'We know there remains a gap between the employment rate of disabled and non-disabled people. We want to ensure everyone has the opportunity to transform their lives for the better by getting into work. That's why, as part of our One Nation approach, we have committed to halving this gap. On current figures, that means getting 1 million more disabled people into work.
>
> I want to be clear – this employment gap isn't because of a lack of aspiration on the part of those receiving benefits ... the poor quality of support they receive leads too many sick and disabled people languishing in a life without work, when work is actually possible for them.'

This was a speech made just as the government was starting a process of substantially reducing crucial support for working people with a sickness or disability under Universal Credit.

Support for Mortgage Interest and the 'zero earnings rule'

Universal Credit also creates problems for working homeowners needing help with mortgage interest payments through Support for Mortgage Interest or SMI.

At present SMI[8] may be paid to those in receipt of income-based out-of-work benefits. This means that claimants may work up to 16 hours per week and still receive some SMI. A new 'zero earnings rule' under Universal Credit means that claimants who are earning *anything at all* will not be eligible to receive SMI support. This will leave many claimants with a difficult question of whether to earn a very small amount of money, and lose help with mortgage payments, or to avoid earning, so as to continue to receive mortgage support. It is worth remembering in this context that David Cameron promised that Universal Credit would make work pay from 'the very first hour you work'[9] – for people paying a mortgage, this could do exactly the reverse.

'Benefits in kind', Universal Credit and 'making work pay'

The issue of 'benefits in kind' (support that is linked to the benefits system but provided in some form other than cash) has been mentioned a number of times in the course of this book. While there are many good reasons to provide benefits in kind, they can create real problems for work incentives. This is because, unlike cash, they normally can't be reduced as earnings increase – you either get them or you don't.

A particularly important example of this is free school meals. These have a significant cash value – around £388 per child each year.[10] Under the Tax Credits system families can normally get free school meals if they are on a low income and are not working sufficient hours to receive Working Tax Credit – less than 16 hours per week if a lone parent and 24 hours if a couple (and earning under around £16,000). If they work more than the maximum number of hours, free school meals are withdrawn.

As can be imagined, this has significant potential to affect work incentives – a family with three school-aged children may receive free school meal entitlements worth £1,164 per year. If parents move into work, this loses them their entitlement to support – they will have to pay for school meals for their children from their own pocket.

At present this problem is addressed by aligning the point at which a family loses their free school meals with the point at which they gain entitlement to Working Tax Credit. Since maximum Working Tax Credit entitlements will almost always be greater than the value of free school meals, the loss of one is outweighed by the gain of the other – so work incentives are maintained.

Following the introduction of Universal Credit, new eligibility criteria need to be created for the new benefits system. One approach that the government has looked at for setting eligibility criteria for free school meals under Universal Credit is to set an earnings threshold above which entitlement is lost. However, this risks creating a substantial benefit 'cliff edge' – a point at which overall household income *falls* despite (or indeed, because of) earnings *increasing*. Unlike under the old system, Working Tax Credit will no longer exist to offset this loss.

If an increase in earnings pushes a family slightly above the relevant threshold at which free school meals are withdrawn, the lost entitlement could mean that the family is left significantly worse off overall – they could effectively be paying for a pay rise. For example, consider the impact that the loss of free school meals would have on a single-parent family with three school-aged children, if an earnings limit of £7,500 per year (£144 per week) were to be introduced for entitlement.

In this circumstance, should family income rise above £144 per week, overall effective household income (including the value of the free school meals) suddenly falls by around £22 per week as a result of the loss of free school meal entitlement. As a result of steep withdrawal rates from Universal Credit as earnings increase, an additional £60 per week of earnings would be needed before the household made up for the loss of free school meals entitlement – meaning that their wages would need to reach around £10,800 per year before they were as well off as when they were earning £7,500.

Put simply, if a parent in this circumstance who was earning £7,500 took on additional hours, not only would they not gain from their extra work, *they would be paying in order to do it.* In fact, they would only start to actually make some money out of their additional labour once their earnings reached £10,800 per year.

This deeply undermines the key intention of Universal Credit – to provide smooth work incentives and remove cliff edges, in a way that 'provides certainty that increased effort will always result in increased reward'.[11] The free school meals problem could instead risk creating one of the largest 'cliff edges' the benefits system has ever seen.

The only real solution to this problem is to provide free school meals to all children in receipt of Universal Credit. Notably, at the time of writing in 2017, the government has, on a temporary basis, agreed to do just that. However, it has been made clear that this is only an interim solution while the Department for Education decides what to do in the longer term.[12]

Providing free school meals to all children in families in receipt of Universal Credit would not eliminate the 'cliff edge' altogether (there would still be a point at which entitlement is lost, and household income overall drops). However, this would happen both at a higher threshold (so that the value of the lost meals would be relatively low in proportion to overall household income) and the cash equivalent of the lost entitlement would also be recovered more quickly as income increases, because deductions from Universal Credit receipt would no longer be taken from any additional earnings (meaning that there would be much less of an impact on work incentives).

Childcare costs and Universal Credit

As discussed in the previous chapter, for many families, help with childcare costs through the current benefits system is often significantly greater than claimants and professionals alike think that it is. The combination of help with childcare costs through Tax Credits and through Housing Benefit and Council Tax

Reduction means that as much as 96% of childcare costs may be paid for through the benefits and Tax Credits system.

Because Housing Benefit is rolled into Universal Credit, it will no longer be the case that additional support with childcare costs is provided through the Housing Benefit system. Instead, Universal Credit will cover up to 85% of childcare costs. Technically, claimants are still likely to be able to claim support with childcare costs through a Council Tax Reduction disregard (although now this in the hands of local authorities, and some may choose not to provide this). However, this means committing to regular reporting of childcare costs to the local authority (in addition to the Universal Credit service). Given this, it is questionable whether parents will consider it worth claiming such support where it only covers an additional 3% of their childcare costs.

The provision of 85% support with childcare costs under Universal Credit has been presented as an increase in support[13] from the current 70% provided through Tax Credits (which was, notably, 80% back in 2010, before it was cut). As one Department for Work and Pensions (DWP) spokesperson put it:

> Universal Credit includes a wide range of additional support that is not offered under the old system, including increased childcare and help to progress into work.[14]

For many families (particularly those not receiving Housing Benefit) it is true that support increases under Universal Credit. However, compared to support currently paid to those receiving a combination of Tax Credits, Housing Benefit and Council Tax Reduction, the 85% rate of support represents a cut.

It is the poorest working families that are most likely to be affected by this cut in support. Analysis for The Children's Society[15] estimated that working families who are living in poverty are around *four times more likely* to be affected by this change than families receiving help with childcare costs through Tax Credits who are not living in poverty.

However, the administration of childcare support can create further problems, which risk being exacerbated by the introduction of Universal Credit. Claims for help with childcare costs under Tax Credits can be made on the basis of predicted childcare costs. Under Universal Credit, help with childcare costs is paid in arrears on the basis of costs incurred.[16] This means that families will have to *pay out their childcare costs before they can get them paid back.*

Many families – and particularly those on higher incomes – will be okay with this. They will be able to afford to pay any upfront costs from savings, and then claim back support in arrears. For many low-income families without savings, looking to make an already risky move into work, the challenge is much more serious. In many cases, it is likely that the consequence of this will be families taking on debt in order to pay childcare costs.

One study in Northern Ireland found that one in four parents regularly used credit cards, loans from family or friends or payday loans to pay their childcare bills.[17] Payday loan companies are already giving childcare as an example of the kind of thing that payday loans may be used to cover:

> Consumers need cash for urgent expenses. A payday loan is not a long-term financial instrument like a credit card or home loan. Consumers might use payday loans for car repair, child care or other unexpected expense.[18]

Such use of high-cost credit to pay for childcare may be all the more common in the future.

Savings limit

Under the old system, different rules apply for how savings affect different benefits. While savings are generally ignored for contribution-based benefits, means-tested out-of-work income replacement benefits (such as Income Support, or income-based JSA) and Housing Benefit have very strict capital rules. For these benefits, each £250 of savings over £6,000[19] is treated as an extra £1 of income each week for the purposes of means testing. In addition, there is a savings limit of £16,000 – households with savings over this amount are not entitled to any support through these benefits.

The rules for Tax Credits are considerably more generous. Not only is there no savings limit but, in addition, only gross income from savings is taken into account for means testing, with the first £300 per year of income ignored. Despite combining both Tax Credits and means-tested out-of-work benefits, Universal Credit will use the savings rules for the latter.

Where under the old system claimants could retain significant entitlement to Tax Credits despite substantial savings, Universal Credit awards will be reduced steeply as savings increase, and in their entirety if these savings exceed £16,000. These strict savings rules will make it very difficult for many working families to save, for example, for a deposit on a house.

Imagine a household has £20,000 of savings in an account with an interest rate of 3%. The income from these savings would be £600 per year. Because the first £300 of this is disregarded, their actual income from savings for Tax Credit purposes is just £300. At the current withdrawal rate of 41%,[20] the amount a working household will actually see deducted from their Tax Credit award is just £123 per year (about £10 per month). Under Universal Credit they would lose their full award on account of their savings.

The rules will particularly penalise working savers who would be entitled to substantial Tax Credit awards under the old system, such as working parents with substantial childcare costs.

For a lone parent with two one-year-old children, working 30 hours per week, earning £12,000 and paying childcare costs of £650 per month, but with no housing costs, their Universal Credit award would be around £1,030 per month (contributing to an overall income of around £2,140 per month). However, if this family had more than £16,000 of savings, they would keep only their earnings and their Child Benefit, a total of around £1,100 per month – or just £450 per month once they had paid their childcare costs.

The 'Minimum Income Floor'

As highlighted in Chapter 6, self-employed Universal Credit claimants may be treated as earning more than they actually are. This is due to the application of a 'Minimum Income Floor' (MIF), which means that they are treated as earning no less than a certain amount (normally the equivalent of 35 hours per week at their relevant rate of minimum wage). This is intended to avoid providing long-term support for failing businesses.

However, the level of the MIF is very high – many claimants have to earn £1,050 per month (after tax) before the MIF no longer applies. This means some claimants may see as much as £660 per month deducted from their entitlement purely as a result of the application of the MIF.

Furthermore, the application of the MIF also penalises self-employed workers with profitable businesses but fluctuating earnings. For example, if income over two months *averaged out* at the MIF level, but the claimant earned more than the MIF in one month and less in the second, the claimant would have their actual earnings taken into account for the first month, but the MIF would be applied in the second – effectively meaning that they are penalised purely for their income instability.

One piece of research, commissioned by the DWP, found that amongst self-employed workers in receipt of Tax Credits even those with relatively high levels of earnings thought that their monthly earnings might fall below the MIF level at some point.[21]

The big problem: Cuts undermining work incentives

All of the problems discussed above undermine the effectiveness of Universal Credit, but the big problem with the effectiveness of the new system in promoting work incentives runs deeper than any individual measure. It is that Universal Credit is being introduced in the context of cuts.

When Universal Credit was first proposed by the Centre for Social Justice, a taper rate of 55% was suggested – this couldn't be afforded, so it was introduced at 65% (although this was later reduced to 63%).

Removal of the ESA work-related activity component has drastically reduced support for sick and disabled people trying to make the move back into work.

The problem of passported benefits hasn't yet been solved, because the Department for Education doesn't have the money to provide free school meals to all children in families on Universal Credit.

Similarly, work allowances under Universal Credit were meant to ensure that when people moved into work they kept a decent proportion of any earnings. But cuts to support have undermined that too. As discussed in the previous chapter, in the Autumn of 2015, the government introduced regulations that would have cut support for working families within the Tax Credits system, but that would also have cut support for working families within Universal Credit.

The Universal Credit cuts introduced significant reductions in the amount that claimants could earn before additional income started to affect their Universal Credit entitlement. While the government backtracked on the Tax Credit proposals, cuts to in-work support in Universal Credit remained unchanged. As the Chancellor said when he announced the government's reconsideration of Tax Credit cuts, in the 2015 Autumn Statement:

> ... the improved public finances allow us to reach the same goal of a surplus while cutting less in the early years. We can smooth the path to the same destination.
>
> And that means we can help on Tax Credits. I've been asked to help in the transition as Britain moves to the higher wage, lower welfare, lower tax society the country wants to see.
>
> I've had representations that these changes to Tax Credits should be phased in. I've listened to the concerns. I hear and understand them. And because I've been able to announce today an improvement in the public finances, the simplest thing to do is not to phase these changes in, but to avoid them altogether.
>
> Tax credits are being phased out anyway as we introduce Universal Credit. What that means is that

the Tax Credit taper rate and thresholds remain unchanged.[22]

The message from the Chancellor was clear. The government would back down on Tax Credits, but the end goal remained the same – savings would be made through cuts to support for working families within Universal Credit. In the long run, nothing was changing.

Before the changes (introduced in April 2016), a single claimant receiving Universal Credit could earn £111 per month before additional earnings started to affect their Universal Credit entitlement. After the changes they couldn't earn anything at all.

The largest cuts were for single parents who own their own home.[23] In these cases a work allowance of £734 per month was cut to £397 – a reduction of £337. This work allowance cut reduces support for working single parents who own their own home by £212 per month (£2,544 per year).

After further pressure in 2016, the government made a small concession to provide better in-work support under Universal Credit – reducing the taper rate from 65% to 63%. While welcome, this measure made only a relatively small difference to support for most working claimants receiving Universal Credit (compared to the losses resulting from the work allowance cuts). In addition, a taper rate reduction is less well targeted than increasing the generosity of work allowances, since it disproportionately benefits those on higher incomes on Universal Credit. This is because a lower taper rate reduces the loss of entitlement for each additional £1 of earnings. So, for example, a household with net earnings of £1,000 per year in excess of their work allowance would receive an additional £20 per year in Universal Credit entitlement as a result of the taper reduction. Another household with net earnings of £30,000 in excess of their work allowance would receive an additional £600 per year.

Universal Credit started to be introduced at a time when benefit cuts were just beginning. The intentions were always right, but it is questionable whether the money was ever there to make Universal Credit a benefits system that really worked. Since then all that has happened has been for Universal Credit to move further and further away from its original intent.

Figure 13.1: Cost to the Exchequer of maintaining the Tax Credit taper and income threshold (£ million)

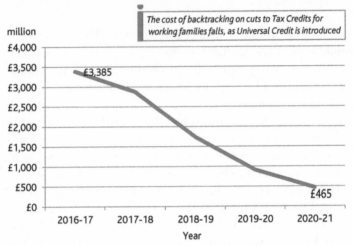

The cost of backtracking on cuts to Tax Credits for working families falls, as Universal Credit is introduced

Increasingly, it has been seen as easier to cut Universal Credit than it has been to cut support in the old benefits system, because – unlike Tax Credits – many people who will be affected by the introduction of the new system aren't yet receiving it, and, as a result, aren't immediately affected. A reform that was genuinely aimed at improving the welfare system has become one that has been an easy target for cuts because of slow implementation.

One important implication of this is that there is now much more economic pressure to introduce Universal Credit quickly. The cost to the Treasury of backtracking on cuts to in-work support under Tax Credits was put at £3.4 billion in 2016, but (as shown in Figure 13.1) by 2020, the cost is expected to be only £500 million.[24] The difference of nearly £3 billion per year must be dependent on the introduction of Universal Credit.

Up to 2016, the DWP was taking its time with Universal Credit implementation (including several delays); now the government's own financial savings commitments rely on its introduction.

Conclusion

The process of welfare reform has been all about fairness to those who work hard to make ends meet – people who often see themselves as supporting those who are out of work and living on benefits.

Universal Credit was meant to play a key role in solving this problem. The DWP, rather optimistically, called the Universal Credit White Paper 'welfare that works'. Certainly some of the changes made are much needed. The system does address some work disincentives: circumstances where people keep just 4p in each extra £1 they earn, or even keep none of their earnings at all (as is the case for many of those in receipt of out-of-work benefits).

But over time, Universal Credit has become a shade of what it was intended to be. Not only was the money never found to make it work in the way that it should, but it has also proved rather easier to cut than the old system when the Treasury wants to find savings.

In order to fulfil Universal Credit's potential, a number of key changes are needed. First, to simplify the system, Council Tax Reduction support should be rolled into Universal Credit. Having a localised system of provision is complex, confusing and undermines work incentives. This measure would take a big step towards making Universal Credit the simpler system it was intended to be.

Second, better in-work disability support needs to be provided in Universal Credit in order to help close the disability employment gap. There are two steps to achieving this. The first is to make Universal Credit work allowances additive, so that disabled people can receive both a work allowance on account of their disability *and* an additional work allowance on account of having children. The second step is to bring back the 'limited capability for work' component of Universal Credit – at least for working claimants.

Third, free school meals should be provided to all children in families in receipt of Universal Credit. Failure to do so risks creating a benefit 'cliff edge' that would deeply undermine the fundamental principle behind the introduction of Universal

Credit, and leave some families losing money as a result of a pay rise.

Fourth, childcare support under Universal Credit needs to be paid upfront rather than in arrears, in order to avoid families unable to make the initial payment getting into serious debt as a result of moving into work.

Fifth, Universal Credit needs to adopt the savings rules for Tax Credits – to enable lower-income working families to save for a home.

Sixth, the level of the 'Minimum Income Floor' for self-employed Universal Credit claimants should be reduced, since the current level of the MIF risks pushing many of those running potentially successful businesses out of employment altogether. In addition, the application of the MIF currently penalises self-employed claimants with fluctuating incomes – in order to avoid this, claimants should be able to average their earnings over a number of months.

Finally, cuts to work allowances under Universal Credit that were introduced from 2016 need to be reversed. These have turned Universal Credit from a positive system to promote work incentives to a way of cutting support, without creating too much upset in the short term. The government reversed pernicious cuts to Tax Credits for working families; they need to do the same with Universal Credit.

Universal Credit can make a real contribution to making sure that work pays for low-income families, and contribute to getting families into employment, but it can only do so if it is backed up with the investment needed to really make it 'welfare that works'.

14

Contribution-based benefits:
The great insurance scam

Contribution-based benefits are built on the principle that people pay in when they can afford to (through National Insurance Contributions), and get additional support back in periods of difficulty (such as sickness, unemployment or old age).

To some degree this works – particularly where people have savings, or a partner who works. In such cases contribution-based benefits can bypass the stringent means testing of income-based entitlements, and provide additional support to those who have paid in. However, for many households, contribution-based benefits can be absolutely worthless. As we will see, in some cases they even be 'toxic' – leaving families worse off overall than they would have been had they not paid National Insurance Contributions in the first place. The introduction of Universal Credit risks making this problem considerably worse.

This cannot be right. When people pay in, they should have the reasonable expectation that the contribution-based benefits that they receive have some value – and certainly that they should never be in a situation where they risk being left out of pocket.

A quick reminder of how contribution-based benefits work

In Chapter 5 we discussed how contribution-based benefits work, and the differences from means-tested provision. While entitlements to income-based benefits are calculated on the basis of household needs and income, contribution-based benefits are an individualised entitlement – with the level of support calculated on the basis of individual income and needs. We saw that this has three consequences:

- More than one member of the household can claim the same contribution-based benefit at the same time (so, for example, two partners could each receive contributory Jobseeker's Allowance [JSA(C)] – while, if they were claiming means-tested [JSA(IB], they would make one claim, paid at a 'couple rate').
- While savings are taken into account in calculating how much someone might be entitled to in means-tested benefits, they are normally excluded in working out contribution-based benefit entitlements.[1] The principle is that having paid insurance, contribution-based benefit recipients are provided with some level of protection from having to dip into their savings in order to pay for living costs during a period of ill health or unemployment.
- Only individual rather than household income is taken into account when calculating the amount of benefit to which the claimant is entitled (so, unlike means-tested benefits, if one partner in a couple is in work and earning a decent level of income, the other may still be able to claim contributory JSA(C) or Employment and Support Allowance [ESA(C)], based on their own circumstances).

This final point is particularly important, since it means that contributory benefits can help to maintain income in a couple-household, where one partner faces a job loss. They also help non-working people in couple relationships to maintain a sense of financial independence and worth.

This makes it particularly worrying that, as discussed in Chapter 10, the introduction of new restrictions on the time for which contribution-based ESA can be received has significantly reduced the number of claimants eligible to receive the benefit.

Why contributory benefits may be worth nothing (and how this is just the start of the problem)

While some people can benefit a great deal from their contribution-based benefit entitlement, in many other cases (and particularly for single claimants), contribution-based benefits do not have any (or have limited) financial value.

This is because many contribution-based benefit entitlements are worth exactly the same as their income-based equivalent. For example, a single, unemployed 30-year-old entitled to contributory JSA (and no other benefits) would receive £73 per week, but they would also receive £73 if they hadn't paid National Insurance Contributions and were reliant on income-based JSA instead. (As explained in Chapter 5, the claimant's contribution-based JSA is deducted in full from their income-based entitlement – where the amounts are the same, this means the claimant receives all of their JSA[C] but no JSA[IB].)

In other cases, contribution-based benefits can be worth less than their income-based equivalent – for example, the contribution-based old State Pension is worth less than Pension Credit guarantee. In these cases (as we saw), if they have no other income or savings, the claimant would normally have their contribution-based benefit 'topped up' to the level of their income-based entitlement.

Where a claimant's contribution-based benefit is not deducted in full from an underlying entitlement to an equivalent benefit (for example, a claimant in receipt of JSA[C] may have no underlying entitlement to JSA[IB] because their partner is in work), non-equivalent benefits may be affected – such as Tax Credits and/or Housing Benefit. In such cases the contribution-based benefit entitlement will be treated in a similar way to earnings and may reduce entitlements to the other means-tested benefits by a proportion of their value (according to the relevant 'taper') – but not pound for pound. In summary, in such cases, the household will keep some of the value of the contribution-based benefit, but not all of it.

As a result, many claimants receive no additional entitlement (or do not keep their full entitlement) as a result of having paid National Insurance Contributions, and receiving contribution-based benefits. However, as we will see in the rest of this chapter, the problem with contribution-based benefits runs deeper than this. For many claimants, receipt of contribution-based benefits may not only leave them with no more than those who are not entitled to this support, but may also leave them with *less*. Having paid a contribution, the 'support' they may end up receiving could be actively toxic to their financial health.

Contribution-based benefits and 'passporting' to other support

The first problem relates to benefits 'passporting'. In certain circumstances receipt of a benefit can ensure that a claimant receives another kind of support – in England,[2] for example, receipt of Income Support 'passports' a claimant to free prescriptions.

Income-based out-of-work benefits (such as Income Support, income-based JSA or income-based ESA) are frequently used as passports to other entitlements (such as free school meals, free prescriptions and Housing Benefit). They are often used to passport to concessionary prices for local amenities as well, such as leisure facilities and adult education courses.

The 'income-based' bit is crucial here – contribution-based JSA and ESA do not typically passport to these entitlements. This is because while means-tested benefit receipt is used as an indicator of low household income, receipt of contribution-based benefits cannot be used as such a proxy (since households in receipt of contribution-based benefits may have a high level of other income or savings).

However, many households in receipt of contribution-based benefits *do not* have any other income or savings, but may still lose out on their entitlement to additional support altogether. This is the case, for example, with Cold Weather Payments that provide £25 of extra assistance with fuel bills in weeks of very cold weather, and can *only* be received by claimants in receipt of certain means-tested benefits. In other cases, the claimant has to go through a full means test in order to get support – which is complex and confusing for claimants receiving contributory out-of-work benefits.

Crucially, the loss of passported benefits can result in people who have paid their National Insurance Contributions ending up worse off than if they hadn't paid in at all.

It should be noted that the problem of lack of 'passporting' for contribution-based benefit recipients is partially solved for those in receipt of Universal Credit. This is because many contribution-based benefit claimants on a low income will also be entitled to receive some Universal Credit.[3] Passporting under Universal Credit does, however, create other (very severe) problems in the new system that risk deeply undermining work incentives. The problems with passporting to free school meals under Universal Credit, for example, were discussed in Chapter 13.

Contribution-based benefits and the tax system

A second problem with some contribution-based benefits (and particularly contribution-based ESA) is their interaction with the tax system. Unlike means-tested ESA (and despite frequently having no greater value), contribution-based ESA is normally treated as taxable income. This is a particular problem, since, while out-of-work benefit entitlements are paid as a *weekly* amount, Income Tax is an *annual* calculation.

The mismatch between the two means that someone who claims contribution-based ESA for the first half of the year, and then moves into work for the second half, would see their contributory benefit added to their earnings to calculate their overall income tax liability for the year.

For example, John claims contribution-based ESA from April to September at a rate of £102 per week – receiving a total of £2,660. He then moves into work and earns £15,000 between October and the following March. His overall income for the purposes of Income Tax (calculated over the course of the whole year) is £17,660 – £2,660 higher than it would have been had he received (non-taxable) income-based ESA.

Overall this costs him £532 over the course of six months (20% of his entitlement) compared to what he would have received on income-based ESA. Rather than receiving £102 per week, John's actual entitlement (after tax) for this period is around £82 per week. In summary, this means that John's National 'Insurance' payments cost him 20% of his out-of-work benefit entitlement.

Notably, unemployed claimants do not face this disparity under the old benefits system, since both income-based JSA and contribution-based JSA are taxable (meaning that a JSA claimant returning to work after a period of unemployment would see their JSA entitlement added to their earnings for the purposes of calculating overall annual income – whether they were claiming income-based or contribution-based JSA).[4]

However, this is no longer the case with unemployed claimants in receipt of Universal Credit. This is because the equivalent support to JSA(IB) provided within Universal Credit is not taxable (since Universal Credit as a whole is a non-taxable benefit). This means that contribution-based JSA(C) can be deducted pound for pound from the claimant's Universal Credit entitlement, and then taxed. Since Universal Credit is not itself taxable, this means that the unemployed claimant in receipt of JSA(C) may be left worse off overall than an equivalent claimant not entitled to JSA(C), and just receiving Universal Credit.

In addition, and as we discuss next, Universal Credit creates a further problem for those in receipt of contribution-based benefits – by extending the circumstances under which their contribution-based award is deducted pound for pound from their underlying income-based entitlement.

Universal Credit and contribution-based benefits as 'unearned income'

As previously noted, in the old benefits system, pound for pound deductions of contribution-based benefits are taken from the equivalent benefit paid through the income-based system. Under Universal Credit (because of the bringing together of a range of different in- and out-of-work benefits) they can also effectively be deducted pound for pound from non-equivalent provision – including from entitlements paid to working households. So, for example, a claimant receiving ESA(C) could in effect have this deducted from help with housing costs or support with children (the equivalent of what would currently be Child Tax Credit) paid through Universal Credit.

This means that where currently contribution-based benefit entitlements would normally provide no additional income for non-working claimants in households with no other income or savings (because they are deducted in full from their underlying income-based entitlement), under Universal Credit *this is also true for low-income working households.* This has a particular impact on claimants in receipt of contribution-based out-of-work benefits but with a partner in low-paid employment, and represents a major transfer of insurance entitlements away from this group.

As with the old system, some contribution-based benefit payments remain taxable – meaning that not only will people be more likely to see no gain from their contribution-based benefits (compared to income-based ones), but they may also face additional Income Tax as a result of their receipt of these benefits.

A range of different contribution-based benefit entitlements is deducted pound for pound from Universal Credit, and is taxable. For example, Widowed Parent's Allowance is a benefit, worth up to about £112 per week, which is paid on account of a parent having lost a partner. The intention is to support widowed parents through a really difficult period of their lives – a period in which they are likely not only to be struggling emotionally, but may also be finding things extremely difficult financially, having lost a wage earner from the family. Widowed Parent's Allowance is only paid in cases where the partner who died had paid in their National Insurance Contributions, making it a contribution-based benefit – albeit one paid on account of a partner's National Insurance Contributions rather than the claimant's own.

As with contribution-based JSA and ESA, Widowed Parent's Allowance is deducted pound for pound from Universal Credit entitlement. Low-income widowed parents in receipt of Universal Credit keep absolutely nothing from it – it goes in one pocket, and disappears from another.

However, for a widowed parent with other earnings, it gets worse. Since not only does Widowed Parent's Allowance count as unearned income for the purposes of Universal Credit, it is also treated as taxable income. So not only is the £112 per week deducted in entirety from the household's Universal Credit entitlement, it is also taxed.[5]

A working widowed parent whose partner had also worked before they died, *and* had paid their National Insurance Contributions, is effectively fined £8 per week[6] for having lost their partner. Just to reiterate, this isn't £8 per week worse off than they would be if they received full Widowed Parent's Allowance. It is not £8 per week worse off than they would have been if they received some kind of equivalent bereavement support through the means-tested benefits system. It is £8 per week worse off than *exactly the same parent, earning exactly the same income, but who had not recently lost their partner.* As it stands, for this group, Widowed Parent's Allowance is a 'toxic' benefit – it is one that costs families money rather than offering them anything. It is a sham, and some of the most vulnerable people in society may be affected by it.

Notably, the introduction of the Bereavement Support Payment (which replaces much of the current system of bereavement payments) will not count as income for Universal Credit, and will be tax free.[7] This is an important change in the structure of the new benefit. However, for some time, many bereaved parents will continue to receive Widowed Parent's Allowance instead.

Contribution-based benefits and pensioners

Through the course of this chapter we have focused on working-age contribution-based benefits. However, perhaps the most important contribution-based benefit is the State Pension.

Many pensioners have independent private incomes, which are topped up through the provision of the State Pension. For this group there is a clear benefit to receiving the State Pension as a top up to other income received.

However, for low-income pensioners, the benefits are not so clear. As with other contribution-based benefits, the State Pension is directly deducted from its equivalent means-tested entitlement (in the case of pensioners, Pension Credit). This means that if a single claimant receiving the Basic State Pension in full doesn't have any other income or savings, they will be no better off receiving this than they would be just receiving Pension Credit.[8]

As with other contribution-based benefits, the State Pension is also taxable. Although receipt of the State Pension on its own would not be a sufficiently high income to pay tax, when combined with another income, some pensioners may both pay tax on their pension and have it deducted pound for pound from their benefit entitlement. As with other contribution-based benefit claimants, this could leave some pensioners on a low income *worse off* on account of their entitlement to a State Pension. This is particularly likely to be the case for mixed age couples in receipt of Universal Credit (see Chapter 19 for more on issues affecting this group).

Conclusion

Contribution-based benefits were meant to provide the core of the benefits system created in the late 1940s. They build on the principle that by making a contribution, we earn the right to support when we most need it.

However, in this chapter we have seen how, for many low-income households, two key problems related to contribution-based benefits undermine this principle. Together, these problems mean that not only are contribution-based benefits worthless in many cases, in the worst cases (and more so under Universal Credit) they can be toxic – actively leaving households worse off on account of receiving them. However, in both cases, there are solutions. If there is the political will to build a more meaningful contribution-based benefits system, it can be done.

Contribution-based benefits do not act as an automatic passport to other benefits in kind as their income-related equivalents often do. This means that people in receipt of contribution-based benefits who are living on a low level of income either have to go through a complicated claims process to get some assistance (rather than getting help automatically), or (as in the case of the Cold Weather Payment) may be cut off from support altogether.

Contributory benefit entitlements are deducted pound for pound from some means-tested benefits and may be taxed. This can leave some claimants worse off overall, and this problem becomes significantly worse in Universal Credit.

In combination, the problems outlined above show that contribution-based benefits are simply a mess. It cannot be right to have a benefits system in which people are fined, including in the most difficult periods of their lives, for working hard and paying in their National Insurance Contributions.

There are a lot of well-intentioned ideas about improving the system of contribution-based benefits and strengthening the 'contributory principle' by increasing their value. However, for many people trapped in this situation, where they are both losing their contribution-based benefits pound for pound and also paying tax on them, this change would make many households still *worse off* under Universal Credit, since they would still lose their contribution-based benefits in full, and would also pay tax on an increased entitlement.

There are a number of ways of resolving these issues. One option (which would work particularly well within Universal Credit) would be to reduce means-tested benefits entitlement against contribution-based benefits according to a taper, rather than by pound for pound deductions. This would have the following advantages:

- The application of a taper to prevent contribution-based benefits entirely 'cancelling out' means-tested equivalents would mean that contribution-based benefit claimants with no other income or savings were safeguarded from losing automatic entitlement to certain passported benefits. Even a small entitlement would have a major impact on overall income by ensuring contribution-based benefit claimants received these other key forms of support.
- By providing an income-based supplement to contribution-based benefit, the taper would ensure that some additional entitlement was kept by lower-income households in receipt of contribution-based benefits,[9] over and above what they would receive if they weren't entitled to these forms of

support. For the reasons discussed above, this is particularly important within Universal Credit.

- The taper would also help to ensure that low-income claimants were prevented from being worse off as a result of their contribution-based benefit entitlement being taxed. (An alternative approach would be to make working-age contribution-based benefits non-taxable, although this would benefit higher as well as low-income earners.) The level at which such a taper was set would need further analysis. One option would be to set it at the same rate as for earnings under Universal Credit (that is, reduce means-tested entitlements by 63% of the value of the contribution-based benefit). To take Glen's example, which we used in Chapter 5:

Rather than being deducted in full, Glen's ESA(C) entitlement of £102 per week is deducted from his Universal Credit entitlement at a rate of 63%. This means that rather than have an overall benefit entitlement of £102 ESA(C) and £110 Universal Credit, his actual entitlement is £102 ESA(C) and £148 Universal Credit – an increase of £38 per week (37% of the value of his ESA(C)).

This would be sufficient to cover any additional income tax liability Glen may incur as a result of his ESA(C) payment, and provide a small amount of additional financial support as well.

Today, it would require significant (although not impossible) reform to make contribution-based benefits provision play the principal role in the working-age benefits system. In particular, time limits in contribution-based unemployment and sickness benefits would need to be scrapped, and a review would be needed of how means-tested benefits for children and (most of all) for rents could be incorporated into contribution-based provision.

However, it would require far more limited reform to ensure that contribution-based benefits play a much fairer and more meaningful role *alongside* means-tested provision than they do today. For example (and regardless of how large a role contribution-based benefits should play in the benefits system), it cannot be right that those entitled to contribution-based provision can, in certain circumstances, receive *less* than they would if they were solely reliant on the means-tested safety net. I would go so far as to say it would seem a reasonable expectation that they should receive at least a small amount *more*.

The introduction of a taper on the treatment of working-age contribution-based benefits for the purposes of calculating means-tested entitlements (rather than making pound for pound deductions) would be a significant step towards ensuring that people are always rewarded – and never penalised – for making a contribution.

Part IV
Chaos, error and misjudgements – Payments and administration in the benefits system

It may be tempting to think that all that matters in the benefits system is getting the level of entitlements right for different benefits; that once you make sure that the values of different benefits are enough to live on, and appropriately reflect the different needs of different household types, then the job's done.

But setting the values of different benefits is only the first part of making the benefits system work. This part of the book is about making sure that the *right people get paid the right amount at the right time*.

This part of the book addresses five key themes. The first is how well the benefits system determines *who* should receive support on account of ill health or disability. This includes (in Chapter 15) the effectiveness of assessments of ill health and disability for the purposes of awarding benefits such as Employment and Support Allowance and the Personal Independence Payment.

Second, even if it has been determined that a claimant is entitled to receive a certain amount of benefit paid at a certain rate, this doesn't necessarily mean that they receive the right amount at the time when they need it. Problems with the administration of the benefits system frequently mean that money gets paid late or not at all, or, as discussed in Chapter 16, that overpayments of benefit lead to families getting into serious and unavoidable benefit debt.

Third, there is a question of whether there are circumstances under which *payments of benefit should stop or be reduced*. Chapter

17 considers the application of benefit sanctions, and raises concerns that too often decisions about sanctions are being made in the wrong way, and for the wrong reasons.

Fourth, this part of the book also considers whether it is best to administer certain benefits at a national or local government level. Chapter 18 looks in particular at two key forms of support that have recently been localised: Council Tax Benefit, and emergency aid now provided through Local Welfare Assistance schemes. There are both potential advantages and risks to local benefit administration, and we also discuss concerns that 'localisation' of benefits may be used as a way of passing across responsibility for cuts to provision from national to local government.

Finally, in Chapter 19, we consider *who should be awarded retirement benefits*, raising concerns that changes introduced in recent years disproportionately reduce the length of retirement for many of those on the lowest incomes.

By addressing some of these issues of administration of the benefits system, we can seek to ensure that not only are the values of benefits set at the appropriate rates, but also that people get paid what they need, when they need it.

15

Reasons to be fearful?: Assessing sickness and disability

It is our intention to protect the most vulnerable, including the disabled. I believe our reforms demonstrate our strong record of supporting disabled people. We introduced the Personal Independence Payment to ensure more support is going to those who need it. More than 700,000 of those who were, once upon a time, stuck on incapacity benefits under Labour are now preparing or looking for work.... Our purpose is to protect the most vulnerable. It has been from the beginning, and it will continue to be. There is, therefore, no reason for people to be fearful....[1]

Within a year of saying disabled people had 'no reason to be fearful' of reforms to sickness and disability benefits, Iain Duncan Smith had resigned from his role as Secretary of State for Work and Pensions over changes to the assessment process for the new Personal Independence Payment, which he saw as a 'compromise too far'.[2]

Underlying his decision was a critical policy issue – how do we fairly assess disability and ill health in order to make decisions about whether, and how much, support to offer someone?

This chapter considers the assessment process for two key sickness and disability benefits: Employment and Support Allowance (ESA) and Personal Independence Payment (PIP) (as well as its predecessor, Disability Living Allowance (DLA)).

Employment and Support Allowance: The 'work capability assessment'

Until 2008, the key out-of-work benefits for people too sick to work were Incapacity Benefit (a contribution-based benefit) and Income Support (which is means tested, and can be received by those who haven't paid National Insurance Contributions). Since 2008 a new benefit has been gradually introduced – Employment and Support Allowance – and with it, a new test of entitlement called the 'work capability assessment' (WCA).

The WCA has two parts. The first considers whether the claimant is able to undertake a series of activities, or whether, as a result of their illness and/or disability, they are normally unable to do so. Points are assigned accordingly. If the claimant receives sufficient points, they are found to have 'limited capability for work'. This test is more rigorous than that for Incapacity Benefit and, crucially, far fewer people are exempt from it. For example, someone who has a deteriorating illness is only exempt from the test if they are predicted to have less than six months to live. Someone who is predicted to have a life expectancy of about 12 months and whose ability to function (walk, stand etc) is limited could still be found fit for work and required to look for employment.

The second part to the WCA is about assessing the claimant's ability to undertake 'work-related activity' (training and other activities designed to prepare the claimant for moving back into work in the future). For this part of the assessment there are a series of statements, and if the claimant is found to meet the criteria for any one of the statements, they are found to have limited capability for both work and work-related activity, and are placed in the ESA support group.

How the test is carried out

When it was first introduced, the contract to undertake WCAs was awarded to Atos Healthcare. Concerns were raised in the first years, however, that many of the assessments conducted by the company were astonishingly poor. There was evidence that many very sick or disabled people were being awarded no points at all – in fact, between 2008 and early 2011, 60% of those who were found to be entitled to the benefit following an appeal *had received no points on the initial assessment.*[3]

Newspaper reports indicated that so many people were unhappy with the way their claim was treated, and that the Tribunals Service (that decides on appeals against bad decisions) had to take on extra staff and open on Saturdays in order to deal with the backlog of cases.[4] Often, expert evidence from a claimant's own GP or consultant was not gathered, or available information was not properly taken into account, when assessing a claim.[5]

Given this, unsurprisingly, the quality of assessments was annoying those who had to deal with the appeals – the tribunal judges themselves. Following one tribunal, a judge independently released a statement on the assessor's report from the WCA, saying:

> The report is misleading, superficial and shallow. It is not fit for purpose.... It is inexcusable that the Secretary of State should seek to justify this report as a basis for making a decision. Sadly there are too many reports of this standard.[6]

The early criticisms led to calls for the full implementation of ESA to be delayed, including from amongst those who had designed it.[7]

Despite the criticisms, the government ploughed ahead with the introduction of ESA, including the reassessment of people who had been claiming Incapacity Benefit and Income Support on account of disability.

Unsurprisingly, many of those who had previously not been found fit for work were being thrown off the benefit, and told that they were ready to move back into employment. One person who had worked on the government's Work Programme (a scheme aimed at helping unemployed benefit claimants into work) felt the wrong decisions were often being made, telling *The Guardian* newspaper:

I had a woman with multiple sclerosis who had
been domestically abused and was suffering from
very severe depression and anxiety, and she had a
degenerative condition and she was deemed fit for
work.... I gave people advice under the radar about
how to appeal ... but it was absolutely not in our
remit to encourage people to appeal.[8]

Following early statistics in 2012 which indicated that more
than a third (37%) of reassessed Incapacity Benefit claimants
were now deemed 'fit for work',[9] Chris Grayling, Employment
Minister at the time, said:

These first figures completely justify our decision
to reassess all the people on Incapacity Benefit. To
have such a high percentage who are fit for work just
emphasises what a complete waste of human lives the
current system has been.

We know that for many it will be a long haul back
to work but it's much better to help them on the
journey than to leave them on benefits for the rest
of their lives.[10]

Not only were these figures – produced on the basis of claimants
failing a poor test – nothing to be proud of, they were also
disingenuous for two reasons. First, they didn't take into account
appeals (of which, as previously indicated, there were many).
And second, many of the early reassessments were undertaken
with those closest to returning to work – at least some of the
cases would probably have been found ineligible for benefit even
under the old regime, simply because the claimant's condition
had improved.

Figures from later in the reassessment process, and once
outcomes of appeals are factored in, show a very different picture.
In the most recent quarter, only around one in twenty reassessed
claims was found to be fit for work – rather a change from the
37% highlighted by the Minister back in 2012. Of course, this
is equally misleading. The later reassessed claims represent those

people on Incapacity Benefits who were furthest from being able to move back into work.

However, taking all reassessments from 2011 through to 2015 – and considering appeals – around 19% of reassessed claimants were found to be fit for work overall, around half the rate highlighted by the Minister. This rate is likely to remain low as the small number of remaining reassessments are undertaken (see Figure 15.1).

Figure 15.1: Outcomes of Incapacity Benefit/Income Support reassessments for ESA each quarter, 2011-15[a]

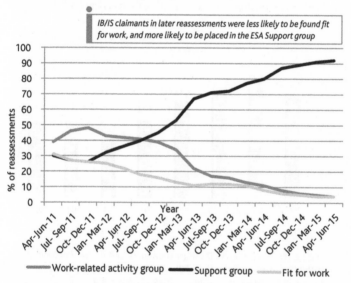

Note: [a] by proportions of claimants referred for assessment each quarter (non-cumulative results)
Source: Analysis of data from DWP (Department for Work and Pensions) (2016) ESA: Outcomes of work capability assessments: Claims made to Jun 2015 and appeals to Dec 2015, www.gov.uk/government/statistics/esa-outcomes-of-work-capability-assessments-claims-made-to-jun-2015-and-appeals-to-dec-2015

As previously noted, reassessments of claims using the old Incapacity Benefit assessment (called the personal capability assessment) would also have found that some claimants were no longer entitled on reassessment, simply because in some instances, *people get better*. For this reason, the actual number of reassessed claimants found fit for work *as a result of the introduction of the new test* is probably somewhat lower than 19%.

Despite the reassessment process, overall numbers of claimants of sickness benefits[11] have not changed hugely over the last five years. In May 2010, there were around 2.46 million out-of-work sickness benefit claimants (excluding those receiving National Insurance credits only, who do not receive any cash support). By May 2015, this had fallen to 2.33 million, a total fall of about 130,000 (see Figure 15.2).

Figure 15.2: Incapacity Benefits[a] claimant numbers, May 2008-May 2015, excluding those receiving National Insurance Credits only (000s)

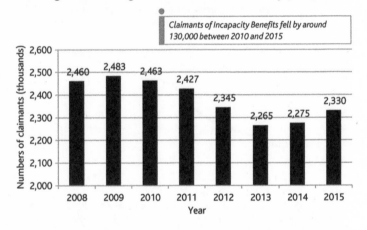

Note: [a] Incapacity Benefit/Severe Disablement Allowance/Income Support/ESA. Source: DWP (Department for Work and Pensions) (2016) *Quarterly benefits summary – Great Britain statistics to August 2015*. London: DWP

There are a number of different reasons for this reduction, but probably the single biggest contributing factor appears to be the decision to limit contribution-based ESA for those in the work-related activity group (WRAG) to a single year's entitlement[12] (rather than the ESA reassessment process).

There is likely to have been some fall in overall claimant numbers as a result of the reassessment process, but it is difficult to disentangle the exact impact of the reassessment process from other changes going on at the same time.

Reconsiderations and appeals of decisions

Given the problems with the WCA, you might expect the government to do whatever they could to support claimants through the process of challenging a decision. However, in 2013, the government made it much harder to go to appeal over an ESA decision, requiring a claim to be 'reconsidered' by the Department for Work and Pensions (DWP) first.

There is no problem as such with the DWP reconsidering decisions before appeal – in fact, such an approach might be welcomed. It should be quicker and easier for a claimant to have their decision reconsidered by the DWP than to have to go to a benefits tribunal to get the right outcome. In fact, in the earliest years after the introduction of ESA, only a very small number of decisions were overturned by the DWP, with around 6% of claimants who ended up in the WRAG having been assigned to that group following reconsideration. By 2014, this had risen to around a third, which may suggest that the DWP was more frequently properly reassessing claims.

However, as well as making this reconsideration a mandatory part of the complaints process, the government also announced that people found fit for work could no longer receive ESA while waiting for their claim to be reconsidered.[13] This means that those who decide to complain about the decision are faced with having no income at all during this period, or making a claim for Jobseeker's Allowance (JSA) or another out-of-work benefit.[14]

If the claimant makes a claim for JSA, this means that they have to accept that they are available for and actively seeking work, even though their appeal is precisely against their ability to do so. It is unclear what the claimant should do if they aren't up to this. As the Citizens Advice website puts it:

> If you feel unable to claim JSA during your reconsideration, for example because you feel too ill to go to the Jobcentre, *you need to think about how you'll manage during this period.* (emphasis added)[15]

While the DWP claims that these reconsiderations will be processed as quickly as possible, their own data shows considerable delays. For reconsiderations requested up to October 2014, a quarter of claimants found themselves waiting more than 30 days for the result of this 'mandatory reconsideration'.[16] This issue is at the heart of the (fictional, but sadly realistic) film, *I Daniel Blake*, in which the main character finds it difficult to cope on JSA while his ESA claim goes through a mandatory reconsideration. As he considers ending his JSA claim, an adviser in a Jobcentre says to him:

> Please listen to me, Dan. It's a huge decision to come off JSA without any other income coming in ... you see, there's no time limit for a mandatory reconsideration.... Please, just keep signing on. Get somebody to help you with the online job searches. Otherwise, you could lose everything. Please don't do this. I've seen it before. Good people, honest people, on the street.[17]

The problems this has caused are likely to get much worse under Universal Credit, since someone who is found fit for work will be considered to be so until their appeal is heard – not just during a mandatory reconsideration of the decision. This could add several months to the period during which claimants challenging a decision about their fitness for work are denied income unless they look for work.[18]

At the same time, specialist support with appealing decisions has been made much more scarce. The Legal Aid, Sentencing and Punishment of Offenders (LASPO) Act took welfare advice cases outside of the scope of legal aid, making it much harder for claimants to receive the support they need with challenging a decision. Gillian Guy, Chief Executive of Citizens Advice, warned that these changes were taking away advice at exactly the time when people most needed it:

> Cuts to legal aid have created an advice gap, stranding people with nowhere to turn. At precisely the time when people's need for specialist advice on issues

such as housing and welfare increased, provision for this support has been slashed.[19]

One Citizens Advice Bureau in the North West of England commented:

> Benefits appeals are failing as clients are unable to pay for supportive medical evidence and/or are attending on their own without submissions. There have been problems with referring clients to specialist advice to challenge decisions on benefit entitlement and overpayment issues, including assembling specialist medical evidence to support ESA and DLA/PIP claims and preparing cases for appeal.[20]

It is likely that this has had an impact on the number of appeals of fit for work decisions being heard – falling from 93,000 in 2011, to 11,000 in 2014 (or from 42% of fit for work cases down to just 12% in 2014). It could be argued that this fall is because of more decisions being made correctly, either the first time, or on reconsideration. However, the evidence on the success rate at appeal suggests that this is not the case – as the proportion of fit for work decisions reaching appeal has fallen, the proportion of decisions heard at appeal being overturned has risen rapidly, from around a third in 2011 to more than a half in 2014 (see Figure 15.3).

This suggests that people are increasingly being put off making an appeal on a bad decision. Increasingly, perhaps, only those whose decisions are the most obviously wrong are able to get support; otherwise, it is left to those who feel able to challenge a decision from the DWP on their own.

Challenging a bad decision should be a right. However, the introduction of mandatory reconsideration with a period of non-payment of benefit, combined with cuts in legal aid provision, has deeply undermined that right.

Following ongoing problems with the ESA assessment process, Atos increasingly became what the Work and Pensions Select Committee called a 'lightning rod for all the negativity around the ESA process'.[21] Atos left its contract early, with the US company Maximus taking over from 2015; one newspaper inevitably reported that Atos had been found not 'fit for work' itself.[22] At the time of writing, whether Maximus will be up to the job is still something of an open question.

Figure 15.3: Proportion of ESA 'fit for work' decisions heard on appeal and proportions of decisions heard on appeal that are overturned

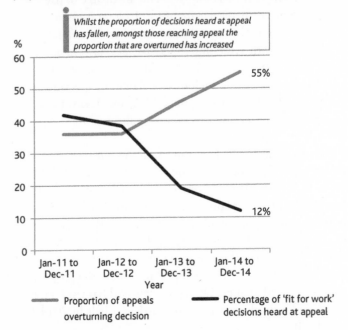

Whilst the proportion of decisions heard at appeal has fallen, amongst those reaching appeal the proportion that are overturned has increased

Legend:
- Proportion of appeals overturning decision
- Percentage of 'fit for work' decisions heard at appeal

Source: Analysis of data from DWP (Department for Work and Pensions) (2016) *ESA: Outcomes of work capability assessments*, www.gov.uk/government/statistics/esa-outcomes-of-work-capability-assessments-including-mandatory-reconsiderations-and-appeals-september-2016

Disability Living Allowance and the Personal Independence Payment

The new Personal Independence Payment (PIP) was announced in the first Budget of the coalition government in June 2010. It was intended to replace Disability Living Allowance (DLA) for 16- to 64 year-olds (under-16s would continue to receive DLA for children, and pensioners would continue to receive

Attendance Allowance). The new benefit was expected to reduce expenditure on the group affected by 20%[23] (producing savings of £3 billion per year by the time it was fully introduced).[24]

It was expected that reductions in expenditure would be produced by a reduction in the number of claimants – from a forecast of 2.2 million working-age DLA claimants in 2015/16, down to 1.7 million PIP claimants,[25] a reduction of nearly a quarter of the claimant population.

PIP was initially introduced for new claimants, but over time, it has been rolled out to working-age DLA claimants (although, as discussed below, the reassessment process has been somewhat delayed).

PIP has many things in common with DLA – it remains a non-means-tested and non-contribution-based benefit (the amount you get is neither affected by income nor National Insurance Contributions), and continues to have components to help with care or 'daily living' needs, and to help with mobility needs. However, it also has a number of crucial differences from DLA, including the assessment process.

First, there is no point-scoring 'test' for DLA (assessments are made on the basis of whether, on the evidence provided, the claimant meets the relevant criteria). There is, however, such an assessment for the PIP. As with ESA, points are scored on the basis of difficulties undertaking certain activities. If a claimant reaches 8 points for either the daily living or mobility component, they receive the standard component for that part. If they reach 12 points, they receive the enhanced component.

Second, the new PIP effectively removed the low rate care component of DLA. While a direct comparison cannot be drawn between the rates of support, the expected reduction in overall numbers of eligible claimants, combined with the removal of the 'lower rate' category, implies that the bar is raised, and the lowest rate claimants would be expected to be squeezed out altogether.

One way in which a claimant could receive the low rate care component of DLA is to pass the 'cooking test', which assesses whether the claimant is unable to cook a meal for themselves. Under PIP, this would not normally be adequate for the claimant to receive the standard daily living component.

Of those DLA claims that had been reassessed by July 2016, around 73% led to an award – meaning that around one-quarter of claimants lost entitlement on their reassessment (around the rate that the government had expected).[26]

However, the new benefit did not reduce the overall number of DLA and PIP claimants (and consequently failed to reduce spending as expected). Following this, the government decided that the test as introduced was not tough enough, and sought to move the goalposts in order to reduce the number of claimants. To achieve this, it was decided (albeit briefly) to change some of the circumstances under which points would be scored in the PIP assessment. The role this played in a rapid backtrack on a key budget measure – and the resignation of the Secretary of State for Work and Pensions – is discussed in more detail below.

Third, the introduction of PIP brings significant changes to the application process. Normally (although not always), DLA claims would be made by a written application only. For PIP, most claimants are expected to undertake a face-to-face assessment. Shortly after its initial implementation, PIP (including the reassessment of existing DLA claims) was causing considerable hardship and upset for many of those affected by it. The Public Accounts Committee found that while the expectation was that around three-quarters of assessments would be face-to-face rather than paper only, in reality, around 97% of cases were requiring a face-to-face assessment, and these were taking longer than expected.

The problems were causing delay and uncertainty for worried claimants, with many facing a wait of more than six months just to see a claim decided, and average waiting times nearly one-and-a-half times as long as the government had initially expected.[27] One claimant told an independent review into the introduction of the new system:

> The process is far too long and slow. We still haven't received any money, even though the date that it should have been paid in on has passed.... It wouldn't be such a large amount if it hadn't taken 11 months to get through the process! It's not just the fact that we haven't been receiving any money for a year, but

all the other benefits that rely on that bit of paper, such as a disabled bus pass, train pass etc and the proof needed to take parental leave.[28]

The Public Accounts Committee found that all of this should have been established through piloting the programme, and meant that many of the most basic assumptions about the new system were wrong,[29] calling the implementation of the new system 'rushed'.

There is even evidence that some claimants have difficulty accessing the centres where the face-to-face assessments take place. One claimant I spoke to was told she needed to attend a medical assessment at 9am. Attending the appointment would have meant she had to leave her flat at 5.45am and take a train, a tube and two buses. When she called the helpline, the adviser refused to change the appointment time, but said they could move it to an equally hard-to-reach location. Deeply upset she hung up; when she called back later she spoke to another person who wondered why the last person she spoke to hadn't offered her a taxi. She got the help that she needed to get to the appointment, but only by having the luck of speaking to someone willing to help, and after considerable anxiety.

In conclusion, the Public Accounts Committee chair, Margaret Hodge, called the implementation of the new system 'a fiasco' that 'has let down some of the most vulnerable people in our society'.[30]

However, despite the chaos and confusion caused by the PIP reassessment process, at the point of writing, the savings the government had suggested would be achieved by PIP have simply not yet materialised. By 2015/16 there were more than 500,000 PIP claimants. Between the introduction of PIP and this date, the number of working-age DLA claims in payment fell by only 300,000, resulting in an overall increase in DLA/PIP claims among working-age claimants (see Figure 15.4).[31]

Taking into account substantial expected savings from the transition between the two disability benefits, the 2013 Budget forecast expenditure on DLA of £11.4 billion and PIP of £2.9 billion by 2015/16. By the Autumn Statement 2015, actual expected expenditure was £13.2 billion on DLA and £3 billion

Figure 15.4: PIP and DLA (working-age) claimants, 2010/11-2015/16

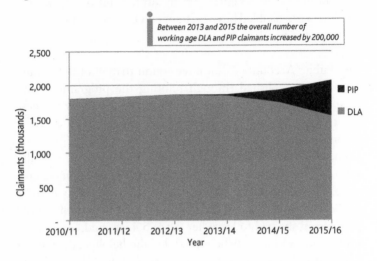

on PIP, meaning that DLA and PIP together were costing nearly £2 billion more than expected.[32] The Public Accounts Committee concluded, with some foreboding, that:

> The Department has yet to achieve the savings it intended to make and will have to seek compensatory savings elsewhere.[33]

One approach to make such further savings from PIP was through the planned (and then chaotically withdrawn) plan to change the 'aids and appliances' rules.

PIP aids and appliances – what was all the fuss about 'aids and appliances'?

Following a consultation, plans to reduce the points awarded for claimants requiring 'aids and appliances' to meet certain daily living needs were announced in early March 2015. Within a week, the announcement would lead to the resignation of the Secretary of State for Work and Pensions, and a backtracking on this key Budget measure.

These 'aids and appliance' changes would have meant that those who required the use of aids to enable them to meet their toilet needs, and for dressing and undressing, would have received 1 point for each of these activities rather than 2 (towards the total of 8 points required for the benefit).

It was believed that the change would affect around 640,000 claimants and would reduce PIP spending by £1.2 billion per year by 2020.[34] The Minister of State for Disabled People, Justin Tomlinson, announced the changes, saying:[35]

> ... it is clear that the assessment criteria for aids and appliances are not working as planned. Many people are eligible for a weekly award despite having minimal to no extra costs and judicial decisions have expanded the criteria for aids and appliances to include items we would expect people to have in their homes already.

The official statement on the proposed change from the DWP further reflected this, noting:

> Many of the aids and appliances for which points are being awarded are likely to be already found in people's homes, provided free by the NHS and local authorities, or can be bought for a low one-off cost.[36]

Infuriatingly, this is based on a fundamental misrepresentation of the reason for awarding points for requiring aids and appliances. The points are not awarded because of the cost of the aids (some of which, as the Minister points out, may well be in people's homes already), but as a way of understanding the difficulty faced by people undertaking those activities – a proxy to indicate a certain level of impairment. So, for example, a food processor may be required in order help the claimant cut up food[37] – the extra points are not awarded to buy a food processor, but because of all the other day-to-day difficulties, and associated costs, someone might face if, as a result of being disabled, they are unable to cut up food with a knife.

As the government's consultation itself described the PIP descriptors:

There are a range of descriptors for each activity, reflecting the ease or difficulty with which a person can carry out the task as a proxy for additional costs.[38]

A good example of the difference is the 12 points awarded for the mobility component of PIP if a claimant 'cannot follow the route of a familiar journey without ... an orientation aid.' The higher rate mobility component of £57 per week that would be awarded if the claimant met this descriptor is not paid to enable the claimant to buy a white stick, which costs just over £20.[39] The vital extra money is paid because of the overall additional mobility costs faced by people with severe visual impairments – additional costs that can hardly begin to be offset by the use of an aid.

Equally misleading was the way in which the Minister described the government's approach to consulting on these changes. As he put it:

> We consulted widely to find the best approach. And this new change will ensure that PIP is fairer and targets support at those who need it most.[40]

It is true that the DWP consulted on the changes, but they don't appear to have taken any account of the 281 responses that they received. Of these, only 11 (or 4%) said that they thought that changes to the aids and adaptation rules were desirable. As the government's own response to the consultation notes:

> The vast majority of respondents who provided a view on the substantive issue of the policy on aids and appliances ... thought that the current policy was preferable to any of the options for change. Many also pointed to the fact that PIP is still a relatively new benefit, arguing that making changes now would be hasty and would create unnecessary uncertainty for claimants.[41]

Perhaps in this context this change was inevitably going to trigger some discontent on the government's backbenches, but the extent of the outrage could not have been predicted. Immediately following confirmation of the PIP aids and appliances changes in the Budget 2016, and a week after the DWP had first announced the introduction of the changes, Iain Duncan Smith resigned from his position as Secretary of State for Work and Pensions. In his resignation letter to the Prime Minister, he said:

> I have for some time and rather reluctantly come to believe that the latest changes to benefits to the disabled and the context in which they've been made are a compromise too far. While they are defensible in narrow terms, given the continuing deficit, they are not defensible in the way they were placed within a Budget that benefits higher earning taxpayers. They should have instead been part of a wider process to engage others in finding the best way to better focus resources on those most in need.

Within a couple of days, a new Secretary of State, Stephen Crabb, had been appointed. In his first speech to Parliament in his new role he announced that the changes to the PIP would not go ahead, adding,

> I am absolutely clear that a compassionate and fair welfare system should not just be about numbers; behind every statistic there is a human being, and perhaps sometimes in government we forget that.[42]

The withdrawal of these further cuts to the PIP helped to prevent many thousands of claimants applying for PIP, or being moved from DLA to the new system, from losing support.

Conclusion

In 2015 Iain Duncan Smith announced that disabled people had 'no reason to be fearful' of the process of welfare reform. Within a year he had resigned as Secretary of State for Work and Pensions over cuts to support for disabled people, which he feared had simply gone too far.

In light of the endless problems with the ESA assessment process, and the implementation of PIP being branded 'a fiasco' by the Public Accounts Committee, it would have been difficult to accept that disabled people truly have 'no reason to be fearful', even before the additional changes to the PIP were proposed.

Disabled people deserve a better assessment process. They deserve an assessment process that takes proper account of the evidence that has been collected over the years on their case by specialists.

They deserve an assessment process that is efficiently organised, and doesn't leave people with lengthy waits before they receive a proper decision.

They deserve an assessment process that actively encourages engagement with poor decisions, rather than one that withdraws support from those who attempt to challenge a decision.

There are perhaps few more concrete tests of how civilised a society is than how it treats those who are sick or disabled. The current assessment process for sickness and disability support falls a long way short of the standard that we should expect in the UK today.

16

'Chaos, error and misjudgement':
The administration of Tax Credits and
Universal Credit

Tax Credits were introduced to provide additional payments to support families, make work pay and tackle poverty,[1] but soon after their introduction in 2003, they were beset by administrative problems. So much so, that in 2005, the then Prime Minister Tony Blair apologised to those who had faced 'hardship and distress'[2] as a result of problems with the system.

The then Shadow Chancellor George Osborne led the charge against the government for problems with the system, even questioning whether the Minister responsible should resign, noting:[3]

> There are serious questions about the future of Dawn Primarolo, who told Parliament the system was working well, when it patently wasn't.

He said two reports on this issue (one from Citizens Advice and the other from the Parliamentary Ombudsman) painted a 'devastating picture of administrative chaos, computer errors and political misjudgements at the heart of the Tax Credit system'.

The problem was to do with the way in which Tax Credits are calculated and paid. While, as we shall see, many of the problems were addressed at the time, they have been rapidly re-emerging in recent years.

Why have Tax Credits been in such a mess?

As explained earlier in Chapter 6, Tax Credits are an annual award – the total amount a claimant is entitled to is calculated for the whole year. However, people, and particularly those living on the lowest incomes, need to receive payments more frequently than once a year. For this reason they are normally paid on a weekly or four-weekly basis, based on an *estimated* entitlement for the whole year. Since Tax Credits are means tested, the claimant's household earnings over the course of the year can affect the overall amount due – predicted annual entitlement is therefore based on what the claimant thinks their income will be for the year.

The difficulty arises at the end of the year, when the award amount is checked against the household's actual income for the year. If the household's income is lower than the estimate, the award may have been underpaid and is topped up to the actual entitlement. If the household's income is *higher* than the estimate, this can result in the award being classed as overpaid and the government asking for some of the money back.

And we aren't talking about small amounts of money – in 2004, at the height of the Tax Credit problems, around £1.9 billion was overpaid to households in receipt of Tax Credits.

To reduce the likelihood of overpayments occurring, the Tax Credit system has a built-in 'buffer zone' (known as the 'income disregard'), which means that a household's income can rise by up to a given amount during a year without affecting entitlement. In the mid-2000s, as a result of the amount of Tax Credits being overpaid, the government decided to increase the income disregard from £2,500 to £25,000. In effect, this meant that if a claimant had been paid Tax Credits for a few months at the start of the year based on their previous year's earnings of £10,000, and then changed job so that by the end of the year they had earned £35,000, their overall Tax Credit entitlement wouldn't be affected.

Some overpayments are, in fact, impossible to avoid without a buffer zone – a household that has a low income for most of the year and then gets a sharp but unforeseeable increase in income may otherwise have already had more than their yearly entitlement before the rise in their income.

As shown in Figure 16.1, following the introduction of this larger buffer zone, overpayment rates (unsurprisingly) fell significantly in the following year. As the Revenue Benefits[4] website put it:

> The effect of the increase was to bring greater certainty for claimants in a system where a major problem had been the sheer unpredictability of what families could expect to receive.

Despite this positive effect, following the 2010 election, the coalition government decided to reduce the size of the overpayments buffer zone – first, from £25,000 to £10,000, and then, to £5,000.

Astonishingly, the coalition government also decided to introduce the reverse of a buffer (an anti-buffer?), which disregarded *falls* in income of up to £2,500 from 2012. This means that when (for example) a worker sees their hours reduced so that they earn £2,500 less than they did the previous year, the earnings figure used to calculate Tax Credits is not immediately adjusted down. Instead, they are treated as if their earnings are the same as the previous year, which could cost them more than £1,000 at a time when they are likely to be struggling.

As the income disregard has been reduced, overpayments (again, unsurprisingly) have increased. As shown in Figure 16.1, a higher proportion of Tax Credit claimants faced overpayments in 2014/15 than during the height of Tax Credit problems in the mid-2000s, with more than one in three claimants facing an overpaid award, and £1.7 billion of overpayments generated in 2014-15. This includes some exceptionally large overpayments – including around 50,000 families overpaid by more than £5,000.[5]

Government responses to this are notable. In 2005, when these problems were first recognised, the then Shadow (and later actual) Chancellor of the Exchequer questioned whether the Minister responsible should resign. The response of the government was dramatic – not only did the Prime Minister apologise, but the large increase in the size of the income disregard was also a direct response.

Figure 16.1: Proportion of Tax Credit awards overpaid, 2003/04-2014/15

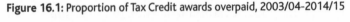

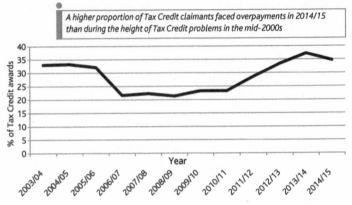

In 2015, when he himself was faced with a similar scale of problems within the system, the response of the Chancellor was to *further reduce* the level of the income disregard, back to the 2003-04 level of £2,500. We don't yet know the impact that this will have on overpayments, but the Chancellor expects to save a quarter of a billion pounds from this measure at its peak in 2018-19.[6]

It is astonishing that in response to this Tax Credits crisis, the government has felt able to act in this way – so opposed to what they called for a decade ago. Perhaps equally astonishing is the lack of public outcry – no calls for ministers to resign, no 'Tax Credit amnesty' campaigns set up[7] in response. The public has perhaps become so accustomed to ongoing cuts to support that overpayments have become largely indistinguishable from the raft of other cuts to support affecting low-income families. There is perhaps a loss of the will to fight;[8] unlike in 2005, benefit problems today simply seem inevitable.

Failing to act on overpayments – allowing them to escalate to the levels they are at today – cannot be an acceptable part of reforming the benefits system. It shows how, far from making the system 'fairer', cutting benefits frequently creates a less fair and more complex regime.

Universal Credit: solving the problem?

A frequent claim is that problems such as these will be resolved in the future as a result of the introduction of Universal Credit.

Certainly, Universal Credit will help to address some of the overpayment problems associated with Tax Credits. Universal Credit is a monthly rather than an annual entitlement, and is paid in arrears based on actual reported income for a given month. This helps to address the problem of incomes changing during the course of the year, and makes it less likely that large overpayment problems will occur.

However, Universal Credit payments are beset by their own problems of administration. First, payments are normally made monthly. Many families are not used to managing income (whether through benefits or earnings) on a monthly basis, being more used to weekly or fortnightly payments. This change is likely to be difficult for some to manage. While the Department for Work and Pensions (DWP) has argued that monthly payments are more like how earnings are paid, for many low-paid workers, this is not the case.

Concerns have also been raised that while, under the old system, different benefits could be paid to different people in a household, all of Universal Credit is normally paid as one sum into one nominated account. While many couples may be comfortable about having all of their Universal Credit paid into one account, others (and particularly newly formed couples) may be concerned about fully sharing household benefit income. For example, suppose a lone parent (not responsible for any housing costs) moves in with a new partner who currently receives Housing Benefit towards rent for a privately rented property. Under the old system, having moved in, the lone parent could continue to be paid support for the children while her partner could continue to receive Housing Benefit towards rent for the home. Under Universal Credit, the amounts for child-related costs[9] and for housing costs are bundled together into one payment. This means that either the lone parent relinquishes full control of the money she receives for her children, or her partner gives up control of the support he receives for housing costs. Having just moved in together, neither partner may be entirely happy to make this step. This could put some partners off from moving in together and forming long-term stable relationships.[10]

It is particularly concerning that this arrangement means that the child elements of Universal Credit will not necessarily go to the main carer of the children. It has been argued that where money intended for children's needs is paid to the person who provides care for them, it is more likely to be spent on the children than if the money is paid to someone else in the family.[11]

The fairest way of resolving a situation like this would be to enable payments to be split between partners – with payments for children going to the main carer, and payments for housing costs going to the person principally responsible for rent. This would also enable other sensible divisions of entitlements – for example, basic personal allowances for adults could be split equally between the joint claimants, and any additions on account of disability could go to the disabled person. While special arrangements do allow for the splitting of payments between partners, these are normally restricted to instances where there is a risk of financial abuse by one partner.

Third, and perhaps most seriously, Universal Credit is intended to be paid a month in arrears, with an additional week to process the application and, normally,[12] with a week's waiting period before the claim even begins. In total, this means that as standard, new claimants will be left with a period of six weeks to cope before they receive their first Universal Credit payment.

In response to this, the government made provision for 'advance payments' of Universal Credit to be made during the six-week period. However, six in ten clients Citizens Advice spoke to about claiming Universal Credit said that they had not been told about these by JobCentre Plus; in many cases, they only found out about them too late to get the help they needed (since they were denied help if asking for it more than three weeks after the claim was first made).[13] Even if an advance payment is made, it will only be for a maximum of half the claimant's total entitlement for a month.

Worryingly, a recent Citizens Advice report found that in a survey of clients who had moved on to Universal Credit, the waiting period was considerably more than six weeks for many, with one in ten respondents having waited more than nine weeks for their first payment and several having waited more than four months.[14]

Lengthy delays are not simply errors, they are a structured part of the Universal Credit system. For example, if someone claims Universal Credit because they have lost their job, they are expected to use their final salary payment to last them through the six weeks they are waiting for their first payment. However, if the employer makes this payment more than a week after the claimant makes their Universal Credit claim, their final earnings are treated as income for their first Universal Credit award period, meaning that their first payment may be delayed by a further month, and they have to wait 10 weeks for a payment instead of six.

Payments in arrears also cause particular problems with help with childcare costs through Universal Credit, since this support is provided on the basis of expenses that *have already been incurred*. This leaves families with the challenge of working out how they are going to manage to cover the upfront costs of childcare in the first place, before they can claim back some of these charges through Universal Credit.

Additionally, even when they are finally paid, claimants may not receive everything they should have been entitled to. In the old benefits system, many claims for support can be 'backdated', which means that if the claimant was entitled to receive support before the point at which they applied for it, they can get a lump sum payment of the money that they should have received. Under the Tax Credits system, a claim can be backdated by up to one month as standard. Universal Credit claims are not automatically backdated at all. Some backdating may be possible in exceptional cases, but only where evidence can be provided that there was a system error that prevented a claim being made at the right time, or because of illness.

One group that is particularly likely to become entitled to Universal Credit for the first time is new parents – both because of higher entitlements as a result of having their first child, and because of reductions in earnings often experienced around that time. Now (and I hope this will be clear for parents and non-parents alike), on the day on which someone's first child is born, it is unlikely that the first thing they will do is log on to the Universal Credit system and make a new claim for benefit.

However, this group is not explicitly exempted from the backdating rule. Perhaps they are expected to get a doctor's note to say that they were too busy giving birth to make a claim, or perhaps they are simply meant to give up on their first few days of entitlement. Either way, it can feel like Universal Credit is a system that too often is designed to make it hard to get the credit that is due.

Conclusion

Talking about how benefits are paid may not seem the most interesting part of welfare reform. It may not feel as much of a crisis as the billions of pounds being cut from children and working-age claimants across the system as a whole, but many cuts to support are the result of snipping away at the edges like this – not just by reducing provision, but also by making it harder to get the remaining support to which people are entitled.

Tax Credits were always problematic, but cuts to income disregards have consciously recreated the high rates of overpayments that existed in the mid-2000s. Universal Credit may help to resolve some problems with the generation of large benefit overpayments, but only at the risk of making it much harder for people to get the support they are entitled to in the first place.

It cannot be this hard to get people the correct amount of benefit at the time they need it. Solving this payments problem would play a major role in fixing the benefits system.

17

Sanctions

Many benefits come with conditions attached. Unemployed Jobseeker's Allowance (JSA) claimants are expected to be doing everything they can to prepare for moving back into work. Claimants receiving sickness benefits may be expected to undertake 'work-related activity' in order to prepare for the move back into employment when they are able. Single parents receiving Income Support while caring for young children may, similarly, be expected to be thinking about a return to work when their child gets older.

If claimants do not meet the conditions imposed on their receipt of benefits, they may face 'sanctions'. The nature of these sanctions varies, but at their heart they involve the withdrawal or reduction of benefit payments for a period of time.

It is right that there are some circumstances under which sanctions can be applied. Where people who should be seeking work are refusing to look for a job, the final threat of a sanction seems a reasonable measure in order to ensure compliance. However, where such an approach needs to be taken, this should be seen as a failure of policy to positively promote employment.

The principal way to move people into work should be to provide helpful support to find employment and clear financial work incentives – and in doing so, reduce the necessity of sanctions. As we shall see, this does not seem to be the direction of travel, and it is some of the most vulnerable groups who are suffering the most as a result.

Who can be sanctioned?

Under the old system, there are three main groups of claimants who may face sanctions for failing to meet certain conditions attached to their benefit. These are unemployed claimants in receipt of JSA, sick or disabled claimants receiving Employment and Support Allowance (ESA) (other than those in the support group), and single parents receiving Income Support on account of looking after a young child. A broader group of those claiming Universal Credit may be affected – the extension of sanctions under Universal Credit is discussed later in this chapter.

Of these groups, it is the jobseekers who (by their nature) are expected to be 'available for and actively seeking work' who face the highest level of work-related requirements, and who are the most likely to face a sanction on their benefits for failing to comply with these conditions.

This group may face benefit sanctions for a range of different reasons, including if they refuse to apply for or accept a job, if they fail to take part in training activities that they are required to, if they leave a job either voluntarily or as a result of misconduct, or if they are not deemed to have spent sufficient time each week looking for and applying for work.

Second, claimants who are placed in the work-related activity group (WRAG) for ESA (but not those in the support group) are expected to undertake work-focused interviews and other training and preparation for moving back into work. If they fail to do what is expected of them, they could face their benefits being sanctioned.

Understandably, many people in receipt of ESA are affected by conditions that would make it difficult for them to comply with the work-related activity requirements being placed on them, either because of physical incapacity (making it difficult to attend a required appointment) or mental health conditions. Too often claimants' health conditions have been found not to be properly taken into account in determining appropriate activities that they could undertake – such as someone whose work capability assessment (WCA) said they couldn't walk 200 metres being expected to walk nearly a mile for appointments.[1]

What benefit is sanctioned, and for how long?

For those claimants who do face benefit sanctions, this may not mean that they receive no financial support at all.

For JSA claimants, the claimant will typically not be paid any JSA during their sanction period.[2] However, to avoid destitution, they can often claim 'hardship payments' that are typically paid at 60% of the rate of their JSA entitlement (under Universal Credit, hardship payments are normally paid as loans that have to be repaid; sanctions under Universal Credit are discussed in more detail below).

For ESA claimants, the amount of benefit that is sanctioned has changed over time. When ESA was first introduced, this sanction was only applied to a small proportion of the claimant's ESA receipt (the work-related activity component), and the sanction ended when the claimant re-engaged with the activities expected of them. From the end of 2012 the sanctions were made considerably tougher – applying to the majority of the benefit[3] rather than just the work-related activity component.

Following the government's decision to scrap the work-related activity component (discussed in Chapter 10), in many cases the sanction will apply to all of their ESA entitlement, just as it would for many JSA claimants.[4] As with JSA claimants, ESA claimants can make a claim for hardship payments during the period of their sanction.

For lone parents in receipt of Income Support, the sanction applied is typically 20% of their 'personal allowance' (around £14.50 per week in 2017).

In all cases, claimants should continue to be entitled to any other benefits that they receive – such as Housing Benefit, Child Benefit and Tax Credits (since these benefits are not sanctioned). However, since Housing Benefit can be 'passported' (as discussed in Chapter 6), from means-tested out-of-work benefits, when payments of income-based JSA or ESA have stopped as a result of a sanction, many claimants have in the past found that their Housing Benefit stopped as well. This shouldn't have been happening, since claimants technically remain entitled to JSA during the period of the sanction (just not any money!), and there are some indications that guidance on this has improved.[5]

The length of the sanctions depend on who they are applied to, and the reason why they are applied. In some cases (particularly for lone parents caring for very young children), the sanction may end once the claimant undertakes the work-related requirements expected of them. At the other extreme, since the 2012 changes to the sanctions regime (which significantly extended the period for which sanctions could be applied), jobseekers who fail to do what is expected of them may face a sanction lasting as much as three years.

How frequently are sanctions being applied?

JSA claimants are by far the most frequent group to face a sanction on their benefit. At their recent peak in 2013, as many as 90,000 sanctions were handed out in a single month – with a total of more than 2 million between October 2012 and March 2016.[6]

One might think that sanctions would be most likely to be applied during periods of high employment, where it is (relatively) easy to find work, and it may be more reasonable to imagine that those remaining on unemployment benefit are not being sufficiently active in looking for work, and need to 'get on their bikes' and look for it. In periods of high unemployment, it might be expected that a higher proportion of JSA claimants are receiving the benefit because of adverse labour market conditions, and so sanctioning would be less common.

In fact, the evidence suggests that the reverse is true – it is in periods of high unemployment that sanctions are most likely to be applied. Figure 17.1 shows the number of JSA claimants and the proportion of them sanctioned since 2000. It indicates that when the number of JSA claimants rises, the proportion of claimants sanctioned also appears to rise shortly afterwards;[7] similarly, when the JSA claimant count falls (as it has – at the point of writing – for the last few years), the proportion of claimants who are sanctioned also appears to fall shortly afterwards.[8]

This makes little sense. A fair sanctions system should only penalise people for refusing to comply with the conditions of receiving their benefit. There is no reason why this should be higher in periods of high unemployment than in periods of low unemployment – and indeed, there may be reason to expect it to be lower.

The figures may, perhaps, be best interpreted as governments seeking to use sanctions as a means of actively controlling rates of claimants during periods of higher than normal unemployment – when unemployment is higher, claimants face increased levels of expectations (backed up with sanctions) around actively looking for work. When unemployment is lower, such expectations may be relaxed.

Figure 17.1: Numbers of JSA claimants, and sanctions applied, as a percentage of JSA claimants (2000-15)

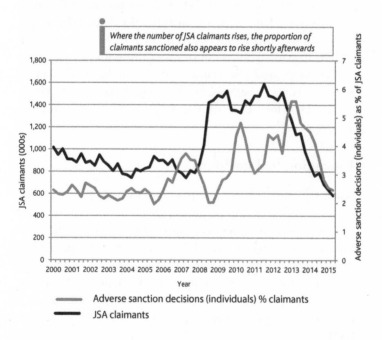

However, it is not only unemployed benefit claimants who can face high levels of sanctions use. Similarly, many claimants (albeit a significantly smaller proportion) in receipt of ESA can also face sanctions.

Between the start of 2013 and the Autumn of 2016, it was decided to apply around 84,000 ESA sanctions.[9] Through much of this period, numbers of sanctions applied rose rapidly[10] – at its peak in 2014, nearly 3,700 ESA sanctions were being applied in a single month.

As with JSA, between the middle of 2014 and the end of 2015, numbers of sanctions applied to ESA claimants were on a downward trend. In part, the reason for this is likely to be the increasing number of ESA claimants being assigned to the support group (who, as a result of being exempted from requirements to undertake work-related activities, do not face benefit sanctions for failing to do so). However, much of the reason appears to be a reducing propensity to apply sanctions, since the proportion applied per ESA claimant in the WRAG also fell in this period. As with JSA, it may be that overall levels of claimants affect the likelihood that claimants are sanctioned.

As shown in Chapter 15, too often the WCAs that determine which group claimants are placed in for ESA have been found to be inadequate. The combination of this with high levels of sanctions use against ESA claimants placed in the WRAG raises the risk of claimants being both asked to undertake work-related activities for which they are not fit, and facing a sanction for failing to comply.

Challenging bad decisions

Concerns have been raised about cases of both JSA and ESA sanctions being levied in the most ridiculous of circumstances. The *Independent* newspaper compiled a list of some of the most bizarre examples, including a claimant sanctioned for missing an appointment after having been hit by a car, someone who had found a job that was due to start in a fortnight being sanctioned for not seeking work in the meantime, and a claimant who was sanctioned for missing an appointment because she was at a job interview.[11]

Where a claimant feels that they shouldn't have been sanctioned, they can challenge the decision on a number of different grounds. For example, they might argue that they actually did the activity that the Department for Work and Pensions (DWP) said that they didn't do, that they were asked to do something that wasn't appropriate to their circumstances (for example, as a result of sickness or caring responsibilities), or that a personal crisis meant that they weren't able to comply (as, perhaps, in the case above of being hit by a car!).

The challenge process has three parts; the first is a review of the decision by the DWP. If the claimant is still unsatisfied with the outcome, they can ask for a further review (known as a 'mandatory reconsideration'), followed by an appeal to an independent tribunal.

Between October 2012 and March 2016 'decision-makers' (the people to whom the original decision about applying a sanction is referred) decided to apply around 2.35 million sanctions to JSA claimants.[12] Of these, just over 600,000 (about a quarter) were challenged, and of these challenges, around 325,000 were successful, leading to the original sanction decision being overturned.

Although in recent years the proportion of sanctions being challenged has fallen (as shown in Figure 17.2), the likelihood of a challenge being successful has risen enormously – from around half in 2013, to around eight in ten by the end of 2015. As a result, the overall picture is of an increasing proportion of initial decisions being overturned.

The rise in the proportion of challenges that are successful may be a worrying sign of declining quality of decision-making, or suggest that as people find it harder to access the process of challenging a sanction, only the strongest cases are being challenged. On the one hand, it is likely that this also indicates that changes to the review process (including the introduction of the second stage review of 'mandatory reconsideration') are having a positive impact, meaning, poorly applied sanctions are more likely to be overturned.

Signs of an improving reconsideration process make access to this process particularly important. However, there are indications that some of the most vulnerable claimants find it most difficult to challenge a decision. For example, recent work by The Children's Society showed that care leavers in receipt of JSA were significantly less likely than other groups to challenge a sanction that had been applied, although, when they did challenge them, they were considerably more likely than other groups to have the decision overturned.[13]

Figure 17.2: Percentage of JSA sanctions challenged, successfully challenged, and percentage of challenges to a JSA sanction which are successful

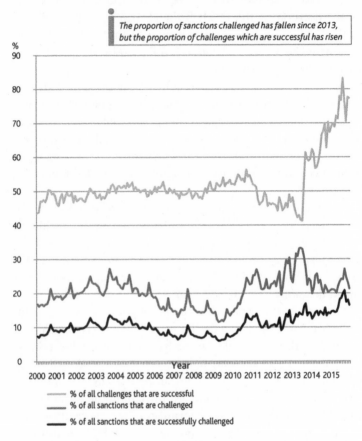

The proportion of sanctions challenged has fallen since 2013, but the proportion of challenges which are successful has risen

— % of all challenges that are successful
— % of all sanctions that are challenged
— % of all sanctions that are successfully challenged

Source: Author's analysis of data from DWP (Department for Work and Pensions) (2016) Stat-Xplore, https://stat-xplore.dwp.gov.uk

The impact of sanctions

Out-of-work benefit rates already represent a level of income that is significantly below a decent 'minimum income standard', and normally well below the poverty line. Unsurprisingly, further cutting someone's benefits for a period of time below even this level can have serious implications on their health and wellbeing.

Many claimants find it impossible to afford even basic living essentials during a period of sanction. One report found a link between areas seeing an increase in the use of sanctions, and higher emergency distribution of food aid.[14] Another report found that 20 to 30% of foodbank users had seen a reduction in their benefit payments as a result of a sanction.[15]

In some cases, the severity of the situation is such that sanctioned benefit claimants may feel that they have to steal to survive. One such claimant gave the following story of his experience of benefit sanctions in *The Guardian* newspaper:

> The sanctions became a vicious cycle as I became too ill to do anything ... feeling like it was my only option, I pocketed a sandwich from a supermarket. I was arrested and fined £80. I had no way of paying and spent a week in prison for non-payment. I lost my flat as I was £1,000 in rent arrears and I had piles of outstanding bills.[16]

The use of sanctions against claimants who are already sick or disabled raises particular concerns about their health impact. Research for the Scottish government highlighted evidence that sanctions can both exacerbate existing health problems and create new ones, including weight loss and disturbed sleep.[17] The stress caused by the imposition of sanctions can also have severe impacts on people's emotional health – some claimants affected by sanctions have been found to seek medication for depression as a result.[18]

The sister of one claimant believed that by leaving her brother without the money he needed to chill his insulin, sanctions contributed to his death. Gill Thompson wrote in *The Guardian* that:

> My brother David was found dead in his flat on 20th July 2013, he died alone, penniless and starving he was just 59. The coroner's report stated there was no food in his stomach. His money had been stopped a month before he died for failing to attend an appointment and by 8 July he had just £3.44 in his bank (you

need at least £5 to draw money out). His electric key had run out and [he] could not chill his insulin and there was no food in the flat.[19]

A rather different impression of the sanctions regime has been given by the DWP. The Department was caught out in 2015 when it was discovered that they had used fictional case studies of benefit claimants receiving incapacity-related benefits in a leaflet on sanctions, including one case ('Sarah') who was reported as being pleased about the outcome of being sanctioned:

> I didn't think a CV would help me but my work coach told me that all employers need one. I didn't have a good reason for not doing it and I was told I'd lose some of my payment. I decided to complete the CV and told my work coach.
>
> I got a letter to say my benefit would go down for two weeks. I was told it was longer than a week because I missed a meeting with my work coach back in March.
>
> My benefit is back to normal now and I'm really pleased with how my CV looks. It's going to help me when I'm ready to go back to work.[20]

Unsurprisingly, the case studies have since been withdrawn.

Of course, the other potential impact of the threat, and use, of benefit sanctions, is that claimants may do a better job of looking for and finding work. In 2016, the then Secretary of State for Work and Pensions, Iain Duncan Smith, was reported as saying that, 'sanctions are the reason why we now have the highest employment levels ever in the UK, and more women in work'.[21]

Certainly research has highlighted that benefit sanctions can lead to reductions in the period of time that claimants remain unemployed, and the proportion of people in employment. However the longer-term impacts are less clear, with sanctions use having been found to be associated with less sustainable employment, as well as lower levels of income in work.[22]

'In-work' conditionality and sanctions

Universal Credit introduces the potential for further changes to the sanctions regime. Under the old benefits system, the separation of out-of-work benefits makes it easy to say at what point a sanction can and cannot be applied – claimants in receipt of JSA, ESA or Income Support (out-of-work benefits) can have those benefits sanctioned for failing to meet work-related requirements. Benefits paid in work (Housing Benefit, Tax Credits, Child Benefit etc) won't be sanctioned. Claimants normally lose their entitlement to out-of-work benefits if they work 16 hours or more per week (or 24 hours for couples), meaning that claimants working over this threshold won't face a sanctions regime.

However, as outlined in Chapter 6, Universal Credit loses much of the distinction between 'in-work' and 'out-of-work' benefits, which has meant that new rules needed to be put in place for the circumstances under which someone could, and could not, face a benefit sanction.

The government decided to set the new work threshold *considerably* higher. In fact, under Universal Credit, single people may be expected to meet certain conditionality requirements (such as interviews and training) if they earn less than the amount they would receive working 35 hours per week at (their relevant rate of) the minimum wage – for joint claimants it is twice that. If they are found not to meet these requirements, their Universal Credit may be sanctioned – normally, by an amount equivalent to their standard allowance.

This means that, where claimants would currently 'escape' the sanctions regime on working 16 or at most 24 hours per week, under Universal Credit, claimants may need to work as many as 35, or even 70, hours (as a couple), or more specifically, earn as much as £13,700, or £27,400 for a couple,[23] before the risk of sanctions is withdrawn.

Of course, since this is an earnings-based rather than an hours-based threshold, this means that the least well-off workers may be expected to look for additional work, and could face sanctions on their benefit when they may be working considerably more hours than a better-paid employee in the same circumstances who faces no level of conditionality.

> For example, Jane is a single mum with one 12-year-old son; she rents a flat costing £150 per week. She works 20 hours per week at the National Living Wage, and earns £7,800 per year. She also receives around £219 per week in Universal Credit.
>
> June is a different single mum, also with one son and a flat costing £150 per week. However, June is Jane's manager, and while she also works 20 hours per week, she earns £14,000. She receives an income top up of around £158 per week in Universal Credit.
>
> In this case, Jane may have to spend up to an extra 15 hours per week in work-related activities; she may be expected to apply for other jobs if they pay more. If she is found not to be complying, she could have her Universal Credit reduced by as much as £73 per week.
>
> June would not be required to do any additional work-related activities, and as a result, could not face sanctions for failing to comply.

This inequitable change also raises questions around the circumstances under which the DWP might require claimants to – for example – apply for and accept another job if they are already working (but earning less than they are required to in order to escape labour market conditions on their Universal Credit). There could be good reasons why someone in Jane's position may not wish to accept an alternative job – they may feel their current job is in a better location, has childcare facilities not offered by another employer, or simply that they enjoy it more and think their future prospects are better by staying.

At the time of writing, reports are just starting to appear of some in-work Universal Credit claimants facing sanctions – including one claimant who said she normally works 30-40 hours per week on a zero hours contract being fined for failing to attend a Jobcentre meeting when she went on holiday. Reportedly, she was told that 'being on holiday was not a valid reason not to look for work'.[24]

Conclusion

Benefits sanctions should be a last resort, used to ensure that those who should be looking for work do so. Their use should be considered a sign of policy failure rather than success.

Perhaps most importantly, they should be applied consistently. However, the tendency to see an escalation of sanctions use when numbers of unemployment benefit claimants rise (and declines when the number of claimants fall) suggests that this may not be the case. Instead, perhaps, when unemployment rises, expectations on claimants similarly increase, in an effort to get the numbers of people out of work down again.

Many of the sanctions that are being handed out are also being found to have been applied wrongly when challenged. However, as we have seen, some of the most vulnerable groups (such as young people who have previously been in the care system), on whom sanctions may have the greatest impact, are among the least likely to challenge them.

In Chapter 3 I argued that governments may use the benefits system to reward and encourage socially desirable behaviours. One such behaviour is making the move into work where one is able to do so. However, the benefits system can be neither fair, nor perceived to be fair, if it changes expectations of claimants when times are the hardest (when unemployment rates are high), or if the most vulnerable find themselves least able to challenge a bad decision.

In this context, it is particularly worrying that in the future, we may see the extension of benefit conditionality and sanctions to increasing numbers of working claimants. This may leave workers feeling like they are being expected to make choices about taking on more work, or even changing jobs, that are not in their best interests. Furthermore, it is likely to further deepen inequities in the application of sanctions – meaning that workers on lower pay may face considerably higher levels of expectation and risk than workers in similar circumstances but on higher levels of pay, even if they are both reliant on the same benefits.

18

Local benefits, local choices

In modern Britain, the vast majority of benefits are provided as an entitlement which applies across the UK. This means that they aren't provided on a discretionary case-by-case basis, but instead, are based on entitlement criteria set down in legislation – meaning that whoever you are, and wherever you live in the country, if you meet that set of criteria, then you can receive support.

Two emerging, and connected, trends this decade have gradually shifted the UK away from this position. The first has been a shift of more decision-making powers over the benefits system to local councils and to the devolved nations. The second has been an increasing role of 'discretion' in determining receipt of support, rather than providing help on the basis of a fixed entitlement.

This chapter looks at three areas exhibiting this trend: the increasing role of Discretionary Housing Payments in the provision of support with housing costs for households on a low income, the localisation of crisis support, and the localisation of support with Council Tax bills through Council Tax Benefit.

Discretionary Housing Payments

Since 2001[1] local authorities have been given additional funding, known as Discretionary Housing Payments (DHP), to help them to support claimants where Housing Benefit payments are not sufficient. As indicated by the name, how this money is used is largely at the discretion of the council. For example, it might be used to provide short-term help for a family struggling with housing costs, to enable them to remain in their home while their child finishes their GCSEs.

This money has become all the more important in recent years. In Chapters 7 and 8 we saw how a number of different reforms have reduced the amount of support that tenants might receive with their rent – leading to significant shortfalls in support received compared to actual housing costs, for many tenants in both the private and social rented sectors.

As a response to this, the government has 'topped up' the amount of money provided to councils for DHP, in order to help local authorities to cope with the impact of various cuts to support within the Housing Benefit system – including the introduction of the Bedroom Tax, the benefit cap and reductions in support through Local Housing Allowance (LHA).

From funding of £20 million for DHP in 2010, this had risen to a peak of £180 million in 2013. The cash amount of the top ups between 2010 and 2016 (along with the reforms they have been intended to help councils cope with) are outlined in Figure 18.1.

Analysis has found that councils struggle to make long-term plans for future use of DHP, because of uncertainties about the future size of the fund.[2] So it was helpful that the Summer Budget in 2015 announced that £800 million of top ups would be paid in total up to 2020 (later reports have put this at £870 million, around £170 million per year), so local authorities could expect funding for this to continue at a relatively consistent rate to the end of the decade.

Except in Scotland (where this cap no longer applies), councils are allowed to spend up to 2.5 times the government allocation on providing DHP. Despite an extremely tight funding environment, in 2014-15 the situation became so desperate that many local authorities found that they were paying additional money from their own resources in order to try to keep people in their homes.[3] Since 2013, councils in Scotland have received additional funding from the Scottish government to supplement DHP allocations from the UK government, including £35 million in 2016/17.[4, 5]

DHPs are completely inadequate to the scale of the problems facing Housing Benefit claimants. It has been estimated that measures introduced since 2010 had cut Housing Benefit expenditure by more than £2 billion per year in cash terms by 2015/16.[6] In comparison, expected DHP of £125 million in that year covered little more than one-twentieth of the shortfall.

Figure 18.1: Discretionary Housing Payments (£ million cash) including additional transitional components to help with different welfare reforms

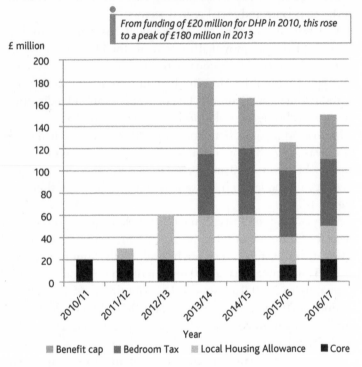

Source: Based on figures from Wilson, W., Barton, C. and Keen, R. (2016) *Housing Benefit measures announced since 2010*, Briefing paper number 05638. London: House of Commons Library

Despite this, the use of DHP is being presented as the panacea for resolving all 'difficult cases'. For example, in responding to a legal challenge that the Bedroom Tax discriminated against certain groups of vulnerable disabled people (including a case of a disabled child who needed an additional bedroom for a carer), the Department for Work and Pensions (DWP) argued:

> We know there will be people who need extra
> support. That is why we are giving local authorities
> over £870m in extra funding over the next five years
> to help ensure people in difficult situations like these
> don't lose out.[7]

This argument appears to misunderstand the core nature of DHP (it is even in the name) – they are discretionary. If you believe that children needing an overnight carer should not be affected by the Bedroom Tax, why not simply exempt them from it? It makes little sense to rely on a cash-limited, discretionary pot of money to provide this help. The DWP lost this case in the Supreme Court, but there are many other examples of people in urgent need having no certainty they will be able to stay in their home.

There is also a constant risk that, because payments are limited by the size of the pot available, the size of this 'pot' will reduce or disappear. For example, in a statement on the benefit cap, the government noted:

> £110 million has been made available to local
> authorities over two years [2013 to 2015] through
> the Discretionary Housing Payment (DHP) fund to
> support people who need extra help.[8]

For the following two years, 2015/16 and 2016/17, the level of additional DHP to assist with benefit cap cases had fallen to £65 million, despite it being set at a lower level from Autumn 2016, therefore affecting many more people.

Crisis support for families

A second example of the trend towards localisation of the benefits system is in the localisation of emergency provision in a crisis.

Sometimes, people simply run out of the money they need to buy basic essentials – to heat their home, or to make sure that they and their children are fed. This may be because of an unexpected expense (such as a boiler breaking down) or a fall in income (such as a sudden reduction in hours or a benefit payment problem). Whatever the reason, in these circumstances, it is the responsibility of any decent society to make sure that people do not freeze or starve. To achieve this, it is crucial that there is some form of safety net, outside of standard provision, which exists to give aid in a crisis.

Until 2013, this support was principally provided through what is known as the Discretionary Social Fund, payments that were made on a discretionary (and normally one-off) basis, to meet immediate needs. The fund was cash-limited, so there was a limit to the amount of support it could provide. This fund was made up of three key components: Budgeting Loans, Crisis Loans and Community Care Grants.

- *Budgeting Loans* were interest-free loans to help with costs that were difficult to budget for on a low income. These loans could help with things like furniture, clothing, removal expenses or travel costs.
- *Crisis Loans* were interest-free loans to help with immediate short-term needs in a crisis. In some cases so-called 'alignment payments' were paid, to help where claimants were waiting for a first payment of benefit (or a first payment of wages after moving into work).
- *Community Care Grants* were non-repayable grants to help people who had spent a period in institutional care, to resettle independently in the community, or to ease exceptional financial pressures facing a family.

In 2012, the government undertook wholesale reform of the Discretionary Social Fund. Some parts were kept (albeit in a different form, so Budgeting Loans are now called Budgeting Advances in Universal Credit, and Crisis Loan Alignment Payments changed to become Short-Term Benefit Advances or Advance Payments in Universal Credit).

However, the government also abolished two key elements of the Discretionary Social Fund: Crisis Loans (other than Alignment Payments) and Community Care Grants. These have been replaced by funding transferred to local authorities (and the devolved administrations) on a non-ring-fenced basis, with the intention that they establish their own Local Welfare Assistance schemes. A report by The Children's Society illustrated the changes as shown in Figure 18.2.

Figure 18.2: Changes to the Discretionary Social Fund

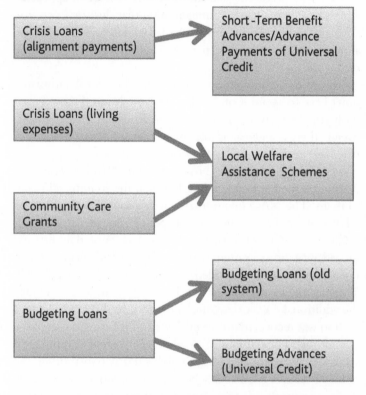

Source: Royston, S. and Rodrigues, L. (2013) *Nowhere to turn? Changes to emergency support.* London: The Children's Society

There have been some benefits to this localisation process. For example, in some cases local authorities have reported being able to use Local Welfare Assistance schemes as an opportunity to identify risk factors in the household, and to provide additional services to help tackle the underlying reason why support was needed.

However, any benefits of localising emergency support have been undermined by a lack of resources. When the government localised Crisis Loans and Community Care Grants, they also made major cuts in the support available to deliver this provision, from about £330 million in 2010/11, down to around £178 million (in real terms) in 2013-14.[9]

After this point the allocation was at risk of disappearing altogether, before campaigning arguing that this was 'a cut too far'[10] persuaded the government to backtrack. As a result, an allocation of £130 million per year (in cash terms) was secured to the end of the decade.

However, the funding is not ring-fenced (so local authorities don't have to spend it on local welfare provision if they do not wish to), and given the pressure on local authority budgets overall, there is understandable concern that much of this money may have ended up being spent on other things.

A National Audit Office (NAO) report in 2016[11] reported that 78% of councils were spending less than the funding allocated to them. The NAO questioned whether some families may be relying on credit for emergency expenses instead.

Changes to Crisis Loans, in particular, have wasted money and moved away from a system that encouraged self-reliance. Crisis Loans were loans – provided at zero interest, but paid back. This enabled them to be recapitalised each year, so as to reduce the additional costs of ongoing provision. In 2011/12, £148.4 million was recovered from paid-back Crisis Loans as part of the Discretionary Social Fund.[12] Analysis at the time that the local schemes were introduced suggested that nearly two-thirds (62%) of Local Welfare Assistance schemes did not provide loans, with a preference towards provision of non-repayable grant awards (whether cash or benefits in kind).[13]

So, at the same time as the then Chancellor announced that no one would get 'something for nothing' any more,[14] reform of the Discretionary Social Fund was doing the reverse – replacing interest-free emergency credit with grants of furniture, food and fuel.

Changes in household outgoings from month to month mean that many people are at risk of simply being unable to pay for something essential from time to time. But inevitably, those struggling with exceptionally tight budgets are most at risk. Although loans may seem less generous, they can be an effective way of allocating a limited amount of money, to ensure that households don't have to turn to high-cost credit in an emergency.

Access to crisis support should be a key component of the welfare system. It is not. The result is that when things go wrong, people either rely on inflexible, often inadequate hand-outs, or turn to high-cost credit in order to get by – risking greater problems in the future.

We return to how the benefits system could provide a better system of emergency support in Part VI.

Council Tax Reduction

Our third example of localisation in the benefits system relates to the reform of Council Tax Benefit – support with Council Tax bills for low-income households.

Until recently, Council Tax Benefit covered the costs of Council Tax in full for those with no income or savings other than an out-of-work benefit such as Jobseeker's Allowance (JSA). From 2013, responsibility for administering the benefit was passed to councils. As a result, each council was asked to produce a local scheme of support (called a Council Tax Reduction scheme).

However, the government also decided to simultaneously reduce the money available to local authorities for providing Council Tax Reduction. Funding was reduced by 10%[15] – the Local Government Association (LGA) found that this meant that there was a £1 billion shortfall between the money needed to retain the pre-2013 scheme and the money actually available to councils for delivering the new schemes.[16]

However, the reduction in support for working-age claimants was significantly greater than this 10% reduction, since councils were told that pensioners had to be protected. The impact of pensioner protection varied across the country, depending on the proportion of older people in the local area. As a result of this protection, in 2013, overall Council Tax support fell by 14% for working-age households.[17]

Unsurprisingly, the combination of localisation and funding cuts resulted in a wide variety of different Council Tax

Reduction schemes being introduced across the country. Some of the main differences between schemes revolved around:

- Whether households with no income other than benefits continued to receive support to cover their Council Tax in full. Shortly after the new schemes were introduced, it was found that about three-quarters of councils no longer covered 100% of Council Tax for households with no other income.[18] A survey of schemes taking this approach found that of those not previously paying Council Tax who started to have to from 2013, half had to pay at least £85, a quarter at least £170 and 10% at least £225 per year.[19]
- The rate at which Council Tax Reduction entitlement was withdrawn with earnings (the 'taper' rate) varied between schemes. One review found that about 20 local authorities increased the taper rate for Council Tax Benefit from the rate applied under the old system.[20] In addition, some councils looked again at what counted as income for the purposes of Council Tax Benefit – for example, counting Child Benefit as income for the purposes of calculating entitlement.
- Similarly, some councils looked at the treatment of savings, and withdrew entitlement from people at a lower level of savings than under Council Tax Benefit.
- Finally, some local authorities opted to take the 10% reduction in Council Tax Benefit funding on the chin, and cover the shortfall in funding from other money available to them. However, by 2014-15 only 46 councils out of 326 continued to provide the same rate of support as was provided prior to localisation.[21]

The impact of this reduction in support has been serious for both claimants and councils. At the same time as Council Tax Benefit was localised and cut, there was a significant rise in Council Tax arrears, and further increases the following year (see Figure 18.3). By 2015 councils faced arrears of £2.7 billion – more than 10% higher than the total arrears in 2013 – just before the localisation of Council Tax Benefit. Analysis from the New Policy Institute found that those areas where support was cut the most also saw the largest increases in arrears.[22]

Figure 18.3: Council Tax arrears across English authorities at 31 March for each year, 2010-11 to 2014-15 (£ millions)

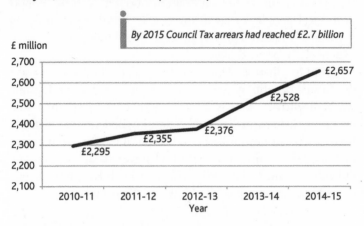

Source: Analysis of data from DCLG (Department for Communities and Local Government) (2015) *Collection rates for Council Tax and non-domestic rates in England, 2014 to 2015*, www.gov.uk/government/statistics/collection-rates-for-council-tax-and-non-domestic-rates-in-england-2014-to-2015

However, this wasn't simply about money not being paid. The localisation of Council Tax Benefit has also been causing considerable stress for those affected. The Children's Society found that in 2012/13 there were a total of 1.9 million court summons for Council Tax debt; following the localisation of Council Tax Benefit, this had increased by a third, to 2.6 million.[23]

Cut and localised Council Tax Benefit is costing councils many millions of pounds each year as a result of reduced collection rates, let alone all the additional costs of chasing payments from people without the money to pay. It is a measure which has created a patchwork of different schemes, resulting in a postcode lottery for claimants who may or may not happen to live in an area able to afford more generous provision.

As with the provision of DHP, the localisation of Council Tax Benefit is an example of additional responsibilities being placed on local authorities without the support that they need in order to provide adequate assistance. Rather than genuine localisation – intended to give local communities more control over policies that affect their residents – localisation in the context of a cut like this only creates an illusion of control for local councils. It forces them to make difficult decisions about how to cut support from local people, or (as in the case of DHP) to fill holes in dramatically reduced provision, without giving them any scope to actively improve things.

Finally, localisation of Council Tax Benefit also serves to make the future benefits system more complex, and to undermine work incentives. This is because, unlike other means-tested benefits (and in particular, unlike Housing Benefit), Council Tax Benefit has not been rolled into Universal Credit. As discussed in Chapter 13, this means that whatever means testing any individual council uses for their Council Tax Reduction scheme, this will come on top of the Universal Credit taper.

Conclusion

A benefits system based on national entitlements provides stability, consistency and some degree of fairness. While the significance of the trend towards local and discretionary support should not be overstated, and it remains the case that the vast majority of benefit payments are based on entitlements set at a national level, the emerging reliance on local, often discretionary, support is a worrying trend.

Despite some potential benefits to local provision – it can, in some circumstances, provide an opportunity to join up financial provision with other local support services to address underlying needs (as may be happening with some Local Welfare Assistance schemes), as seen in this chapter, local provision also carries a number of risks.

There is a risk that a postcode lottery of support is created, with some areas providing a more generous package of assistance than others (as can be seen with the variation between Council Tax Reduction schemes introduced across the country).

There is also a risk that local authorities are unable to provide the best value for money, because administrative complexities make it more difficult to deliver local provision in the same way as was possible at a national level (for example, local authorities are likely to find it difficult to provide the kind of interest-free loan scheme that was available through Crisis Loans).

If people do not receive support as an entitlement, there is even a risk that a non-ring-fenced pot of funding can disappear altogether – invested in other areas by local authorities facing major budget pressures.

But perhaps the biggest risk is that 'localisation' is used as a way of passing the buck for the impact of cuts. This may be done by cutting funding for provision, and handing over responsibility for the difficult task of creating a new, lower-cost scheme to councils (as was the case with both Council Tax Benefit and Local Welfare Assistance).

Alternatively, this may be done by giving inadequate, discretionary funding to local authorities, with which they are expected to patch up holes left by larger cuts to support to national entitlements (as with the temporary increases in DHP). In neither case is this true 'localisation'.

Localisation should mean the empowerment of local areas in making decisions to improve communities, not just passing responsibility for making difficult, unpopular choices on how to cut provision.

19

Making 'older people' older: Changes in the pension age

Although, as we saw in Chapter 11, the value of benefits for pensioners is increasing, the group of people entitled to receive them is becoming more restricted. Until 2010, the State Pension age for women was 60 and for men it was 65. This was the age from which people could receive the State Pension, and was also the age of entitlement for Pension Credit.

Since then, the State Pension age for women has been rising in order to align it with that of men (a process that will be completed in 2018). Then, from the end of 2018, the State Pension age of both men and women will rise to reach 66 by October 2020. From 2026 the State Pension age will rise again, to reach 67 by 2028.

This chapter is about why this is happening, and how some of the lowest-income older people are losing out the most as a result.

Why is the State Pension age being increased?

There are two main changes to the State Pension that have started to be introduced since 2010. The first is the alignment of the State Pension age for women with that of men. The second is the further increase in the State Pension age for everyone.

Plans for aligning the State Pension age between women and men were first introduced as far back as 1993.[1] The then Chancellor Ken Clarke justified this partly on the basis of the changing role of women in the economy, and partly on the basis of cost, international comparisons and competitiveness:

We believe that it is right to equalise at 65 because, first, women are increasingly playing a role equal to men in the economy. They live longer and can expect to work as long as men. Secondly, equalising at 65 will improve the future support ratio between those working and those on a State Pension. Lastly, throughout the world, countries are equalising upwards or increasing pension ages for both sexes.[2]

Increases in the State Pension age for both men and women (which were first legislated for in 2007) are principally justified by increases in life expectancy. Even taking into account increases in the State Pension age, the length of time the average pensioner may expect to receive the pension may be considerably greater than it has been in the past. Life expectancy at birth in the UK rose between 2000 and 2014, from 75.3 to 79.1 years for men and 80.1 to 82.8 years for women. For those who reach 65 (and so are likely to receive a State Pension), UK life expectancy from that age increased from 15.2 years in 1998 to 18.5 years in 2014 for men. For women, the comparable increase was from 18.5 years to 20.9 years.[3]

An extra three years of life expectancy at 65 over a 15-year period is a simply enormous increase and, as one government impact assessment put it, 'increasing life expectancy is good news, but comes with a cost'.[4] Without corresponding changes in the State Pension age, both the number and proportion of pensioners in the UK would be likely to increase substantially, putting further pressure on expenditure on the State Pension, both as an absolute amount, and as a proportion of GDP.

As a result, either the pot of money available to fund the State Pension has to increase to cover an additional period of provision for the average claimant, or the State Pension age has to rise. For this reason, aligning the State Pension between men and women, and then increasing both – first to 66 and then to 67 – can be argued to have a strong rationale.

The increase in the total number of State Pension recipients gradually slowed between 2010 and 2015 (as a result of the increase in the State Pension age for women). Forecasts indicate that between 2015 and 2020, the number of State Pension claimants will decline (when the State Pension age for both women and men will have risen to 66) (see Figure 19.1).

Figure 19.1: State Pension claimants, 2005-20[a]

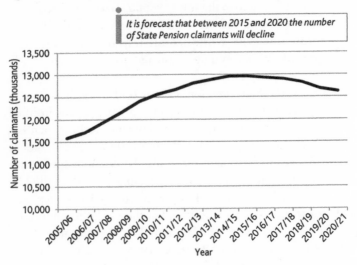

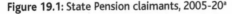

It is forecast that between 2015 and 2020 the number of State Pension claimants will decline

Note: [a] Numbers are forecasts from 2016/17 to 2020/21
Source: Department for Work and Pensions (2017) *Benefit expenditure and caseload tables - outturn and forecast Spring Budget 2017*. London, Department for Work and Pensions, https://www.gov.uk/government/uploads/system/uploads/attachment_data/file/603005/outturn-and-forecast-spring-budget-2017.xlsx

The government has signalled that further increases in the State Pension age will be linked to increases in life expectancy. In the 2013 Autumn Statement, the Chancellor said that the expectation was that people should spend up to a third of their life in retirement:

> … [we] have to guarantee that the Basic State Pension is affordable in the future, even as people live longer and our society grows older. The only way to do that is to ensure the pension age keeps track with life expectancy.
>
> We think a fair principle is that, as now, people should expect to spend up to a third of their adult life

in retirement. Based on latest life expectancy figures, applying that principle would mean an increase in the State Pension age to 68 in the mid 2030s and to 69 in the late 2040s.[5]

Inequalities in life expectancy

Increasing the State Pension age has been seen as an important measure in controlling expenditure over time. However, what makes sense on the face of it looks rather less fair when inequalities in life expectancy are considered.

Life expectancy varies a great deal across the UK and between different social groups. The coalition government's own *State of the nation* report in 2010[6] found that those living in the poorest neighbourhoods in England die an average of seven years earlier than people living in the richest neighbourhoods. The report went on to highlight that the gap in terms of disability-free life expectancy is even larger – with the average difference between those living in the poorest and richest neighbourhoods being 17 years.

In addition, inequality in life expectancy has been growing. The greatest growth in life expectancy at birth for males between 1982-86 and 2002-06 was experienced by those in the lower managerial and professional class, such as school teachers and social workers, at 5.3 years. The smallest growth in life expectancy at birth was experienced by those in the two least advantaged classes, at around 3.8 to 3.9 years.[7]

The consequence of this is that we may expect an increasing proportion of spending on the State Pension to go towards provision for wealthier older people who live longer over the State Pension age. In so far as support for pensioners grows as a proportion of the overall welfare budget, so we might similarly expect a gradual shift towards increased spending on better-off households.

The widening of the gap in life expectancy between better-off and poorer households is not over – inequalities in life expectancy are expected to continue to grow in coming years. One study found that inequalities in life expectancy between the most and least deprived 1% of districts across the UK would reach 8.3

years by 2030.[8] Furthermore, the report raised concerns that rising inequalities are being exacerbated by austerity policies.[9]

So, the gradual increase in the State Pension age, which may seem like a reasonable measure in light of increases in average life expectancy, starts to look rather less fair, when it is considered that this increase occurs regardless of background.

However, not only is the life expectancy of the most disadvantaged people rising more slowly than that of the most well-off, *their effective retirement age is also increasing much faster than that of other groups.* This is because of an aspect of welfare reform affecting older people that we have not yet discussed in detail – Pension Credit.

Pension Credit

While there has been a great deal of discussion about the rights and wrongs of increasing the State Pension age, its less glamorous cousin, Pension Credit, has received rather less attention.

As discussed in Chapter 4, Pension Credit is an income-based benefit, paid to older people living on a low level of income. This may be either because they are not entitled to receive the State Pension, or because while they do receive a Basic State Pension, they don't have substantial other income to rely on in retirement – meaning that Pension Credit 'tops up' their pension income to a minimum level.

Until 2010, claimants (both men and women) could claim Pension Credit from the age of 60. This both significantly increased incomes for the over-60s, and exempted them from having to look for work. At that point, Pension Credit (rather than the State Pension) effectively set both the age of retirement and the level of retirement income for many low-income older people – and particularly those in manual work, and with deteriorating health. As a result, the difference between the age at which Pension Credit could be received, and the age at which men could receive their State Pension, helped to address inequalities in life expectancy between more and less disadvantaged households.

Since 2010, the age at which people can claim Pension Credit has risen in line with the State Pension age for women

– increasing from 60 to reach 65 by 2018. The Pension Credit age will then rise in line with the State Pension as it increases further over time.

This means that while for men on a higher level of income, the effective retirement age (using the State Pension as a proxy) will have risen by one year by 2020, for low-income workers (using Pension Credit age of entitlement as a proxy), the age of retirement will have risen by *six years* over the same period.

All in all, we may expect that men from a more privileged background, with a life expectancy rising more rapidly, and a slower increase in their retirement age, may see their expected period of retirement continue to lengthen despite the increase in the State Pension age.

At the same time, a slower increase in life expectancy, combined with a rapid increase in their retirement age between 2010 and 2020, means that the most disadvantaged workers may expect to see their overall period of retirement shorten significantly over the course of this decade.[10] The lucky ones from this group will still expect to receive some – shorter than average – retirement. The unlucky ones will never reach retirement – or, if they do, they may be too worn out from a lifetime of labour to enjoy any quality of life through this period.

Sixty- to 66-year-olds on a low income

The question then remains, if low-income 60- to 66-year-olds will not be able to receive Pension Credit in 2020, what support will they receive instead?

Some will try to hang on in work until they reach State Pension age. Others will find themselves too old, sick and tired to work – but instead of being able to retire on Pension Credit, this group will find themselves claiming either unemployment or sickness benefits.

The impact of this increase in the Pension Credit age can already be seen as it has crept up since 2010. Over-60s have increased substantially as a proportion of both the Jobseeker's Allowance (JSA) and Employment and Support Allowance (ESA) population[11] – from 1% to 7% of JSA claimants, and from 5% to

13% of ESA claimants. By the summer of 2016 there were around 350,000 ESA and JSA claimants aged over 60 (see Figure 19.2).

Not only does that mean that they have to meet the work-related requirements imposed on both JSA and ESA claimants, but it also results in a substantially lower level of income for this group.

> For example, Michael is a 63-year-old man. He is too sick to work – he receives ESA at a rate of £73 per week (with the work-related activity component removed). Were he a year older[12] and entitled to receive Pension Credit, he would receive £158.

In addition, while ESA will remain frozen to 2020, Pension Credit is expected to rise at least in line with earnings, taking the expected value to around £167 by the end of the decade.[13]

The increase in the Pension Credit age means that instead of spending the last years of their life with a decent level of income, and without being required to seek work, people like Michael may spend the final years of their life with less than half of a proper retirement income, and continuing to be expected to prepare for employment.

This isn't how people should spend the last of their lives, as the former Labour Pensions Minister Malcolm Wicks put it (with reference to the increase in the State Pension age, rather than that of Pension Credit):

> These are people in the main who left school at 15 or 16 and have been in the labour market ever since. By their 60s many of them are worn out and simply need the rest that retirement can offer.[14]

However, as inequalities in life expectancies grow, and as the State Pension age increases (pushed up by the longer lives of the better-off), this is the 'retirement' that can be expected for increasing numbers of the least well-off people in society.

Figure 19.2: Over-60s as a proportion of ESA and JSA claimants, 2008–16

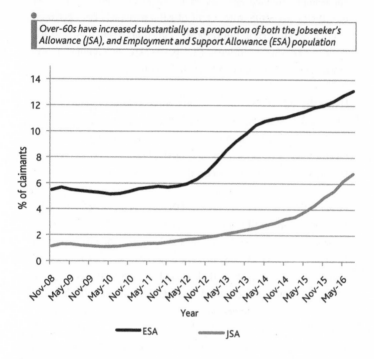

Over-60s have increased substantially as a proportion of both the Jobseeker's Allowance (JSA), and Employment and Support Allowance (ESA) population

Mixed age couples

This problem is exacerbated under Universal Credit. Under the old benefits system, if one partner in a couple is over Pension Credit age and the other is under Pension Credit age, then the couple would normally be entitled to receive Pension Credit (based on the age of the older partner).

Under Universal Credit, if either of the partners are under Pension Credit age, the couple will be required to claim Universal Credit rather than Pension Credit (effectively they will both be treated as being of working age).[15] This will have an enormous impact on their income.

In addition, since the State Pension is a contribution-based benefit treated as 'unearned income' for the purposes of Universal Credit entitlement, any pension received by the older partner will be deducted in full from the couple's Universal Credit entitlement (as described in Chapter 14), so the claimants won't gain anything from this benefit either.

For example, Amanda, aged 66, and Dennis aged 62, are a couple who rent their own home, with a rent of £100 per week. They get their Council Tax covered in full through Council Tax Reduction. Amanda receives an old State Pension of £122 per week; Dennis is not currently in work, but not old enough to claim his pension.

Under the old system, Amanda and Dennis receive a top up of £121 to Amanda's State Pension through Pension Credit, plus they also receive £100 per week in Housing Benefit to help with their rent (giving them a total income of around £343 per week, or £243 to live on after paying housing costs).

Under Universal Credit, Amanda and Dennis will be expected to claim the new benefit until Dennis reaches Pension Credit age. Amanda's pension is deducted in full from their Universal Credit entitlement. In total they receive £122 in State Pension income, and £93 in Universal Credit entitlement, making their overall income £215 per week, or £115 after housing costs are deducted. *This is about half what they would have to live on at present.*

In such a case, someone in Amanda's position could have to wait a number of years *above pension age* before receiving a proper retirement income. It is notable that this treatment of mixed age couples only affects older people on a low income who need extra help with rent and living costs through the benefits system.

Conclusion

Despite the increase in the State Pension age, and as a result of increasing life expectancy, the number of recipients of the State Pension is still forecast to be about the same in 2020 as in 2010. This is the result of a rise between 2010 and 2015, and subsequent fall between 2015 and 2020.

Although there are expected to be the same number of claimants at the start and end of the decade, the triple lock means that the overall cost of the State Pension is forecast to rise substantially over this period – costing an additional £18 billion in real terms by 2020 compared to 2010.[16] Budget forecast tables allow us to derive that the average cost of the State Pension per claimant will rise in real terms from around £6,200 per year in 2010, to more than £7,650 per claimant by the end of the decade.

The costs of increasing the value of the State Pension are paid for in significant part by increasing the State Pension age and the age of Pension Credit entitlement, and by reducing entitlements for people below that age. The focus of policy on providing a *higher* level of income to an *older* age group means that the gains can be expected to accrue disproportionately to better-off households, who can expect an increasing amount of their life to be spent above the State Pension age.

Put simply, rises in the State Pension age, combined with the triple lock on the State Pension, increasingly target higher levels of support at a relatively more advantaged group with a longer life expectancy.

It was fair of the former Chancellor to say that people should spend up to around a third of their adult life in retirement. However, adjusting the State Pension age to reflect average life expectancies means that many people from the most disadvantaged households, with lower than average life expectancies, get an awful lot less than that.

Between 2010 and 2020, for many of this group the pension age has gone up not by one year, but by six, as the age at which Pension Credit can be claimed has increased from 60 to 66. Many of this group of low-income older people can expect to see little or no time in healthy retirement after that age.

At the same time, older partners in mixed age couples may expect to have to wait even longer to receive a retirement income, as changes under Universal Credit push low-income pensioners in this group back into the working-age benefits system.

One way of addressing the inequalities of life expectancy would be to reintroduce a distinction between the age at which Pension Credit can be claimed and the age at which the State Pension can be claimed. Savings from ending the pensions triple lock could be re-invested (in part) in decoupling the age at which claimants can receive Pension Credit from the State Pension age. Alongside reviewing the State Pension age, the government should look at what the appropriate age of entitlement for low-income pensioners should be – for example, based on life expectancy for the poorest 10th of households (rather than average life expectancy). The age of Pension Credit entitlement could then be set to ensure that this group was able to spend a third of their adult life in retirement.

At the same time, it must be ensured that all those who do reach their appropriate retirement age receive a proper retirement income – even if their partner is not yet a pensioner.

Any civilised society must ensure that it provides for a decent retirement for its elderly, but that provision must be one that is shared by all citizens, rather than being reserved for the more privileged.

Part V
The 'new settlement' – Benefits in 2020

This will be a Budget for working people.

A Budget that sets out a plan for Britain for the next five years to keep moving us from a low wage, high tax, high welfare economy; to the higher wage, lower tax, lower welfare country we intend to create.

This is the new settlement.[1]

Until 2015 you might have believed that cuts to the benefits system were an economic necessity, designed to reduce the deficit. The 2015 Budget changed that.

Following the 2015 General Election, the then Chancellor took the opportunity to make the case for a new phase in the welfare reform agenda. For the coming five years, changes to the benefits system were about more than reducing the deficit; they were to play a key role in a shift in the whole economy – a rebalancing intended to take us from a high tax, high welfare economy to a low tax, low welfare one.[2] This was to be the 'new settlement'.

Previous chapters have looked at both the current benefits system and the challenges faced to 2020 as a result of the process of welfare reform. They have looked in detail at a number of measures that the government are taking to reform the benefits system and to introduce the new settlement. The key question now is just what will this new settlement look like?

This part of the book has two chapters. In Chapter 20 we consider some of the cumulative impacts of welfare reform. This includes looking at benefits spending between 2010 and

2020, reviewing differences in spending between groups, and considering some example household types, to see just how much they could be affected by welfare reform over the decade.

Reductions in spending only matter because they have a real impact on people's lives. In Chapter 21 we look at what some of those impacts might be, including on poverty and living standards, on homelessness and housing insecurity, on fairness and inequality, on health and educational outcomes, on incentives to move into work, and on social isolation.

These are the real reasons why welfare reform matters, and why it is so important to fix our broken benefits system.

20

Understanding the 'low tax, low welfare' economy

Previous chapters have looked at particular parts of the benefits system, and reviewed specific changes made within it between 2010 and 2020. In this chapter, we take a step back to look at the system as a whole, and in particular, what the overall package of changes means for welfare spending – and overall household incomes – over the course of the decade.

We do this in two ways. First, we look at changes in benefits expenditure between 2010 and 2020 – both overall spending and expenditure targeted at different groups (and in particular, the differences between spending on pensioners and working-age benefit claimants). Second, we look at individual household types, exploring the cumulative impact of welfare reforms (as well as other changes) on family incomes.

Benefits spending, 2010-20

Despite all of the measures that the government introduced to reduce it, welfare spending in real terms didn't fall at all between 2010 and 2015. In fact, as noted in Chapter 1, overall welfare spending across Britain was at its highest ever (in real terms) in 2015, at £218 billion overall.

However, looking at overall benefits expenditure can be misleading, since it is affected by more than just the generosity of the benefits system, including (for example) population size. A growing population has higher benefits expenditure since there are simply more people to receive it (as well as, potentially, more people contributing to taxes to pay for it) (see Figure 20.1).

Figure 20.1: Benefits expenditure (GB), 2010-20 (£ billion, 2017–18 prices)[a]

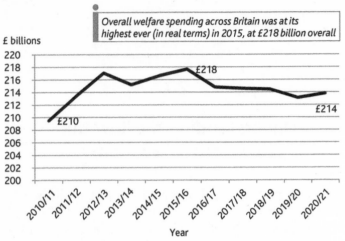

Note: [a]2016/17 to 2020/21 are forecasts
Source: Analysis based on data from Department for Work and Pensions (2017) *Benefit expenditure and caseload tables 2017*, https://www.gov.uk/government/uploads/system/uploads/attachment_data/file/600929/outturn-and-forecast-spring-budget-2017.xlsx

An alternative approach is to look at benefits expenditure per household, or as a proportion of GDP. Again, it is notable that, on either measure, benefits spending did not fall significantly over the first half of the decade. Across Britain, spending per household decreased (very slightly) by an average of £52 per household per year,[1] between 2010/11 and 2015/16 (from £8,185 per household, to £8,133 per household). There was a small fall in spending as a proportion of GDP, which fell by 0.7% from 11.6% to 10.9%, suggesting that as the economy was recovering from the recession, benefit spending consumed a reducing proportion of overall economic output.

The forecast for welfare spending to 2020 looks significantly different. As can be seen above, welfare spending overall is expected to fall by about £4 billion per year between a peak of £218 billion in 2015 and £214 billion in 2020. However, despite this, overall benefits spending is still expected to be around £4 billion per year greater in 2020 than it was in 2010.

Spending as a proportion of GDP is expected to fall considerably further – from 11.8% of GDP in 2010, down to 10% in 2020, the lowest rate since the start of the century. This means that the share of overall economic output taken up by benefits spending is planned to reduce by nearly one-sixth over the course of the decade.

This is only part of the story. Separating out spending on people of working age and children from that on older people reveals a divide in the balance of cuts and spending.

What happens when you take out pensioners from the equation?

In Chapter 11, protections for pensioners through the State Pension and Pension Credit were discussed. As a result of these, overall benefit expenditure for those of pension age, compared to people of working age and children, looks very different indeed.

While 2015 saw the highest ever real terms benefits spending at £218 billion, all of the increase (and more) from the start of the decade came from additional spending on pensioners. Between 2010 and 2015, while spending on pensioners increased by around £11 billion per year, real terms spending on working-age people and children fell by £3 billion. This divergence is expected to continue over the second half of the decade, with pensioner spending expected to remain around the same in 2020 as in 2015, while spending on working-age people and children falls by a further £4 billion per year.

Despite overall benefits expenditure being expected to be around £5 billion higher in 2020 than in 2010, real terms spending on benefits for those of working age and children is expected to have *fallen* by around £7 billion per year across the same period (see Figure 20.2) – or 7% of welfare spending on this group.

At the same time, expenditure on benefits for children and those of working age as a proportion of GDP is expected to fall rapidly, from 5.7% of GDP in 2010/11, down to 4.4% by 2020/21. That's a projected fall of nearly a quarter in the proportion of GDP spent on benefits and Tax Credits for working-age people and children. It reduces the proportion of

GDP spent on welfare provision on this group to around the same level as towards the start of the 1980s (see Figure 20.3).

Figure 20.2: Overall benefit expenditure (GB), 2010-20 on pensioners and working-age people and children (£ billions, 2017–18 prices)[a]

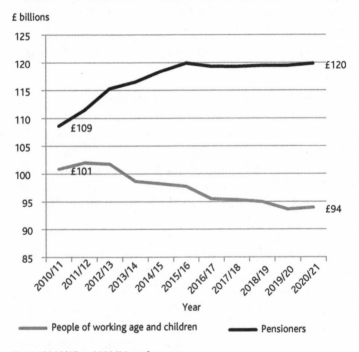

Real terms spending on benefits for those of working age and children is expected to have fallen by around £7 billion per year between 2010 and 2020

£ billions

People of working age and children ——— Pensioners

Note: [a] 2016/17 to 2020/21 are forecasts
Source: Analysis based on data from Department for Work and Pensions (2017) *Benefit expenditure and caseload tables 2017*, https://www.gov.uk/government/uploads/system/uploads/attachment_data/file/600929/outturn-and-forecast-spring-budget-2017.xlsx

Figure 20.3: Benefits spending on working-age people and children as a percentage of GDP[a]

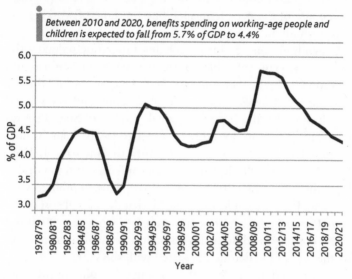

Between 2010 and 2020, benefits spending on working-age people and children is expected to fall from 5.7% of GDP to 4.4%

Note: [a]2016/17 to 2020/21 are forecasts

Source: Analysis based on data from Department for Work and Pensions (2017) *Benefit expenditure and caseload tables 2017*, https://www.gov.uk/government/uploads/system/uploads/attachment_data/file/600929/outturn-and-forecast-spring-budget-2017.xlsx

What is most startling is that despite it all, this is not achieving any reduction in real terms benefits spending at all. In fact, the overall benefits bill will have increased over the course of the decade, from £209 billion in 2010 to £214 billion in 2020.

So where are the savings going?

If overall welfare expenditure isn't falling, but spending on benefits for children and people of working age is falling significantly, it is pretty clear where the savings are going – savings made from cuts are being recycled into spending on pensioners. In fact, *all* of the £7 billion reduction in spending on working-age benefits is expected to be consumed by a £11 billion rise in expenditure on pensioners.

Spending on pensioners as a share of GDP is expected to decline slightly over the course of the decade, but only at around a third of the rate of the decline in spending on those of working age and of children.

Expenditure on pensioners is being limited by reducing the number of claimants able to receive the State Pension and Pension Credit, by increasing the State Pension age and the age of entitlement for Pension Credit. As a result (and as discussed in Chapter 19), the increase in total number of State Pension recipients gradually slowed between 2010 to 2015, and is now expected to decline to 2020. Despite the increase in State Pension age, overall, the number of recipients is still forecast to be slightly higher by 2020 than in 2010. This, combined with the State Pension 'triple lock', means that the overall cost of the State Pension is forecast to continuously rise between 2010 and 2020, costing an additional £18 billion per year over inflation by the end of the decade compared with the start.[2]

As discussed in Chapter 19, increasing the value of the State Pension, and paying for it by increasing the State Pension age and reducing benefit entitlements for those below that age, will mean that gains will accrue disproportionately to the least disadvantaged, who can expect a higher proportion of their overall life to be spent above State Pension age. Meanwhile, people on low incomes aged 60-66 are being removed from low-income pensioner benefits, and moved on to out-of-work benefits for working-age claimants, leaving hundreds of thousands of older people trapped on either Employment and Support Allowance (ESA) or Jobseeker's Allowance (JSA).

Benefit cuts among working-age households

The axe has fallen hard on people of working age and on their children. We can certainly expect that reductions in support will fall disproportionately on those on lower levels of income, simply because lower-income households receive more in benefits, and so have more that they can lose.

Figure 20.4 shows average annual cash benefit receipt in 2013/14 for non-retired households in different income bands. As can be seen, the poorest households tend to receive the most (notably, this is not true if pensioners are factored in, because of the high reliance on benefit receipt among all groups of pensioners).

When looked at in terms of the proportion of overall gross household income coming from benefit receipt, the distinction between groups is all the more clear. The poorest 40% of working-age households have around a third of their overall income paid in cash benefits. This compares to around 3.5% among the wealthiest 40% of working-age households.[3]

Figure 20.4: Average cash benefit receipt by income quintile (non-retired households), 2013/14

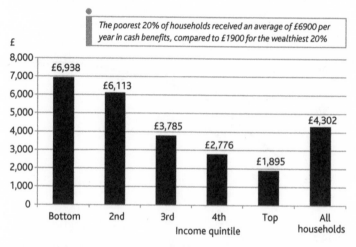

Source: ONS (Office for National Statistics) (2014) The effects of taxes and benefits on household income, 2013/14 – reference tables (table 7), www.ons.gov. uk/file?uri=/peoplepopulationandcommunity/ personalandhouseholdfinances/incomeandwealth/datasets /theeffectsoftaxesandbenefitsonhouseholdincomefinancialyearending2014 /2013to2014/etb201314workbooktcm774087693.xls

Analysis from the Institute for Fiscal Studies (IFS) confirms that the poorest working-age households (particularly those with children, who are likely to be more reliant on benefit receipt than equivalent households without children) are expected to lose the most from tax and benefit reforms to 2020. Their findings, following the 2017 Budget, indicated that the poorest

10% of working-age households with children were expected to see their income fall by nearly 18% as a result of tax and benefit changes between 2015 and 2020. In comparison, the wealthiest half of households are expected to see little or no change at all in household income (see Figure 20.5).

Figure 20.5: Impact of tax and benefit reforms on household income, 2015-20 (as % of net income), by income decile and household type

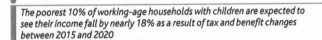

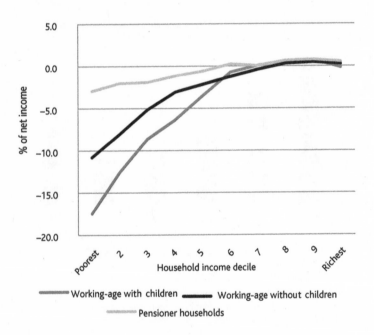

Source: Waters, T. (2017) *Distributional analysis*. London: Institute for Fiscal Studies

This remains true in cash terms, with the IFS suggesting that the poorest 10% of working-age households with children would lose an average of around £3,200 per year as a result of tax and benefit reforms between 2015 and 2020 (and the second poorest nearly £3,000), while the richest 10% lose around £100 per year. The second richest tenth gain more than any other group, ending up better off by 2020 by around £500 per year.[4]

So, broadly, we have an idea of the kind of households losing out the most in the new settlement – it should be no surprise that these are of working age (not protected by the pensions triple lock), living on a low income, and particularly those with children.

'Household level' impacts of welfare reform

However, even among the group of low-income, working-age households with children who are likely to lose the most as a result of welfare reform, the impact is not remotely homogenous.

We have seen throughout the previous chapters how receipt of different packages of benefits and Tax Credits, along with different levels of income, can combine to create a huge variety of different household circumstances for benefit recipients. As a result, even slightly different households can be affected in very different ways by changes to entitlements.

For the same reason, we can't simply 'add up' the different cuts to support outlined in previous chapters to understand how a number of different policy changes affect a household. Different combinations of benefits, Tax Credits, earnings and tax liabilities interact in a way that prevents this.

Looking at different individual household types, and the impact that welfare changes may have on them, can help to address this, showing the impact of different reforms after they interact and combine with one another.

The following case studies bring together a number of the different changes that have been discussed in previous chapters. They consider a given household type making a claim for Tax Credits and other benefits in 2010-11, and compare it to the same household type making a new claim for Universal Credit and other benefits in 2020-21.[5]

Case 1: Lone parent aged 30 with two children and £500 per month rent, Council Tax £65 per month, earning the National Living Wage (30 hours per week) working as a shop assistant.

This first case study considers the impact of reforms to provision for a parent, in the context of the introduction of the National Living Wage from 2016.

In 2010, this parent is receiving the National Minimum Wage (worth £5.93 per hour); by 2020 it is expected that an equivalent worker on minimum wage rates of pay would receive £9 per hour. The earnings gain from the introduction of the National Living Wage is significant (the family sees their net earnings increase by nearly £150 per month in real terms by the end of the decade). However, as a result of the 63% withdrawal rate on their Universal Credit entitlement, around £95 of this is lost through reductions in benefit entitlement.

The family gain from the increase in the Income Tax personal allowance (from £6,475 in 2010 to a planned £12,500 in 2020), since their earnings by 2020 are over the proposed allowance. However, since Universal Credit is calculated net of tax (as discussed in Chapter 6), again, they lose nearly two-thirds of the gain from this from their Universal Credit entitlement.

It is worth a reminder that in neither case is this process in which benefit entitlement is reduced as a result of higher earnings a benefit 'cut' exactly – this is just the standard process of tapering entitlements for benefit claimants as earnings increase. Both cases help to show why measures aimed at increasing pay and reducing tax liabilities are more closely targeted at higher-income households (outside of the benefits system) than those who receive in-work benefits and Tax Credits.

In addition, the family is also affected by a number of other reductions in entitlement. First, the family is affected by a reduction in their rate of 'work allowance' for Universal Credit (discussed in Chapter 13). This means that they face a withdrawal rate of 63% on earnings over £192 per month (whereas only earnings over £263 would have affected entitlement prior to April 2016).

In addition, the family is affected by the four-year freeze on benefit entitlements (following on from other below-inflationary increases).

Along with other living costs, it is assumed that their Local Housing Allowance (LHA) rate is frozen between 2010 and 2020 (so they claim for £500 per month in help with rent in

2010 and in 2020), but it is assumed that, along with other living costs, rental costs increase in line with the Retail Price Index (RPI). The assumption that LHA support is frozen across the decade, rather than falling, is generous given the reductions in LHA rates imposed in the first half of the decade.

In combination, reductions in entitlement greatly outweigh gains from increased earnings through the National Living Wage. Overall a household like this is expected to be worse off by around £6,036 per year by 2020.

2010 monthly income (and equivalent value in 2020):		
Tax Credits:	£720	(£972)
Child Benefit:	£146	(£197)
Housing Benefit:	£260	(£351)
Net earnings:	£694	(£937)
Total income:	£1,820	(£2,457)

Actual 2020 income:		
Universal Credit:	£716	
Net earnings (projected):	£1,088	
Child Benefit:	£149	
Total income:	£1,954	

However, if the claimant was a single parent under the age of 25, their situation would be considerably worse. This is for two reasons: first, they are not entitled to receive the National Living Wage, and second, because they receive a lower rate of standard allowance under Universal Credit as an under-25 (while a young single parent within the current benefits system would receive the over-25 rate; see Chapter 9 for further discussion of this).

Notably, of these two factors, the more significant is the lower rate of standard allowance, costing them around £66 per month, while the reduced rate of minimum wage leaves them around £51 worse off each month. This is because, whilst the net earnings of the over-25 year old are around £137 per month higher than the younger claimant, they lose 63% of this in consequent deductions from their Universal Credit.

If aged 24 (National Minimum Wage uprated from 2017 rate of £7.05 with inflation):	
Universal Credit:	£737
Net earnings (projected):	£951
Child Benefit:	£149
Total income:	**£1,838**

In total, in this case, they are left worse off by £7,430 per year, nearly £1,400 more than the same parent over the age of 25.

Case 2: Young disabled person, aged 23, receiving mid-rate care component of Disability Living Allowance (DLA), rent £400 per month, Council Tax £60 per month.

The second case study is of a young disabled person, living independently. The claimant is out of work and claims Employment and Support Allowance (ESA) (for which they are in the work-related activity group); they also receive the mid-rate care component of DLA.

In 2010, as a result of receiving the mid-rate care component of DLA, they also receive the Severe Disability Premium as a top up to their ESA.

By 2020, a new claimant would see the work-related activity component on their ESA gone, the Severe Disability Premium gone, and their Universal Credit standard allowance reduced from the full rate to the young person's rate (a reduction of around £15 per week). In addition, the small amount of ESA they are entitled to receive will have been substantially reduced in real terms as a result of years of freezes and below-inflationary uprating. In fact, as can be seen below, overall, their ESA entitlement reduces by around two-thirds.

In addition, the assumption of a freeze in LHA rates across the decade, and a reduction in Council Tax support following the localisation of Council Tax Benefit (in this case, we assume they face a 10% reduction), leave this claimant significantly worse off.

This type of claimant is expected to be worse off by around £775 per month (£9,300 over the course of a year) in 2020 compared to 2010. As discussed in Chapter 7, the government promised to protect the disabled from below-inflationary uprating. However, in this claimant's case, it is only their mid-rate care component of DLA that is protected. While this does leave them a little better off than they would otherwise be (by around £25 per month[6]), this is less than a thirtieth of their overall loss of income – hardly the kind of protection this young disabled person might hope for.

2010 monthly income (and equivalent value in 2020):		
ESA (including Severe Disability Premium:	£630	(£851)
Housing Benefit:	£400	(£540)
Council Tax Benefit:	£60	(£81)
DLA:	£208	(£281)
Total income:	£1,299	(£1,753)

Actual 2020 income:		
Universal Credit (standard allowance):	£252	
Universal Credit (housing component):	£400	
Council Tax Benefit:	£72	
Personal Independence Payment:	£254	
Total income:	£978	

Case 3: Couple with three children (one disabled, in receipt of low-rate care component of DLA); own their own home, mortgage £600 per month; one partner working as army corporal earning £27,000 per year.

In the case of this family, on the assumption that their gross earnings increase in line with inflation, the value of their earnings after tax increases by around £44 per month as a result of increases in personal allowances for Income Tax. However, the overall losses for this kind of family are enormous.

As can be seen, 2010 Tax Credit entitlements have a 2020 value of around £759 per month. However, making a claim in 2020, a family of this type would not be expected to have any Universal Credit entitlement at all. This is the result of a combination of factors.

Since they have three children, they lose a child element from their maximum entitlement – this is a loss of £2,780 per year from their maximum Tax Credit entitlement.

Since one of their children is disabled but not in receipt of the high-rate care component, the value of the disability addition within their Tax Credits/Universal Credit entitlement is reduced by half through the introduction of Universal Credit.

They are heavily affected by reductions in rates of work allowances and tapers within Universal Credit introduced between now and 2020.

They lose a significant proportion of the value of their means-tested benefit receipt as a result of the four-year benefit freeze (this also affects their child benefit entitlement; it also affects DLA because of the decision to switch from uprating benefits by RPI to – the normally lower – CPI).

In total, a family of this sort would expect to be around £9,500 per year worse off making a claim in 2020 than they would have been making a claim in 2010, a loss of more than a quarter of their overall income.

2010 monthly income (and equivalent value in 2020):		
Tax Credits:	£562	(£759)
Child Benefit:	£205	(£277)
DLA:	£82	(£111)
Net earnings:	£1,713	(£2,313)
Total income:	£2,562	(£3,460)

Actual 2020 income:		
Universal Credit:	£0	
Net earnings (projected):	£2,357	
Child Benefit:	£209	
DLA:	£100	
Total income:	£2,666	

Case 4: Couple, one aged 67, receives full rate of State Pension (but no additional pension); other (male partner) aged 62; £435 per month rent (privately renting), £87 per month Council Tax, no children or disabilities.

In the 2010 scenario, one partner receives the 'old' State Pension; however, the couple's income is topped up through a combination of Pension Credit, Housing Benefit and Council Tax Reduction. In total, they would have expected to receive around £1,400 per month (or £1,890 in 2020 prices).

In comparison, in the 2020 scenario, the older partner receives the higher 'new' State Pension (expected to be worth around £734 per month by 2020). However, since (in 2020) her 62-year-old partner is below the Pension Credit entitlement age, they are what's known as a 'mixed age couple'. As a result, the couple's support is topped up through Universal Credit rather than Pension Credit. Their maximum Universal Credit entitlement is £934 per month (including a £435 housing component), the same as an equivalent working-age household.

The older partner's State Pension is treated as 'unearned income' and deducted in full from the couple's Universal Credit entitlement. This means that the couple's joint income is no higher than had they been an equivalent working-age couple. Significantly, this means that in 2020, the personal allowance they receive will have been affected by the four-year benefit freeze.

Since they are renting in the private rental sector, we also assume that their housing support has been frozen at 2010 levels, while their actual rent has risen in line with costs of living.

In total, this couple would expect their actual 2020 income to be around £1,050 per month, around £840 per month (or more than £10,000 per year) less than the value for the same kind of family in 2010.

2010 monthly income (and equivalent value in 2020):		
State Pension:	£424	(£572)
Pension Credit:	£455	(£614)
Housing Benefit:	£435	(£587)
Council Tax Benefit:	£87	(£117)
Total income:	£1,401	(£1,890)

Actual 2020 income:		
State Pension:	£734[7]	
Universal Credit:	£200[8]	
Council Tax Reduction:	£117	
Total income:	£1,051	

For many low- to middle-income households, incomes change a great deal between 2010 and 2020 as a result of changes to the tax and benefits system. The extent to which they do (and whether for better or worse) will depend on the individual family type, their personal circumstances, rates of inflation, and the circumstances in which they make any claim for benefit (for example, whether they claim in the current benefits system or Universal Credit, and whether they are an existing or new claimant).

However, there are some notable trends that are illustrated by the case studies above:

- Households in receipt of benefits or Tax Credits are likely to be significantly affected by below inflationary uprating. The impact of this depends on the size of their benefit receipt as a proportion of their overall household income, and the rate at which prices increase in the coming years.
- For many families the introduction of the National Living Wage will not provide sufficient protection from cuts in support through the benefits system – as discussed in Chapter 13, for families in receipt of Universal Credit, up to 63% of any gain from higher wages will be lost through reductions in Universal Credit entitlement.

- Young parents are likely to lose out as a result of a number of different measures – most notably, the combination of reductions in the standard allowance for Universal Credit, and exclusion from the National Living Wage.
- People affected by sickness and disability are likely to be among the hardest hit by cuts in support. This is true in part because of direct reductions in many forms of disability and sickness benefits, and partly because of higher than average reliance on benefits that are not paid on account of disability or ill health.
- Sixty- to -66-year-olds on a low income will be extremely heavily impacted by the loss of Pension Credit entitlement. Older pensioners could also lose out significantly through changes to the treatment of 'mixed age couples' if they have a younger partner.
- Being in work will not prevent income reductions so long as claimants receive some amount of in-work benefit receipt – in many cases, working families may lose out more than other households as a result of cuts to in-work support. Higher-earning households (with low levels of current benefit entitlement) are likely to lose out less.
- Combinations of a number of different circumstances can lead to exceptionally large overall impacts.

In addition, it is worth remembering that changes to the *amount* of benefits to which people are entitled on their own only tell part of the story of the overall impact of welfare reform, or of what the 'new settlement' looks like. Increasingly, through the previous chapters, we have seen the role that benefits administration plays in determining outcomes. For some households, the amount of benefits that they should receive is a moot point – poor administration and mismanagement can mean that the amount that they may actually receive is very different indeed.

Conclusion

The 'new settlement' is not a good deal for many low- to middle-income working-age households, particularly those with children. Despite this, while it is a settlement that aspires to reduce the overall benefits bill, it has not yet delivered this. Instead, the settlement has rebalanced social security payments away from working-age adults and children (and lower-income older people before they reach their late sixties), towards older, better-off, pensioners.

The settlement is one that is built on the presumption that the impact of cuts to benefits will be offset by delivering higher pay and lower taxes for people of working age. It is a presumption that is completely wrong. As can be seen in these case studies, for many people on a low income, gains from increased pay and reduced tax bills are relatively small as a proportion of overall income to start with, and then most of the gains that they do receive are simply deducted from benefit entitlements. For many of those households that need extra support the most, these small gains are massively overshadowed by cuts to benefit entitlements.

However, the long-term effect of benefit reform is deeper than the direct impact on family incomes. The next chapter is about the social impact of the 'new settlement'.

21

The social impact of moving to a 'low welfare' economy

As the gears of government grind ahead towards the 'new settlement', it becomes increasingly clear what the impact of this might be on the incomes of different types of household. As we have seen, welfare reforms between 2010 and 2020 are likely to have an enormous impact on incomes for many groups, and it should be no surprise if this has a profound effect on people's lives, and on the communities in which they live. This chapter considers what the social impact of the 'new settlement' might be.

The impact on poverty

Broadly, there are three main approaches to understanding poverty. The first is to see poverty as living below a fixed income threshold (uprated each year with inflation to reflect changes in costs of living) – this is known as an *absolute poverty measure*.

The second approach is to measure poverty according to whether someone is missing out on a certain set of key essentials necessary for a decent standard of living in modern Britain. This *material deprivation* approach has the benefit that it captures actual living standards for people living in the UK. It has the limitation that material needs keep changing, and vary between groups, making it hard to give a fixed or consistent definition.

The third approach is to say that someone is living in poverty when they are living on an income below a given proportion of that of the average household. This is known as a *relative poverty measure*. Someone is often understood to be living in relative income poverty if they are in a household with less than 60% of average income.[1]

All three measures are important ways of understanding poverty; each has its own benefits and limitations. All three metrics need to be monitored, and action needs to be taken to address them. Often it is the relative poverty measure that is referred to as the 'headline' measure when talking about poverty rates. Before entering government, David Cameron was always clear that he recognised the importance of addressing this 'headline' poverty measure. In 2006 he delivered a lecture as leader of the Conservative Party, setting out his stance on poverty, saying, 'I want this message to go out loud and clear: the Conservative Party recognises, will measure and will act on relative poverty.'[2]

In 2010, 13 million people lived in relative income poverty in Britain,[3] a similar number to the year 2000. By 2020 the number of people in poverty is expected to increase by 20% – from 13 to 15.6 million.[4]

One area of particular concern has been child poverty. In early 2010, all three main political parties agreed to set down in legislation a target to end child poverty in the UK by the end of the decade. But within just a few years, the Conservative Party in government decided to repeal the target (and it was only as a result of public campaigning[5] that a statutory commitment to continue to at least *measure* the number of children in poverty was retained).

There is evidence that on current trends the target would probably have been missed by some way. By the end of the decade, the number of children in poverty[6] is expected to increase to levels not seen since the start of the millennium. By 2020, 5 million children are expected to be living in poverty – 1.4 million more than in 2010 – making up a majority of the overall projected rise in the numbers of people living in poverty (see Figure 21.1).[7]

At the same time it is notable that, despite the large amount of money spent on the triple lock, pensioner poverty rates are *also expected to increase* over the course of the decade – suggesting that (for this purpose at least) the money may not have been targeted particularly well. This issue is discussed further in the next section.

Figure 21.1: Numbers of people in poverty, including forecasts to 2020[a]

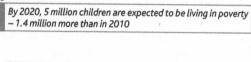

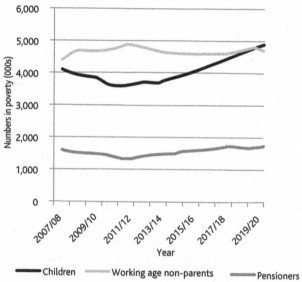

[a]Forecasts are from 2015–16 to 2020–21
Source: Hood, A. and Waters, T. (2017) *Living standards, poverty and inequality in the UK: 2016-17 to 2021-22.* London: Institute for Fiscal Studies

The impact on living standards

Faced with declining levels of support, many families who were already struggling with the cost of essentials have had to make further cut-backs on basic living costs.

One 2015 survey found that one in five families with children had reduced spending on food, and a similar proportion had cut back on heating their home, because of benefits increasing below inflation.[8]

In some cases the consequences of benefit problems and cuts to support can be particularly extreme, including to the point of people requiring emergency aid to ensure that they do not go hungry. An inquiry by the All Party Parliamentary Group on food poverty found that at the end of 2014 there were more than 800 food banks running across Britain.[9] The then Welfare Reform Minister Lord Freud got into hot water in 2013 for suggesting that a five-fold increase in food bank use over a two-year period might be supply-led, since 'there is an almost infinite demand for a free good'.[10]

This may be something of a lesson to politicians to avoid applying poor economic arguments to social issues. Aside from anything else, to suggest that there is no 'cost' to food bank use is insensitive, and implies little understanding of the personal difficulty and trauma many people face in using a foodbank.

Of course, Lord Freud may have been right to suggest that not all of the increase in the use of food banks may be led by benefit cuts, maladministration and sanctions. For example, the localisation of Crisis Loan provision led many local authorities to offer 'in kind' support (such as food parcels) to families facing crisis rather than providing cash assistance, as would have been the case with Crisis Loans. (One piece of analysis found that 81% of local authorities were replacing cash support at least in part with benefits in kind, including food aid.)[11] However, the Department for the Environment, Food and Rural Affairs did commission further research to understand why food bank use has risen. The authors concluded that:

> We found no evidence to support the idea that increased food aid provision is driving demand. All available evidence both in the UK and international points in the opposite direction. Put simply, there is more need and informal food aid providers are trying to help.[12]

A further study from the University of Oxford found that food bank use was linked to unemployment rates, benefit sanctions and benefit cuts. As one of the authors put it:

> We found clear evidence that areas of the UK facing greater unemployment, sanctions and budget cuts have significantly greater rates of people seeking emergency food aid. This pattern is consistent even

after adjusting for the possibility that some areas have greater capacity to give support than others.[13]

This appears to provide some of the evidence that the then Welfare Reform Minister was unable to find. Writing off the rising use of food banks as if it provides no indicator of rising need should always have seemed implausible.

The impact on household debt

Reform of the benefits system can have an impact on household debt in two different ways. First, inadequate financial support or problems with payments can lead to families falling into arrears on rent or other household bills, or having to take out consumer credit to make ends meet. Second, problems with payments and administration of benefits can lead to families getting into debt *on their benefits themselves* (as a result of having been 'overpaid' or having to borrow from future payments, and then having to pay these back).

There is growing evidence on the impact of cuts to benefits on debt. For example, in Chapters 7 and 8 we saw how it has grown increasingly likely that Housing Benefit will not cover the full amount of rent for a benefit claimant, even if they have no independent income to rely on. The government's own evaluation[14] of Local Housing Allowance (LHA) reforms found that nearly half of landlords renting to people receiving LHA said they had seen an increase in rent arrears.

Perhaps most worrying is the increase in arrears associated with people moving on to Universal Credit. One piece of research[15] found that in the Autumn of 2016, 86% of council tenants in receipt of Universal Credit were in rent arrears. All respondents said the six-week waiting period (discussed in Chapter 16) was either 'very frequently or frequently' a contributing factor.

Similarly, as shown in Chapter 18, reductions in support with Council Tax following localisation of the new system have contributed to rising Council Tax arrears, and increasing numbers of people summoned to court for failing to pay.

Similarly, many people have been turning to credit to top up inadequate levels of income. Research from the disability charity

Scope in 2012 found that around half of disabled people had used credit to pay for basic items like food or clothing in the previous 12 months.[16] In some cases, the use of high-cost credit has been actively encouraged by parts of the loan industry. The day after the 2016 Budget, one payday loan broker ran a blog titled: 'As welfare gets cut, payday loans step up'.[17]

Benefit claimants affected by sanctions are particularly vulnerable to falling into debt. As one claimant put it, following a sanction without warning: "the only two options at the end of the day are to borrow money or commit a crime." The claimant took out a £100 loan requiring a repayment of £160.[18]

As shown in Chapter 16, benefit payment problems are also pushing people into debt that they never chose to take on. One Tax Credit claimant I spoke to told me that she never used credit cards or other forms of credit; she always prioritised paying her rent on time, even if it meant having to use food banks to make ends meet, as it did for about a month-and-a-half in 2015. However, HM Revenue and Customs (HMRC) had told her she was £8,000 in debt as a result of Tax Credit overpayments. She has simply no idea how these debts came about, and even less idea how she could possibly ever repay them – she told me that some of the debt is as much as a decade old.

As the level of income disregard in the Tax Credits system is further reduced, we may expect more people to unintentionally get caught in a Tax Credit debt trap.

While Universal Credit may help with reducing overpayments, the debt problems caused by benefit delays are likely to continue. The introduction of a six-week waiting period before the first payment of benefit is likely to leave many claimants with little option but to turn to credit to help them through. Inadequate and difficult-to-access advances on payments do not solve this problem. Citizens Advice reported how one single parent with a young child described her move from the old system to Universal Credit. She explained how she went from a position of just coping with payments on a small amount of debt to 'a frightening position when she moved onto Universal Credit and almost all her income stopped (just Child Benefit remained), she was worried about how she could feed her children and threatening letters from creditors started to come'.[19]

At the same time, as shown in Chapter 13, claimants may also be expected to get into debt in order to make the move into work. In particular, the payment of childcare costs in arrears under Universal Credit is likely to result in many families being forced to take out credit in order to pay for childcare costs upfront.

The impact on health

There is a great deal of evidence that low income has a profound impact on both physical and mental health.

Where people live in cold, damp homes the likelihood of developing health problems – including respiratory, circulatory and mental health problems – is considerably increased.[20] Such circumstances are made more likely where Housing Benefit no longer fully covers the cost of a decent home, and the risk is exacerbated as a result of the four-year benefits freeze, which means that benefit rates no longer reflect changes in living costs, such as a sudden rise in fuel costs.

Poverty is also recognised as a cause of poor diet and malnutrition.[21] In children this can affect both physical and mental health, as well as undermining academic performance.[22] Since food is a relatively 'elastic' commodity – one on which people can adjust their spending according to their budget – reductions in food affordability have been found to be linked to people 'trading down' to a cheaper, less healthy diet, or cutting down on the amount consumed altogether.[23] In other cases, and as highlighted previously, some households are finding it altogether impossible to afford to feed themselves without additional help, relying instead on emergency provision (including from food banks). This may be particularly likely in cases of sudden reduction in income, such as the imposition of a benefit sanction, or a problem with benefit payments.

At the same time, there is evidence that it is not just the absolute amount of income people have available that affects their health – overall income inequality is also a driver of poor health. As shown by Wilkinson and Pickett in *The spirit level*, not only does income inequality drive poor health in those on the lowest incomes, it also reduces health expectations of higher-income households.[24] Welfare reform that drives inequality may be bad for all our health.

Perhaps the greatest injustice of health inequality between social groups is the impact that this can then have on overall life expectancy. In her first speech in Downing Street in 2016, Prime Minister Theresa May committed to:

> ... fighting against the burning injustice that, if you're born poor, you will die on average nine years earlier than others.[25]

In previous chapters we have discussed the inequity of the effective retirement age of those on the lowest incomes going up considerably faster than those on higher levels of income, while their life expectancy increases more slowly. By risking further undermining their health, ongoing reductions in provision for low-income, working-age households may perpetuate a widening gap in life expectancies between the rich and the poor.

The impact on education

As well as the health impacts of poverty, there is also substantial evidence that poverty undermines educational attainment. For example, in 2015, around 61% of children not in receipt of free school meals received at least 5 grades A*-C (including English and Maths) at GCSE. Among children receiving free school meals, this was just 33%.[26]

Disadvantaged pupils have also been found to be under-represented at the high-achieving end. Fifteen per cent of non-disadvantaged pupils achieved an A or above in English and Maths at GCSE,[27] compared to just 4% of disadvantaged pupils.[28]

This gap continues into higher education. As Theresa May herself put it in her first speech as Prime Minister, 'If you're a white, working-class boy, you're less likely than anybody else in Britain to go to university'.[29]

This may not be surprising, given poverty has been found to reduce the ability of families to afford to participate in the kinds of activities children need in order to succeed, as well as creating a stigmatising environment. One survey found that nearly two-thirds of children in families that reported they were 'not well off at all' said they had been embarrassed because they could not afford the day-to-day costs of school. More than a quarter said they had faced bullying as a result.[30]

The impact of benefits reform on homelessness and housing insecurity

As shown in Chapters 7 and 8, it is increasingly the case that even if benefit receipt is their only form of income, Housing Benefit is insufficient to cover the cost of a family's rent. This means that many households are, in effect, expected to find at least some of the costs of their housing from other money they have available, which was not intended for paying housing costs but for other living expenses.

Reductions in support with housing costs for households in the private rented sector is of particular concern. In 2010 private renters already faced many of the limitations on support with housing costs that have caused a great deal of alarm as they have been extended to the social rented sector, and since then, they have faced many more cuts to provision. This group has always lacked the security of tenure of those in the social rented sector, but when this is combined with shortfalls on help with housing costs, the impact can be enormous.

I talked to one claimant who reported having to pay as much as £200 per month from her out-of-work benefit income in order to cover a Housing Benefit shortfall for a privately rented house that her council itself had helped her to find. Only prioritisation of her rent over every other payment going out enabled her to avoid falling behind on payments.

The impact of cuts to support with Housing Benefit can be put starkly when we look at the comparison of repossessions by mortgage providers (from home owners repaying mortgages) and by landlords (from tenants). Since the financial crisis, numbers of home repossessions from mortgagees have plummeted to their lowest rate since the start of the century. In the rental sector we have seen exactly the opposite, with a surge in landlord repossessions from those renting their homes (see Figure 21.2).

Figure 21.2: Comparison of mortgage and landlord repossessions by county court bailiffs, 2000–16 (England and Wales)

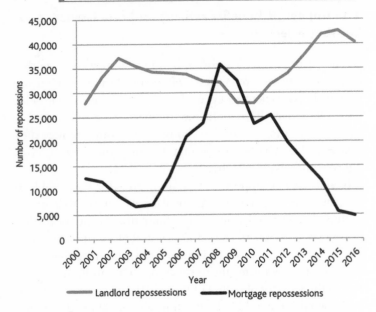

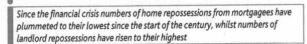

Since the financial crisis numbers of home repossessions from mortgagees have plummeted to their lowest since the start of the century, whilst numbers of landlord repossessions have risen to their highest

Source: Ministry of Justice (2017) *Mortgage and landlord possession statistics October to December 2016*, www.gov.uk/government/statistics/mortgage-and-landlord-possession-statistics-october-to-december-2016

Between 2003 and 2009 the number of homeless households fell rapidly. Unsurprisingly, perhaps, the number of homeless households has been rising ever since. In 2009, local authorities determined that 65,000 households in England were homeless; by 2016 this had risen by more than a third, to around 89,000.[31] It is difficult to imagine that these numbers will not continue to rise as the four-year freeze on LHA rates sees average private sector rents drift further and further from the Housing Benefit available to cover them.

As homelessness was rising in 2011, the then Housing Minister Grant Shapps launched a scathing attack on the media for ignoring the problem of homelessness:

> It's almost impossible to get the outside world to take any notice of homelessness at all. You won't have seen this information in a single national newspaper this morning and if I have a criticism of homelessness in this country ... it's about them lot out there who just don't seem to care about it; even when, as we did this morning, we announced £37.5m for the Homeless Change programme which will help 37 homeless hostels around the country.... I suspect even if I did press release it, no one outside this room would give a damn.[32]

But welcome interventions like this have been nothing compared to the decade of cuts to housing-cost support through the benefits system. While such crisis interventions are important, Housing Benefit provides the safety net that prevents people getting to this point.

Regional variations in shortfalls on Housing Benefit entitlements are leading some to call the reforms a form of 'social cleansing' from higher-cost communities to areas with lower levels of housing cost. One piece of analysis used geographical variations in changes in numbers of free school meal-entitled families to show that while the number of entitled families has fallen by 3% across England as a whole, it has fallen by 16% across Inner London, indicating large numbers of very low-income families moving to other areas.[33]

The impact of cuts to help with housing costs goes beyond homelessness. Many people faced with losing their home will do anything they can in order to make up their rent. This may mean families cutting back on food, heating, travel or other costs in order to top up inadequate provision. Cuts to support with housing costs make it impossible for people on the very lowest incomes to budget effectively. Where previously income might normally be separated into Housing Benefit for rent, Council Tax Benefit to pay Council Tax and other benefits for 'everything else', this is no longer the case, with other pots having to be dipped into simply in order to prevent families falling into rent or Council Tax arrears.

Cuts to help with housing costs are a cut in basic living standards, hidden behind a pretence that the families affected can simply move to a more affordable home.

The impact on social isolation

Perhaps one of the most pernicious effects of benefit cuts is the impact they may have on social isolation, particularly among some of the most vulnerable people in the country.

In Chapter 10 we discussed the potential impact of the loss of the Severe Disability Premium on severely disabled people with no one to provide care for them. Perhaps the most worrying possibility is that people like this disappear from view altogether – no longer able to be involved in normal activities such as going to the shops, pubs or cafes. It would be all too easy (it already is too easy) for them to remain behind closed doors, out of sight and out of mind.

One piece of research from the disability charity Sense found that nearly a quarter (23%) of disabled adults said that cuts to benefits and access to social care had made it harder to make and sustain friendships.[34]

And it is not just disabled people who face this risk. As children's centres and other services for children and families reduce[35] following cuts to local authority budgets, increasingly, the main provision available for families is through paid-for activities – which low-income families are likely to find harder and harder to afford.

Similarly, there is evidence that low income can lead to social isolation among children. One study found that missing out on the same material goods and clothes as their peers, and being unable to take part in the same social and leisure activities, led to children experiencing bullying and fearing stigma and social isolation.[36] Another report found that children from low-income families could be excluded from school activities because they couldn't afford the cost. As one child told the authors:

> There was a history trip to the Big Pit in Wales, I didn't go on that. It was too expensive to go, Mum couldn't afford it at the time, it was twenty-something

pound. I come home and talked to Mum about it and we couldn't afford it…. It felt bad when everyone come back and said how much an amazing time they had.[37]

The impact on work incentives

The government promised that the 'new settlement' would represent fairness for working people. However, the reality is that the majority of people affected by many of the cuts to support are in working households.

At the heart of the 'new settlement' is a promise to shift from provision of benefits to providing financial support through lower taxes and higher wages. As has been shown in Chapters 12 and 13, as well as in the case studies provided in the last chapter, this approach simply does not work for many working families in the benefits system. This is for two key reasons.

First, a worker only gets paid once, but earnings have to be shared between all members of the family. As a result, each member of a larger family benefits less than a single person would from the same increase in pay.

Second, and crucially, reductions in tax liabilities and higher pay serve to increase incomes for the purposes of calculating entitlements to means-tested benefits. This results in benefit deductions that reduce the overall gain. As we saw in Chapter 12, many families keep as little as 4p from each extra £1 that they earn.

For these reasons, a focus on reducing tax and increasing pay (even to the extent that it is within the gift of public policy to increase pay) inevitably favours higher-income households – those with incomes too high to receive benefits. This is particularly true when (as has happened recently) cuts on the basic rate of Income Tax are passed on to high-rate taxpayers as well.

Notably, this is even true with the introduction of the National Living Wage. Statistics from the Office for Budget Responsibility (OBR)[38] indicate that among those households affected by the National Living Wage, those who gain most are low-earning workers in high-income households – who are likely to be minimum wage workers with a high earning partner. This is presumably at least in part because these households have earnings too high for the increase in pay to affect their benefit receipt.

Astonishingly, the OBR go so far as to say that around half the cash gains in household income from the introduction of the National Living Wage may accrue to the top half of the household income distribution.

There are ways to avoid this. In previous chapters we have suggested that if work allowances rise in line with increases in minimum pay and tax allowances, it can be ensured that low-income working families with some reliance on the benefits system gain just as much from pay increases and tax decreases as other families.

The exact opposite has been happening. While the principles behind Universal Credit – and the intention to improve work incentives – are the right ones, cuts to work allowances (as described in Chapter 13), along with the failure to address other earnings incentive problems (like free school meals), have deeply undermined any promise the new system had to improve work incentives for many of the lowest-income workers in the country.

Sadly, the increasing representation of low-income working households among those living in poverty has been a long-term trend. In 1996, two-thirds of those living in poverty were in non-working households, with around a third in working households. By 2015, the majority of those living in poverty were living in low-income working households (see Figure 21.3).

While much of this is the result of substantially reducing the risk of poverty in out-of-work households (and particularly the risk of poverty among pensioners), analysis of the official statistics shows that the risk of an individual in a working household living in poverty has also grown over the last 20 years – with 17% of people in working households living in poverty in 2015 compared to 13% in 1996.

Figure 21.3: Percentage of individuals living in poverty who are in working- and non-working households

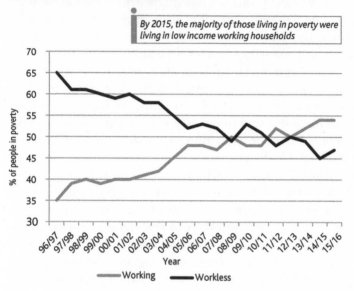

Source: Author's analysis based on data from DWP (Department for Work and Pensions) (2017) *Households Below Average Income: 1994/95 to 2015/16*, www.gov. uk/government/statistics/households-below-average-income-199495-to-201516

The impact on benefit complexity

The coalition government promised to reform the benefits system in order to make it simpler and easier for people to engage with. However, this doesn't appear to be how reform of the system has worked in reality.

Temporary complexity is perhaps an inevitable part of a process of reform of the benefits system. With the introduction of Universal Credit, families with children may receive means-tested benefits for children through any one of three different systems – Child Premiums within Income Support, Child Tax Credit or child elements in Universal Credit. For out-of-work sickness benefits, four systems are running in parallel – Severe Disablement Allowance, Incapacity Benefit and Income Support on account of sickness and disability, Employment and Support Allowance (ESA), and limited capability for work and work-related activity within Universal Credit.

Perhaps there is a lesson here that governments should try to finish introducing one benefits system before moving on to the next one. However, not all of the complexity in the benefits system that has been introduced in recent years can be put down to temporary transitional complexities. In many cases, additional complexity has been introduced as a direct result of cuts to provision. For example, reductions in earnings disregards the Tax Credits system, and, as outlined in Chapter 16, make it more likely that claimants will face Tax Credit overpayments.

Similarly, the introduction of the zero earnings rule for Universal Credit claimants receiving help with mortgage payments (discussed in Chapter 13) means that some home-owning households will have to think carefully about accepting any work at all – far from the former Prime Minister's guarantee that Universal Credit would ensure that every hour of work pays.

At the same time (and as described in Chapter 14), it is now the case that for some claimants, receipt of contribution-based benefits can risk leaving you worse off than if you didn't receive anything in the first place. There is simply no way that the vast majority of people could find their way through knowing what they should and shouldn't claim. Universal Credit makes these problems even worse than they are at present.

Part of the problem is that benefit complexity has been thought through too much from the point of view of the system rather than the point of view of the claimant. There are aspects to the benefits system that *shouldn't be simple* in their own right – the system is complicated because it needs to respond to people's complex and changing lives. What is crucial is that the system is simple *from the user's perspective*. We come on to what this might mean in practice later, in Chapter 25.

The impact on fairness, community and social solidarity

Some forms of benefit can play a role in promoting a sense of common identity within the benefits system. Until 2010, even high-income families could claim Child Benefit and a small amount of Tax Credits (through the family element) – since then, the working-age benefits system has become more targeted on those on lower levels of income, pushing others out of the benefits system altogether (such as through the introduction of the high-income Child Benefit charge, the removal of the family element of Child Tax Credit, or through savings limits in Universal Credit).

At the same time, fairness in the system has been undermined through reductions in the value of contribution-based benefits for working-age claimants – through, for example, the time limiting of contribution-based ESA (as discussed in Chapter 10), and through absurd cases where people are left worse off overall as a result of receiving contribution-based benefits rather than their means-tested equivalents. It is also undermined when those who have worked all their lives and paid contributions then develop a serious illness, but are told they are 'fit for work'.

When the benefits system seems broken and unfair, and when some groups are pushed out of the system altogether, it is unsurprising to see support for social security reduce. Where this happens, it risks setting a direction of travel towards still further cuts to provision.

People view the NHS very favourably because it is seen as a system for everyone, not just the poor – we pay into it when we can, and it is there when we need it. This was the vision for the benefits system as well. There would be times in our life when we were working and didn't have dependents, when we could pay into the system, and periods of our lives when we needed to draw out of it – when we had young children depending on us, or at times of sickness or in retirement. This vision needs to be restored.

It is important to make the benefits system work, not just to improve the circumstances of the current claimants who rely on it, but because it is by showing that it *can* work that it will secure the support needed to survive in the future.

The impact on intergenerational inequality

In Chapter 11 we discussed the sharp division between reform of the benefits system focused on older pensioners, and reform focused on children and people of working age. Every single penny (and more) of the reductions in spending on working age claimants and children over the first half of the 2010s was reinvested in additional spending on pensioners. Working-age benefit cuts, introduced as austerity measures, may, at least in part, be instead seen as 'rebalancing' provision – away from working-age adults and children, towards those above pension age.

So why has social security policy tilted so far away from provision for those of working age, and so strongly towards older people?

One answer might be a 'lag' in policy development. Until the 2000s pensioners were more likely to live in poverty than many other social groups. Significant additional investment in older people changed this for the better – where in the 1990s the proportion of pensioners in poverty was significantly higher than the average (although notably still lower than the proportion of children in poverty), over the course of the early 2000s this fell steeply. However, policy may still act as if the landscape of pensioner incomes was as it was at the start of the millennium.

However, this explanation itself has limitations. For a start, the rapid increase in the Pension Credit age (as discussed in Chapter 19), combined with the exclusion of Pension Credit from the triple lock, and the treatment of mixed age couples under Universal Credit, deeply undermines support for a significant group of low-income people in their early- to mid-sixties. A focus on non-means-tested provision for older, older people (to the exclusion of those 60-somethings too frail to work and with lower incomes and lower life expectancies) does not suggest a poverty alleviation focus.

In fact, official statistics suggest that despite a large fall in pensioner poverty between 2000 and 2010, reductions in pensioner poverty have since stalled, despite the triple lock on the Basic State Pension – and (as noted earlier in this chapter) are expected to rise to the end of the decade (see Figure 21.4).

A second reason for this inequality in investment might be electoral – since pensioners form a large proportion of the electorate (and one significantly more likely to vote than other groups), the impact of this group's political preferences is a significant determinant of the direction of social policy. At the same time, since the State Pension is non-means-tested, it may be that it generates some of the social solidarity across different pensioner groups that is missing from the working-age benefits system.

Figure 21.4: Pensioner poverty rates, 1996-2015

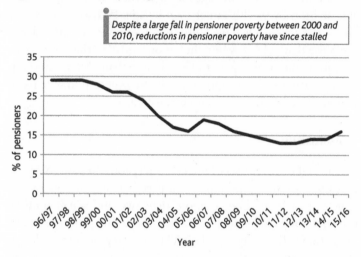

Despite a large fall in pensioner poverty between 2000 and 2010, reductions in pensioner poverty have since stalled

Such an account might explain why recent policy has been more focused on increasing incomes of older pensioners (regardless of wealth) than providing further targeted income supplements to the poorest older people, in order to continue to reduce pensioner poverty.

Regardless of the reason for it, the emphasis on increased spending on pensioners is introducing a worrying, and widening, intergenerational divide. It is difficult to know where this divide could lead, but with the triple lock in place, and life expectancy (at least among the better-off) continuing to rise, this gap in the treatment of different generations may be expected to continue to open in coming years.

It is worth reiterating once again that rising support for 'pensioners' does not benefit all older people. The removal of Pension Credit from younger-older people – those between 60 and 66 – is leading to many lower-income older people receiving little or no retirement at all. Rather than gain from the rapid increases in entitlements targeted at older pensioners, this group has instead seen their benefits cut as they see themselves reclassified as people of working age.

The focus of these Pension Credit changes on lower-income older people means that the difference in how welfare reform is treating those of working age and pensioners may best be seen as a division by wealth rather than by age. Perhaps those of us who can expect to live well into retirement ourselves may have the sense that at least we might get our 'turn' in the future, but for those who may expect to die younger than average, and for whom retirement was supposed to be their period in receipt of Pension Credit, there is no such reassurance.

Conclusion

What might the 'new settlement' society look like by 2020?
It is one in which the number of people living in poverty is expected to have risen by more than two-and-a-half million over the course of a single decade. Despite the promises made in the (now effectively repealed) Child Poverty Act, it is children in low-income families (who are among the most reliant on support through the benefits system) who are forecast to be the most affected.

It is one in which housing insecurity among low-income households is likely to continue to grow as ever larger numbers of families are living in privately rented accommodation – and LHA becomes increasingly inadequate to cover the costs.

It is a society in which the health and educational prospects of people from disadvantaged backgrounds are likely to suffer as a result of inadequate income. Increasing numbers may require emergency food, or other kinds of crisis support, to protect their health and safety, often as a result of sanctions or problems with benefit payments.

It is a society in which the gap between old and young – and more fundamentally, between rich and poor – opens further. It is a divided and insecure society.

Perhaps none of these things are that surprising. However, it is also worth emphasising the following:

First, the 'new settlement' undermines provision for the lowest-income working families who most need extra support.

Despite the government's promise that the new settlement would be for 'working people', the proportion of people in poverty living in working families has been rising in recent years. Reductions in work allowances in Universal Credit (along with reductions in other forms of in-work benefit provision) may be expected to lead to many more low-income working households falling into poverty.

Second, while pensioners have been protected from the impact of benefit cuts, those close to retirement age are among the very hardest hit. In particular, simultaneous increases in the age of Pension Credit entitlement from 60 to 66, and reductions in working-age benefit support, pull the rug from those likely to struggle the most as they move towards pension age.

Notably, despite the amount spent on the pensions 'triple lock', poverty rates among older people are expected to rise over the course of the decade.

Third, some of the most pernicious impacts of welfare reform are likely to be the result of not just cuts to entitlements, but also changes to the way in which claims are managed. As we have seen, spiralling overpayment rates on Tax Credits have led to real payment difficulties for some families, causing stress and anxiety among claimants. In the future, more households are likely to be pushed into debt as a result of a six-week (or longer) wait for an initial payment of Universal Credit, and by childcare costs being paid in arrears under the new system.

At the same time, inaccurate health assessments have led to many people being inappropriately found 'fit for work', or denied disability benefits.

As we established, many of these problems are themselves the result of a programme of benefits cuts – for example, Tax Credit overpayments are likely to have been increased by money-saving cuts to levels of earnings disregards (as discussed in Chapter 16).

Finally, despite all of this, the failure of the 'new settlement' to make any actual reduction in the benefits bill is simply stunning. As we have seen, in 2015-16, spending on benefits was at its highest rate in history, with much of the savings from working-age benefits, reinvested into rising spending on pensioners.

There has to be a better way of doing things – a different settlement is needed.

Part VI
Better benefits

One thing seems beyond doubt – the benefits system needs fixing. It is a clunky mess of a machine, with bits and bobs taped on over time, creating further problems when they interact with other parts and processes, often causing them to simply fail altogether. It is poor both in design and in operation, often leaving people without support when they most need it. Too often cuts to provision are just making this worse. The question remains, what needs to be done?

This part is divided into four chapters, reflecting ways in which our broken benefits system could be repaired in order to meet different goals.

Providing a basic minimum standard of living. The first goal of the benefits system must be to provide a safety net that prevents households becoming destitute. Too often it fails. This chapter looks at changes to policy that could be made in order to provide a better safety net.

Responding to different levels of need – too often the benefits system has been seen as *only* intended to provide a safety net to prevent destitution. As discussed in Chapter 23, in reality it is more than this. The benefits system also helps to correct for inequalities caused by differing levels of household need, particularly where such corrections cannot be made within the labour market. This chapter looks at how the benefits system could better serve this core function.

Supporting socially desirable behaviours – previous chapters have explored how the benefits system either fails to reward behaviours that may be perceived as socially desirable, or in some cases, seems to actively punish them. Chapter 24 looks at what needs to be done in order to change this.

Building a simpler system from the claimant's perspective – a simple benefits system often appears to be the holy grail for welfare reform – it is, for example, the foundation on which Universal Credit is built. However, while simplicity is certainly needed within the benefits system, the conception of this has been misguided. In Chapter 25 it is argued that instead of trying to simplify the system, the goal should be to create a system that is simple *from the claimant's perspective*. What this means, and what changes could help to meet this goal, are addressed in this chapter.

These four chapters identify priorities for reform and make concrete recommendations for starting to fix the benefits system in these four key respects. Some of these recommendations would need additional funding, while others either have little or no cost, or rebalance existing spending within the system.

22

Preventing poverty and destitution

What can be more important than building a benefits system that prevents the most vulnerable from falling into outright destitution, and provides them with emergency support if they do? As discussed in Chapter 2, ensuring that there was an effective safety net to provide a basic minimum standard of living to those who needed it (while not discouraging people from earning and saving for themselves) was at the heart of William Beveridge's vision for the post-war benefits system.

However, from removing key support for the social inclusion of sick and disabled people, through to risking families facing homelessness by cutting housing support, many of the welfare cuts made in recent years undermine the safety net that social security provides.

While prevention is always the best approach to tackling poverty and destitution, there will always be some cases where people simply do not have the money they need to survive. In such circumstances, help is also needed to meet emergency costs. This chapter deals with both issues – reforming the benefits system in order to better *prevent* poverty and destitution, *and* to provide emergency provision where a crisis does occur.

Preventing destitution among those affected by disability or ill health

While a number of measures have been introduced that risk poverty and destitution among those affected by disability or ill health, this section focuses on two in particular – the loss of the Severe Disability Premium under Universal Credit, and the introduction of non-payment of Employment and Support Allowance (ESA) during the mandatory reconsideration process.

Chapter 10 showed how the loss of the Severe Disability Premium within Universal Credit will cost £62 per week for some of the most severely disabled people at the very highest risk of social isolation – those who do not have a non-disabled partner, or another person receiving Carer's Allowance, to look after them. This change alone could cost those affected as much as a third of their income after housing costs.

While it has been suggested that it would be better for social care services to cover many of the costs associated with the Severe Disability Premium, there has been no additional funding made available in order to ensure that these costs are met. As discussed, only a small proportion of those likely to be affected by the change are receiving a significant level of provision from social care services. It would be surprising if most social care services are aware of this change, let alone ready to provide the significant additional level of support that will be needed in order to address it.

It is reasonable to suggest that the impact of the loss of this support may be outright destitution for some of those affected. When The Children's Society and Citizens Advice surveyed claimants likely to be affected by this change, they regularly talked about cutting back on food and heating or staying in bed for longer to save money, their homes falling into disrepair because they were unable to pay for simple jobs that non-disabled people would be able to tackle on their own. In some cases claimants talked about homelessness or even suicide.

The solution to this is simple. The Severe Disability Premium needs to be restored within Universal Credit as a matter of urgency. The costs of providing additional care to disabled people is understood and addressed through Carer's Allowance (and the carer's premium within Income Support and income-based Jobseeker's Allowance [JSA]) – similarly, it needs to be understood that there are even greater costs faced by those without a carer, who have to pay for even simple jobs to be completed.

An alternative approach would be to pay a new 'self-care element' in Universal Credit to those who meet the eligibility criteria to have someone receive Carer's Allowance or a carer element to look after them, but do not. This would clarify the role of this element as mirroring provision for those who receive help with their care needs through payment of Carer's Allowance to someone who provides them with support, enabling them to cover equivalent costs in other ways.

While the 'self-care element' would affect a larger group of claimants (since the eligibility rules for the Severe Disability Premium are restrictive), this could be offset by paying it at the same rate as the carer premium (which is paid at a lower rate than the Severe Disability Premium).

Further risk of hardship for those with poor health or disability is caused by the introduction of mandatory reconsideration for ESA decisions prior to appeal – combined with the decision not to allow ESA to be paid during this period.

Mandatory reconsideration means having to ask to have the decision looked at again before you can appeal the decision. Once a claimant appeals, they are entitled to the basic rate of ESA, but while waiting for the mandatory reconsideration, if they have no other source of income, they will have nothing to live on while they wait, unless they claim JSA. For many claimants who believe themselves to be too sick to meet the requirements imposed by JSA – even for a limited time – the consequence may be trying to get by without either benefit. Concerns have also been raised that some claimants may be being put off from claiming JSA because they are worried that it will affect the decision on their ESA claim.[1] Where people are deciding not to claim benefit, they may be faced with a considerable period without support. As shown in Chapter 15, in a quarter of cases reconsidered up to October 2014, it was taking more than a month to get a decision.

It was also seen how this period could be far longer under Universal Credit – since, if someone is found to be 'fit for work' in a work capability assessment (WCA), and this decision is not changed on mandatory reconsideration, they will continue to be treated as fit for work until their appeal is heard.

Ensuring that the Department for Work and Pensions (DWP) reconsiders ESA decisions before they go to appeal makes sense – it is a good thing to prevent poor decisions having to go to a tribunal if this can be avoided. However, the government should change its position and allow ESA to be paid during this period. As noted by the Work and Pensions Select Committee, the decision to withdraw ESA is not only unlikely to save much money,[2] but it may actually *cost money* because of the administrative expense of switching a claimant from ESA to JSA, and then potentially back again following the reconsideration.[3] Similarly, under Universal Credit, claimants should not be expected to seek work while they are waiting for mandatory reconsideration, or an appeal to be heard.

Preventing homelessness

Many of the reductions in support introduced in recent years have been targeted at support with housing costs. While the 'Bedroom Tax' affecting claimants in the social rented sector has received the most attention, many of the most severe measures have been targeted at private renters – including (as described in Chapter 7) through long-term restrictions on increases in Local Housing Allowance (LHA) rates, so that they no longer keep track with typical local rents.

This focus on reducing the amount of support for those renting privately is a particular concern since, in England, more households now rent privately than live in the social rented sector – with the proportion of privately renting households doubling since the start of the century. At the same time, the proportion of people living in social rented accommodation, as well as the proportion of homeowners, have declined since 2000 (see Figure 22.1).

Analysis from PricewaterhouseCoopers forecasts this trend continuing – with social rental households continuing to decline, and around a quarter of households living in private rental accommodation by 2025.[4]

There are a number of possible reasons why support with housing costs has been particularly targeted by benefit cuts, but one in particular is likely to be the impact of the move across to Universal Credit. Under Universal Credit, help with housing costs will no longer face the steep means test that it does through Housing Benefit, and support effectively continues until the point at which the claimant loses Universal Credit assistance altogether. This is a good thing – as shown in Chapter 12, the old approach to means testing of Housing Benefit has played a key role in undermining work progression incentives for low-income working families. However, this will substantially increase the number of claimants receiving support with housing costs.

Figure 22.1: Percentage of English households by tenure, 2000-13

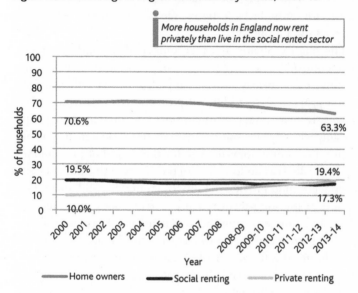

Note: Analysis of data for DCLG (Department for Communities and Local Government) (2016) *Tenure trends and cross tenure analysis (table ft1101)*, www.gov.uk/government/statistical-data-sets/tenure-trends-and-cross-tenure-analysis. In 2008 changes meant that since then this data was recorded by financial rather than calendar year.

Without imposing restrictions on the amount of housing support claimants can receive (and with a rising proportion of households renting, and so eligible for Housing Benefit), it would be likely that under Universal Credit, payments of support with housing costs[5] would rise considerably.

However, reducing LHA rates is only one way of bringing down the cost of benefits that help with housing costs, and one which comes at a high social cost. As shown in Chapter

21, this approach to reducing the Housing Benefit bill is being accompanied by rising homelessness, and reductions in basic living standards for those who are able to keep their home. A better approach would be to address the high costs that result in families requiring high Housing Benefit entitlements in order to find a place to live. This might be done by either increasing the volume of social rented housing stock (so that fewer people need to rent privately), or by reducing rents in the private rented sector (for example, by 'capping' the amount of rent that can be charged for a property).

The charity Shelter has recommended 'second generation rent control'[6] whereby, when a house is made available for renting, rental prices are not capped; however, when tenants rent a property, two additional protections are provided. First, tenants receive longer-term contracts. At present most people renting privately take out an Assured Shorthold Tenancy. While their rents cannot normally rise for the period of this contract, this typically lasts no longer than 6 or 12 months. Longer-term contracts would provide stability of tenure. Second, during the period of the long-term rental contract, rent cannot increase above inflation, ensuring that it is maintained in real terms.

This approach – used in Germany and France – combined with lifting the freeze on LHA rates, might ensure that low-income tenants received the support they needed to prevent them becoming homeless.

Regardless of whether soft rent controls of the sort Shelter outline would work, the LHA freeze should be lifted. The cost of the benefit system should not be reduced by making families homeless, or by squeezing their basic living costs.

Benefit sanctions

As raised in Chapter 17, the extensive use of benefit sanctions presents further risks of destitution for vulnerable claimants. Evidence suggests that use of sanctions is strongly connected to people requiring emergency food aid, and may be linked to health problems.

As we have seen, the proportion of unemployment benefit claimants sanctioned appears to be strongly related to the overall number of claimants. This can't be right – the decision to sanction someone should be based on their unwillingness to undertake reasonably required activities, not the labour market conditions. The government needs to explore why this is happening (and has been for some time), and what could be done to address it.

Where a sanction is considered, this needs to be more responsive to individual circumstances. As we have seen, sanctions use can be higher with some of the most vulnerable groups, who may be the least able to cope. More consideration should be given to how variations in applicable sanctions levels may be used to reduce the impact of sanctions on these groups (for example, by only applying 'low-level' sanctions to care leavers).

The prospect of extending sanctions use to working claimants under Universal Credit is a real concern. Many claimants have good reasons not to look for or accept a job just because it has longer hours or pays more, which may not be recognised by employment advisers. Sanctions should be restricted to those working less than 16 hours per week.

In addition, earnings rather than hours worked will set thresholds for the application of sanctions under Universal Credit. This is unjust to low-paid workers who would have to work a larger number of hours than higher-paid workers to obtain an equivalent level of income – the sanctions threshold should be set according to hours worked, not earnings received.

Delays in benefit payments and payments in arrears

There has always been a concern about delays in payments being processed and paid, and this can have a profound impact on claimants' lives. With the introduction of Universal Credit, many of these problems are set to become much worse. As outlined in Chapter 16, the payment of Universal Credit a month in arrears, combined with a week's 'waiting period' and a processing period, as well as the way in which earnings are treated for new claimants, leaves many people who are claiming Universal Credit after leaving employment waiting six or more weeks before their first payment. This is far from Iain Duncan

Smith's promise that Universal Credit would 'make it easier for people to get the help they need, when they need it'.[7]

One particular problem (highlighted in Chapter 16) is the way in which late payment of final wages from employment can count as income for a claimant's first month of entitlement to Universal Credit – meaning they may have to wait 10 weeks for a payment of benefit, rather than the usual six weeks. Citizens Advice recommend that claimants leaving employment should have their final earnings treated as being paid on the day they finish work, and employees who are paid early in a month should be treated as having those earnings paid on their normal payday.[8]

Better advertising of the availability of so-called 'advance payments' (Universal Credit payments made in advance of a normal payment date) would be helpful to ensure claimants can get some help when they are waiting to receive support, but advance payments are far from an ideal solution to lengthy delays in payments. The six-week wait for benefit at the start of a Universal Credit claim needs to drastically reduce.

In addition, while many low-income employees are paid on a weekly basis, it makes no sense that the benefits system pays monthly – claimants need to be offered the opportunity to be paid weekly, fortnightly or monthly.

One further area where addressing delay is important is around provision of free school meals. At the moment, free school meals are provided solely on the basis of receipt of certain benefits. This can create problems where there is a delay in a claim being processed. Some other benefits in kind – such as free prescriptions – can be obtained based on living on a 'low income' (rather than having to be passported from a particular benefit entitlement). This can be used in circumstances where there is a problem with claiming a benefit. While such an approach should not replace entitlement to free school meals linked to benefit receipt, it could be used to supplement this for households affected by benefit delays.

Simple measures such as these would be a major step towards ensuring that benefit claimants get the right amount of benefit paid when they need it.

Responding to a crisis

Reintroducing the Severe Disability Premium in Universal Credit, paying ESA during mandatory reconsideration periods (and not expecting Universal Credit claimants to look for work while awaiting an appeal on their ability to do just that), ensuring that Housing Benefit covers the full cost of a reasonable rent, a more effective approach to sanctions and ensuring that Universal Credit payments are paid at the right amount and at the right time – all of these measures would be a big step forwards towards ensuring that benefit claimants are protected from destitution.

However, there will always be times when things go wrong – when a family hits a crisis and is unable to keep their home warm, or to put food on the table. That's why, in addition to providing the best protection from destitution, the benefits system also needs to be able to effectively provide help in an emergency.

As discussed in Chapter 18, much of this support used to be provided through the national system of Crisis Loans – interest-free loans that were typically repaid through deductions from benefit entitlements. Following localisation, 150 or so different schemes popped up across the country – each a bit different, and in many cases leaving people in need of support with no idea where to go for help. Since the money is not ring-fenced, in many areas, no effective emergency support scheme is in place at all.

As well as creating confusion, the change made little financial sense – instead of a scheme that paid for itself in significant part (through repayment of the loans), now the scheme largely works on the basis of providing non-repayable grants and benefits in kind to those in the most desperate need.

There is still some loan provision in the national benefit system through what are known as 'budgeting loans' (or 'budgeting advances' for those on Universal Credit) – but the pot for providing support is small, demand high, and the eligibility criteria extremely tight.

A new government-sponsored loan scheme would be a better, more cost-effective, approach to providing support in an emergency than the plethora of local schemes currently in place. Such a scheme could provide interest-free loans (similar to the old Crisis Loans and ongoing Budgeting Advances), repaid either through cash or by direct deductions from benefits.

A new scheme like this could provide real help to those facing the highest levels of need – who are struggling to manage a budget from day-to-day, and unable to meet an additional expense that turns up unexpectedly.

The scheme would require initial capitalisation (and would need topping up each year to reflect unpaid loans and increases in costs of living). However, the ongoing costs of such a scheme would be paid for in significant part through repayments on previous interest-free loans. As with Crisis Loans, a reasonable success in repayments could be secured through recovering loans through benefit and Tax Credit payments where necessary.

Not only would this help to ensure that people were able to cope through an emergency; it would also help to reduce reliance on the high-cost short-term credit often turned to in times of crisis, and which too often just further engrains problems.

Benefits should not be paid in order to service sky-high interest on unaffordable loans. It is impossible to calculate what proportion of the benefits bill goes towards bolstering the profits of high interest lenders, but taxpayers should be furious that a single penny has to. At the same time, it should not be the case that those families least able to afford high interest rates are those most likely to be paying them.

Importantly, as with Crisis Loans, government-sponsored loans should be made available to all who need them – including working claimants – not just those on the very lowest levels of income. Both Budgeting Advances and, in some areas, Local Welfare Assistance schemes have eligibility rules which mean that they cannot be used by most low-income working claimants.

An interest-free savings scheme such as the one proposed would help to complement the (welcome) new 'Help to Save' scheme recently introduced by the government, through which low-income working benefit claimants who save up to £50 per month can receive a top up of 50% of the savings after two years. (Interestingly, this scheme is very similar to the Labour government's 'Saving Gateway' programme that the coalition government scrapped in 2010.⁹)

Not all households can either afford to save small amounts or to borrow, even at zero interest and with repayments made through ongoing benefit payments. There are likely to still be cases where a final safety net of urgent support is needed. It makes sense for such provision to be made as benefits in kind (such as fuel vouchers or direct food aid), but at the same time, in such cases, households relying on such support need to be linked in to social care provision to address underlying causes of their difficulty – something that some councils have sought to do through the provision of Local Welfare Assistance. For this reason Local Welfare Assistance should be retained, and the opportunities this provides to link crisis support to other local authority services should be further developed.

However, this is a consistent need across the country, and it should not be possible for some councils to simply opt out (as some effectively have) from providing Local Welfare Assistance – for this reason, money allocated to councils for providing support in a crisis needs to be effectively ring-fenced to ensure that it is spent on providing an emergency safety net.

Conclusion

Too often households in the UK face outright destitution – unable to keep a roof above their head or food on the table. In some cases this is because of cuts to provision. In other cases, extreme poverty can be caused not by inadequate overall levels of support but by destitution being used as punishment for poor behaviour (as with sanctions) or by maladministration being structured into the benefits system (as with delayed payments in Universal Credit).

Much more could be done to ensure both that the benefits system prevents poverty and destitution, and that it effectively provides emergency relief in a crisis. The recommendations in this chapter would start to move the system towards one that provided a more effective, consistent, and responsive 'safety net'.

However, as discussed in earlier chapters of this book, the benefits system is too often understood as purely being about providing a safety net. It does much, much more. Crucially, as discussed in Chapter 3, it helps to respond to differences in financial need between households. How the system can do a better job of this is the subject of the next chapter.

23

A system that responds
to household need

Throughout this book it has been argued that the benefits system should be understood as providing more than a basic safety net. It also enables a distribution of resources across society that is more reflective of individual and household *need* than would be the case without cash transfers.

Most importantly, it corrects inequalities that cannot be addressed through employment and pay – which principally reflect the market value of a worker's labour, rather than the level of their need. Nor, with some exceptions,[1] could the labour market realistically seek to do much differently – paying people on the basis of (for example) numbers of children in a household, or whether anyone is disabled, would create a considerably more complicated job market.

Recently, the benefits system has been affected by the imposition of 'hard' cash limits on benefits provision, failure to ensure that entitlements reflect changing costs of living, and failure to address inequalities in life expectancy in the design of retirement benefits. Changes such as these have significantly undermined the ability of the system to respond to variations in need between households and over time.

This chapter outlines a number of measures that could be taken to reaffirm the redistributive function of the system.

Limited welfare?

Central to the government's approach to welfare reform since 2010 has been the principle that limits need applying to the benefits system.

Chapter 2 showed that 'limits' in the system are not new – they are the basis on which the benefits system operates. However, these are needs-based limits – which apply in order to distribute resources more evenly on the basis of household resource requirements.

For example, if an individual in a household has a disability, they may receive a higher rate of support than they would if no one in the household was disabled. In such a case, one household has a lower 'limit' on their entitlement than the other.

Needs-based limits on provision are not what the government has been seeking to introduce. Instead, since 2010, a number of hard, cash-based limits have been imposed on benefit receipt. As shown in Chapter 8, these include the introduction of caps on maximum Local Housing Allowance (LHA) rates, an overall cap on benefit entitlements for out-of-work households, and the introduction of a 'two-child limit' on the child element of Child Tax Credit (and Universal Credit equivalent). The application of such limits is similar to the 'wage stop' that existed until the 1970s, which was imposed to prevent out-of-work entitlements exceeding in-work provision. The wage stop wasn't an effective mechanism for limiting entitlements in the past, and it is unnecessary now (as a result of the introduction and tapering of in-work entitlements).

The artificial limits placed on receipt of benefit by the introduction of an artificial overall cap on benefit receipt and by the introduction of the 'two-child limit' have a disproportionate impact on children. We have also seen how the use of such limits can discourage people from making the best choices for themselves and their family – such as the choice for a parent facing domestic violence to flee the family home, or for two loving single parents to move in together.

A more nuanced approach to limiting benefits is needed. This should take three parts: reduce rental costs for private sector tenants; review how household costs increase in line with family size; and finally, if concerned that some families do not spend their child-related benefits on the needs of their children, consider ways to ensure that those payments are spent appropriately.

Reduce rental costs for private sector tenants

One key thing that could be done to reduce the amount of benefit paid to low-income families would be to reduce rental costs for this group – and as a result, reduce entitlement to Housing Benefit or support with housing costs in Universal Credit.

The government's approach has been to cut the benefits that can be paid to help with housing costs for those in the private rented sector, but, as we saw in Chapter 7, this has mainly just led to LHA entitlements drifting further from actual rents.

The best way to achieve lower rental prices would be to get a higher proportion of low-income tenants into social housing – reversing the current trend towards higher proportions of private rental tenancies. This is a long-term goal. In the shorter term (and as suggested in the previous chapter), second generation rent controls for private rental tenants need to be seriously considered, in order to limit increases in private sector rents in those areas where they are growing the fastest.

At the same time, the removal of LHA caps (and freezes on increases in LHA rates) are needed to ensure people can afford a place in which to live.

Review how household costs increase in line with family size

It may be the case that there are cost-saving 'efficiencies' associated with increases in household size (for example, costs of fuel do not increase in direct proportion to household size, because the family still only has one home to heat). This may mean that the costs of having a fourth child are lower than the costs of a third child. If this was the case, it would provide an argument that additional per-child benefits should depend on the number of children in the family, so that the amount of support received reduces per child, as household size increases.

However, it is definitely not the case that the additional costs reduce to nothing. A review of the actual costs of living for different household types (such as the approach taken by the Joseph Rowntree Foundation's 'Minimum Income Standard' project[2]) could help to establish what an appropriate additional benefit amount would be per child in larger families, in order to maintain living standards at the same level regardless of household size. The blunt approach that has been taken in simply capping benefits per child at two children makes no sense at all.

Review child-related benefit payments to ensure that these are spent appropriately

If the government is concerned that in some cases children's benefits are not being used to meet the needs of children, it could review how these are paid. For example (as outlined in Chapter 16), ensuring payments of child-related benefits are made to the main carer could help with this.

In the most extreme cases, where there are serious concerns about whether money paid for children's needs is being spent appropriately, some portion of the payments could be made in kind – for example, through direct payments (such as vouchers) towards fuel or food costs. This should only be considered as part of a wider programme of intensive support for the family.

One approach could be to pay benefit payments that exceed the level of the benefit cap as benefits in kind. This would certainly be more sensible than arguing that because the money isn't being used to meet the children's needs, the money shouldn't be paid to the family in the first place.

Responding to price and earnings rises

One way in which household needs are drifting away from the level of support provided is through the decoupling of benefit increases from rises in costs of living – including through a four-year freeze on most benefits for children and people of working age. As described in Chapter 7, such freezes will be responsible for a significant decline in living standards by the end of the decade.

At the same time – as a result of the triple lock on the State Pension – non-means-tested support for pensioners has increased well above the rate of inflation.

Such a difference in the treatment of working-age and pensioner benefits cannot be justified on the basis of addressing poverty for two reasons – first, investment in Pension Credit (rather than a triple lock on the State Pension) would have been a much better approach to addressing pensioner poverty, and second, pensioners now have a lower poverty rate than either children or working-age adults.

Nor can they really be justified on the basis of protecting those least able to support themselves – the group most likely to be affected by the benefit freeze are children – who are completely dependent on others (their parents and the state) for the level of provision that they receive.

There isn't any clear logic to the provision of the triple lock (and in particular, the guarantee that the State Pension should rise in line with 2.5% regardless of growth in earnings or prices). The cost of the triple lock is also exceptionally high, and (as shown in Chapter 11), by 2015, was around *six times higher* than expected in 2010.

I have no desire to be a 'siren', to use Steve Webb's term, calling for a return to high levels of pensioner poverty. However, the way in which savings from austerity measures over the past five years have been absorbed into a single policy, which is itself a cost-ineffective way of reducing pensioner poverty (and which some of the most disadvantaged older people do not live to benefit from at all) is hard to justify.

The State Pension should be increased in line with earnings, to more closely reflect the expectations of those of working age. Should an uplift be required in periods of low or negative earnings growth (as happened around 2011), this should be applied on a case-by-case basis. This would align the State Pension with the typical uprating approach taken for Pension Credit.

At the same time (while a strong case could be made that benefits for children and those of working age should also rise in line with earnings), it should at least be the case that the freeze on benefits for children and for those of working age should be ended, and support increased in line with prices. This would help to ensure that the benefits system responds to rising costs of living.

Tax, pay and benefits

A third area where the benefits system provides a poor response to different levels of household need is in the interaction of the benefits system with tax and pay.

Increases in personal tax allowances are hailed as assisting those working but on low levels of earnings, but, as we saw in Chapter 12, actually benefit those on higher pay much more. This is principally because, for those in receipt of benefits (including Universal Credit, but notably not Tax Credits), increases in net income resulting from tax cuts just mean higher income for the purposes of means testing, and thus a lower benefit payment.

The same problem exists for increases in pay – for many people living in low-income households, and particularly for those with children, an increase in pay can make very little difference to living standards, because the vast majority of the additional money paid just comes off their benefit entitlements. As shown in Chapter 12, among those gaining from the introduction of the National Living Wage, those gaining the most are those in the highest-income households.

Both of these issues can be addressed through the benefits system (particularly through targeted work allowance increases to ensure that increases in pay, and reductions in tax liabilities, are passed on to low-income workers). Detailed recommendations on this are left to the next chapter, where issues related to 'making work pay' are discussed in more detail.

Retirement

Through provision of pensioner benefits (including the State Pension and Pension Credit), the benefits system plays a major role in making the distribution of both retirement length and income more equitable. Without this provision, people with adequate private pension provision would receive a decent period of retirement, but those without the means to save for retirement would face a choice between working until they are at death's door and a 'retirement' spent in penury.

However, the age at which retirement benefits are paid has never properly responded to people's different needs regarding their health and life expectancy. Unfortunately, recent changes to the benefits system (introduced by a number of different governments) have further entrenched this inequality.

Former Chancellor George Osborne said that a 'fair principle' was that people should expect to spend up to around a third of their adult life in retirement. Based on average life expectancies, this is expected to mean ongoing increases in the pension age – up to 69 by the late 2040s. However, individual life expectancy varies greatly from the average, and most worryingly (as Theresa May noted in her first speech as Prime Minister), tends to be much lower for those born into poverty.

For many people living on a low income, their expectation is to spend significantly less than a third of their adult life in retirement (if any time at all). Despite this (as shown in Chapter 19), many people in this group have seen their effective retirement age rise the fastest. This is because for many in this category, their age of retirement is set by the age at which they can receive Pension Credit, rather than the age at which they can receive the State Pension. Since the Pension Credit age is increasing in line with the State Pension age for women, by 2020 it will have risen six years – from 60 to 66. As highlighted in Chapter 19, many people in this group are already facing much of their sixties on JSA or ESA.

Variations in retirement age could help to respond to variations in retirement 'need' according to health and life expectancy. However, it may be unwise to set one retirement age for one group and another for a different one – such variation in provision would have the potential for a great deal of unfairness and maladministration.

A better way of dealing with this problem is to reintroduce the distinction between the age at which Pension Credit and the State Pension could be claimed – enabling Pension Credit to be claimed from 60 as it was until 2010.

This would represent a kind of 'stepping down' from working-age benefit provision to pensioner provision – with Pension

Credit providing a means-tested safety net for those needing to retire at 60 and who are unable to provide for themselves. This would avoid them having to claim inappropriate sickness or unemployment benefits. The State Pension would continue to provide non-means-tested provision from the state retirement age.

Earlier it was suggested that the pensions triple lock should be ended. Reinvesting part of the savings from this in earlier Pension Credit provision would be a considerably more effective approach to ending poverty among older people – and help to ensure that low-income pensioners were able to enjoy a period of retirement.

Reducing the Pension Credit entitlement age to 60 is suggested because this would reset it to where it was in 2010. However, the principle behind George Osborne's suggestion that people should spend around a third of their adult life in retirement was a fair one – just one that needs adjusting to reflect inequalities in life expectancy. For this reason, the government could look at setting the appropriate age of entitlement for Pension Credit at whatever age would be required to enable typical claimants to spend a third of their adult life in retirement – this could be done by basing the entitlement age on life expectancy for the poorest 10th of people, rather than 'average' life expectancy.

Mixed age couples

In Chapter 19 we saw that under Universal Credit, low-income older couples may only receive a retirement level of financial support when *both* partners reach State Pension age. Until then, many will effectively receive the same rate of support as a non-working couple of working age. This could effectively make the State Pension worthless for pensioners in low-income couples, if their partner has not also reached State Pension age.

There would be a relatively simple way to address this problem under Universal Credit. Under current rules, a partner who has reached State Pension Age, in a couple in receipt of Universal Credit, would have no work-related requirements. This means that, while they may not get any more money, at least this group of pensioners are treated as being unable to work!

However, unless they also have an illness or disability, this group will not receive the 'limited capability for work and work-related activity' component of Universal Credit (as discussed in Chapter 10, this is the Universal Credit equivalent of the support component of ESA, and is included in the Universal Credit award of those too ill to work or to undertake work-related activities).

Providing the older partner in a mixed age couple with this component of Universal Credit would keep the couple in the Universal Credit system (and ensure that the younger partner continued to face some work-related requirements where this was appropriate). However, it would also ensure that the couple received some level of additional income on account of the older partner having reached pensionable age.

Conclusion

The benefits system has a crucial role to play in correcting for needs-based inequalities of provision. Too often, attempts have been made to address these inequalities through tax and pay – and in most cases, have either made little difference, or (as in the case of increasing personal allowances for Income Tax) have further engrained these inequalities.

At the same time, blunt cash-based limits on provision have recently been introduced that have made it all the more difficult for the benefits system to respond to individual needs. The approach that has been taken to their introduction has harmed those least able to provide for themselves (most notably, children), and in the worst cases, has been downright nonsensical (such as the couple penalties introduced by the 'two-child limit').

Changes are needed to enable the benefits system to respond effectively to differences in individual and household needs. Such changes should include replacement of hard cash limits on entitlements with a review of how living costs vary according to household size; ending the freeze on key benefits and Tax Credits and ensuring that they rise in line with living costs; ensuring gains from increases in personal allowances for Income Tax are passed on to low-paid workers; and reducing the age of entitlement for Pension Credit to reflect the lower life expectancies of those on a lower level of income.

The benefits system provides a safety net for those in need of support, and also helps to redistribute resources according to need. However, as discussed in Chapter 3, the benefits system may be seen to have a further role – to encourage socially desirable behaviours. How it can do this better is the subject of the next chapter.

24

Supporting 'socially desirable' behaviours

As discussed in Chapter 3, the benefits system has the capacity to provide financial reward for those exhibiting what may be considered socially responsible behaviours (and the reverse for behaviours considered irresponsible).

Of course, defining 'socially desirable' behaviours can be challenging, as is finding a balance between rewarding them and ensuring that the benefits system serves its purpose in providing support on the basis of need. Some issues related to this are extremely contentious – for example, the extent to which it is appropriate for the benefits system to encourage couple parenting (thereby providing relatively less support for single-parent families).

However, on at least some behavioural issues there is widespread agreement. For example, most people think that if someone works, they should be at least somewhat better off than if they do not.

Similarly, most people would think that if someone makes National Insurance Contributions, they should be provided with better protections as a result.

However, as we have seen throughout this book, despite the rhetoric from a series of governments, about the importance of certain behaviours such as work, saving and making a contribution, many policies introduced over recent years have actively undermined this support.

This chapter is about how the benefits system needs to get rid of the absurdities and contradictions that undermine faith in the system as a whole.

'Making work pay'

In Chapter 12 we saw how, while most people are better off on first moving into employment, work progression incentives can be very poor, with many of the lowest-income working families keeping as little as 4p in each extra £1 that they earn. It's not fair, and undermines both the kind of behaviour that the benefits system should encourage, and belief that the benefits system is fair to the different groups who rely on it.

The benefits system needs work incentives to be super-charged. This was how Universal Credit was intended, but a number of issues with its structure, along with repeated and ongoing cuts to provision, have prevented it from working this way in practice. Very few disagree with the goal that the benefits system should support, rather than inhibit, people moving into work or taking on additional hours – the question is how this can be made a reality.

Removing cliff edges in the benefits system

Universal Credit was meant to ensure that the benefits system provided clear and smooth incentives both to move into, and progress in, work. As shown in Chapter 13, this laudable goal has been deeply undermined by the creation of 'cliff edges' in the system – points at which sudden withdrawal of benefits results in overall income falling, as a result of earnings increasing.

At the time of writing a decision had still not been reached about the long-term future of free school meals within the Universal Credit system. As shown in Chapter 13, were a fixed-income threshold introduced, so that those with incomes over that threshold lost their entitlement to free school meals, this would present a substantial benefits cliff edge and work disincentive. In many cases, parents would end up significantly worse off as a result of an increase in pay.

The biggest step that the government could take towards removing cliff edges within the new benefits system would be to provide free school meals for all children in families in receipt of Universal Credit.

This would not remove the entitlement cliff edge altogether. There would still be a point at which free school meal entitlement was lost and parents were left worse off when earning slightly above that threshold. However, it would shift this threshold to a higher income point (meaning that, as a proportion of overall household income, the loss is significantly smaller).

This approach would also better reflect different levels of household need than a fixed income threshold (and in particular, variations in need related to the number of children in the household), since the larger the family, the higher the earnings point at which Universal Credit entitlement is lost.

Most importantly, the increase in earnings that would be necessary to overcome the 'cliff edge' (that is, to earn back the value of free school meals) would be hugely reduced. This is because (as previous chapters have shown), once families earn enough to not receive Universal Credit, they no longer face two-thirds of any net earnings increase coming off their benefit entitlement.

For these reasons, extension of free school meals to all families in receipt of Universal Credit would significantly reduce the significance of the benefit cliff edge.[1]

Passported benefits are always a tricky problem when it comes to work incentives. They are made all the more so because the government department responsible for delivering the passported entitlement (in the case of free school meals, the Department for Education) is often not the same as the one delivering the benefit from which it is passported, which can lead to conflict between departmental agendas. This is just one reason why closer cross-departmental action is needed to ensure an internally coherent benefits system is in place. Social security policy should not just be a matter for the Department for Work and Pensions (DWP), HM Revenue and Customs (HMRC) and the Treasury.

As outlined in Chapter 13, a further cliff edge in Universal Credit is created by the introduction of the 'zero earnings' rule for Support for Mortgage Interest (SMI), whereby help with mortgage interest payments is lost in entirety when a claimant earns anything at all. This could make it impossible for homeowners with a mortgage to take on small amounts of paid work. The government should remove the zero earnings rule, and allow homeowners to take on small amounts of paid work without putting their home at risk.

Investing in work allowances, not tax cuts

Through the course of this book, we have shown how the government's preferred approach to improving work incentives is to reduce the tax burden on households (in particular, by increasing the personal allowance threshold for Income Tax) and to try to increase pay (for example, through the introduction of the National Living Wage). However, we have also seen how this simply does not work as a fair approach to improving incomes for low-earning families – and particularly those with children.

Increases in personal allowances are not a fair approach to increasing in-work incomes because, for those in receipt of means-tested benefits calculated on the basis of net income, paying less tax just means more money to be deducted from benefit entitlements. As a result, the gains from reduced tax liabilities accrue disproportionately to those higher up the income scale, and those with comparatively lower levels of household need (who are more likely to have escaped this benefits 'trap').

For example (and as shown previously), increasing the Income Tax personal allowance from £10,600 to £12,500 (as set out in the 2015 Conservative Party election manifesto) means that a worker who earns too much to receive Housing Benefit or Council Tax Reduction (or Universal Credit if on the new system) gains around £380 per year. Those receiving Housing Benefit and Council Tax Reduction keep as little as 15% of their £380 – just £57 per year (or around 16p per day).

Since increases in tax allowances least help those workers with the highest levels of need, they are poorly targeted and cost-inefficient measures. Increasing the generosity of in-work benefits is a much more equitable approach to providing additional support for working households than tax cuts.

However, should policy-makers wish to invest in raising personal tax allowances, there is a way of doing this that is considerably more equitable than current approaches. Increasing personal allowances for Housing Benefit and Council Tax

Reduction (and work allowances in Universal Credit) in line with increases in personal allowances for Income Tax would help to ensure that low-income workers in receipt of these benefits gain as much as workers outside of the benefits system. This would be achieved because net income gains from personal allowance increases would effectively be ignored for the purposes of calculating means-tested benefit entitlements.

This would, of course, cost money (the overall cost of increasing personal allowances for Income Tax is currently lower than it would otherwise be, as a result of consequent reductions in benefit entitlements), but personal allowance increases should not be bought at the cost of lower-income working families. Instead, the rate of Income Tax personal allowance increases should be restricted to what can be afforded *alongside* an increase in allowances for relevant in-work benefits – these should be considered part of the package.

This approach would help to improve the benefits system on two counts. First, it would help policy respond to different levels of household need – by ensuring that those with the highest needs do not receive the lowest reward from work. Second, it would also help to actively reward those seen to be 'doing the right thing' by moving into employment – especially if the level of earnings achieved from doing so is relatively low.

Sadly (as outlined in Chapter 13), the government has recently decided to take exactly the reverse approach – while Income Tax personal allowances are rising, work allowances in Universal Credit are being cut. This decision needs to be changed.

Reinvesting savings from increases in the minimum wage back into working people

A similar problem occurs with policies aimed at increasing pay. As earnings increase, claw-backs from benefit entitlements mean that low-income working families typically keep only a small proportion of any gain.

As we have seen, this means that those higher-income households affected tend to benefit the most from the new National Living Wage. This is because where one working partner in a couple earns enough to lift a family out of the benefit system altogether, a minimum-wage second earner partner will keep the benefits of the National Living Wage in full.

In some cases, the interaction of the National Living Wage with the benefits system could leave low-paid workers *worse off* overall. This may be the case where employers attempt to claw back the costs of higher pay through other forms of provision (such as free lunches during shifts) that do not typically affect benefit entitlements. The gains from the National Living Wage may be so small for some people who receive a pay increase as a result, that it would take only a small reduction in these 'perks' to leave these low-paid workers out of pocket.

As with gains from increases in personal allowances, the resultant savings from reduced benefit entitlements accrue to the Treasury. This isn't right – the National Living Wage is meant to benefit workers, not to act as an additional tax on employers, with much of the higher payments from employers going to the Exchequer through reduced benefit entitlements.

Of course, it is right that employees are paid fairly and well, and some low-income groups gain a great deal from higher pay (this is particularly true of workers without children, who are less likely to receive benefits, even on a low rate of pay). However, when employers do pay more to low-income workers, they expect this to end up in their employees' pockets, not in the Treasury coffers following benefit deductions. This is particularly true when this additional pay is offered voluntarily in order to improve workers' living standards (as with payment of the voluntary 'Living Wage', as promoted by the Living Wage Foundation[2]).

As with increases in personal allowances for Income Tax, there are alternative ways of approaching increases in pay for low earners. The simplest approach might be to use whatever Exchequer savings are generated from increases in the minimum wage to fund increases in work allowances – so reinvesting the savings in lower-income workers. This would not ensure that all the money was reinvested in those working on a minimum wage, since all working Universal Credit claimants would benefit, but it would at least ensure that the benefits of increasing the minimum wage are accrued to a greater extent by lower-income workers.

Alternatively, a more targeted approach could be taken by ignoring (in certain circumstances) additional pay for the purpose of calculating a worker's benefit entitlement. For example, if an employer chose to pay the voluntary Living Wage, in order to give their workers a higher standard of living, these earnings could be disregarded for benefit purposes.

Either way, such a Living Wage guarantee could be used to ensure that additional money that employers spend on providing a Living Wage actually gets to their workers. This would help to ensure that those on the lowest levels of pay, and who have the highest levels of need, receive as much from a pay rise as a better-off household.

Providing additional support for disabled people entering the labour market

Without additional financial support, many disabled people find it extremely difficult to move into sustainable employment. For this group, providing additional benefit payments on moving into work is both fair (because it responds to a level of additional need) and also encourages the kind of behaviours that lead to socially desirable outcomes (as we saw in Chapter 10, reducing the disability employment gap has recently been a key policy goal).

Within the Tax Credits system, the principal assistance to help with the additional costs of work for disabled people is through the disability element of Working Tax Credit. However, as shown in Chapter 13, under Universal Credit, this support no longer exists. Instead, additional in-work support for disabled people in Universal Credit was *initially* intended to be provided through a combination of in-work payments of the limited capability for work element, and a higher rate of work allowance.

However, as discussed in Chapter 10, it was later decided to scrap the limited capability for work component, and the additional work allowances provided to disabled people are only available if they do not have children (since you can either receive an enhanced work allowance on account of having children, or you can have it on account of having a sickness or disability – but you can't have both).

This means that under Universal Credit, in many cases there is no additional support with the costs of employment for disabled people, provided through the benefits system.

The work allowance problem would be relatively simple to resolve (although clearly it would cost money to do so) – by making work allowances in Universal Credit additive, rather than exclusive. This would mean that a disabled parent claimant could get an additional work allowance on account of their disability, as well as one on account of caring for a child.

Such an approach (even if work allowances were reduced in order to pay for it) would be fairer than the current approach, since it would better respond to the level of need in the household.

In addition, the limited capability for work component in Universal Credit should (simply) be restored. However, even were the government to take this step, there would still be a key problem – unlike in the Tax Credits system, under Universal Credit sick and disabled claimants would only be able to get this additional in-work support if they were found to have 'limited capability for work'. Given the frequency with which even some of the sickest claimants have been found 'fit for work', it is somewhat difficult to imagine that many will still be found to have limited capability for work once they have moved into employment.

For this reason, the disabled worker element of Working Tax Credit should be mirrored by creating a disabled worker component of Universal Credit, which would be paid to working claimants who had previously received the limited capability for work component, so long as they continue to have a disability that puts them at a disadvantage in the labour market.

This approach would create a lower threshold for the disabled worker component than the limited capability for work component, and would recognise that there is a group between those who have limited capability for work and those who have full capability. This group are able to move into work, but are still at a disadvantage in the labour market, and need additional support to ensure they are able to meet the demands of a job. This principle is recognised in Working Tax Credit, and should be in Universal Credit as well.

Supporting working claimants to save

Benefit claimants can save small amounts of money without this affecting their entitlement (in fact, schemes like 'Help to Save' actively encourage claimants to put away small amounts of savings). However (as shown in Chapter 13), for working households with higher levels of savings, the introduction of strict new rules under Universal Credit (compared to the previous rules under Tax Credits) means that money put away can have a major impact on entitlements – including losing entitlement to Universal Credit altogether. This could make it harder for working households to save towards a deposit for a house, for example.

The savings rules for Universal Credit should copy those of Tax Credits (rather than Income Support and Housing Benefit), at least for working households. This would ensure that savings incentives continue to be promoted in the new system.

Support self-employed workers with fluctuating earnings

It is often said that small business is the life-blood of the economy, but the application of the 'Minimum Income Floor' for self-employed workers under Universal Credit (discussed in Chapter 13) risks shutting some small businesses down altogether.

It is reasonable to expect self-employed workers to show some indication that their business will make a profit in the longer term, but the current level of this floor is set too high.

Furthermore, if a self-employed worker has average earnings above the level of the floor then the introduction of the MIF risks penalising them for fluctuations in their earnings between months. It cannot be fair that if someone earns more than the MIF in one month, and then less in the next month, they receive less support than if they had earned the same amount overall but their earnings were distributed evenly across the period.

In making an assessment of earnings, self-employed claimants should be allowed to average their earnings over a number of months – the MIF would only apply if *average* earnings fell below the level of this floor.

Providing information about in-work support available

On some occasions, it is not simply additional financial provision that is needed in order to support people to move into and progress in work, but also *additional information about the in-work support that already exists.*

For example, in Chapter 12 we discussed the problem of people being unaware of the amount of childcare costs they get help with through the benefits system (and in particular, through the disregard of childcare costs for calculating Housing Benefit entitlement and Council Tax Reduction). In this case, lack of knowledge about their entitlement to help may affect parents' choices about employment. Just helping parents to understand the full amount of assistance they can receive with childcare costs could play a significant role in improving parental employment – particularly among those low-income families who may have up to 96% of their childcare costs covered through benefits and Tax Credits.

A fair contributory benefits system

A further change needed to ensure that the benefits system properly rewards the right behaviours is to ensure that when people pay National Insurance Contributions, they feel that they get something back as a result. We need to reinforce the 'contributory principle'. However, problems with the current structure of the contributory benefits system (and in particular, its interaction with means-tested benefits) mean that simply increasing the value of contribution-based benefits is not necessarily the best way to go about this.

Contribution-based benefits are built on the principle that people pay in when they can afford to, and get additional support back in periods of difficulty (such as sickness, unemployment or old age). As we have seen, to some degree this works – particularly where people have significant savings or a partner who works, bypassing the stringent means testing of income-based benefits can provide additional support to those who have paid in. However, in Chapter 14 we saw how, for many low-income households, two key problems related to contribution-based benefits deeply undermine this principle. Together, these problems mean that not only are contribution-based benefits worthless in many cases, in the worst cases (and more so under Universal Credit), they can be toxic – leaving households worse off on account of receiving them:

- Contribution-based benefits do not act as an automatic passport to other benefits in kind, as their income-related equivalents often do.
- Contributory benefit entitlements are deducted pound for pound from some means-tested benefits *and* are taxed.

In Chapter 14 it was suggested that reducing means-tested benefit entitlement against contribution-based benefits according to a taper, rather than by pound for pound deductions, could be an effective way of addressing both of these problems – helping to ensure that paying contributions is always rewarded, and never penalised.

Addressing couple penalties

Whether or not the benefits system should actively encourage couples to stay together is a controversial question – however, few people believe that the benefits system should pay loving couples (and particularly those with children) who want to live together, in order to keep them *apart*.

As shown in Chapter 9, this is effectively exactly what a number of the policies introduced since 2010 achieve – to the point where (commenting on the introduction of a 'two-child limit' on the child element of Universal Credit) a coalition of faith leaders called the reforms 'fundamentally anti-family'.

In the previous chapter we highlighted a number of measures that could be introduced in order to take a more needs-based approach to limiting welfare provision. It is worth emphasising that these approaches would also help to reduce some of the worst 'couple penalties' that have ever been introduced into the benefits system.

Conclusion

It is inevitable that policy decisions made about the provision of financial support will encourage some choices and discourage others. This has the potential to create a great deal of unfairness if misapplied, but it can also be used (relatively non-controversially in some circumstances) to encourage choices that are generally seen as ones that society should support.

I have attempted to show throughout this book that there are some aspects to the benefits system that are patently unjust in punishing positive behaviours. Perhaps the best example is the reduced level of support that some claimants in receipt of contribution-based benefits may receive, but others, such as benefit 'cliff edges' that can leave people paying for working longer hours, can be found throughout the system.

In other cases, the 'rewards' for the right behaviours are so minimal that they strongly discourage them – this is the case with deduction rates of up to 96p for each extra £1 of income earned that are faced by some benefit claimants.

Rather than reducing the 'unfairness' of the benefits system, cuts to support – including those targeted at in-work entitlements, and those imposing arbitrary limits on provision – have made many of these inequities even more pronounced.

There is much more that can be done to ensure that the benefits system really does reward the 'right' behaviours – a good start would be improving work incentives, reforming the structure of the contribution-based benefits system and addressing some of the worst couple penalties.

25

Simplicity from the claimant's perspective

I have argued that the benefits system needs to provide an adequate safety net, that it needs to respond to the different needs of different people, and that it needs to support positive behaviours (and certainly to avoid punishing them).

However, the level of support provided through the benefits system matters little if problems with delivery mean that people don't get what they have claimed, or if they are so bamboozled by what they might or might not be entitled to that they don't claim anything in the first place.

This chapter is about how we can build a genuinely simpler benefits system – one that inspires confidence rather than trepidation in those who rely on it.

Despite simplification of the benefits system being given much attention by policy-makers in recent years, it often appears that things do not get any better.

Part of the problem is confusion over the *kind* of simplicity needed in the benefits system. The benefits system is complicated – it has to be. It needs to be able to meet the goals set out in the last three chapters (setting an adequate safety net, responding to varying needs, and providing incentives for socially desirable behaviours). There are many different circumstances in which people can live, to which the system needs to respond.

In addition, each part of the system that provides support to an individual or household interacts (often, as we have seen, dysfunctionally) with other parts – not only of the system itself, but also of the world around it, such as the tax system or education policies (as in the case of free school meals).

However, complex systems can still function. In some cases, a complex system can function superbly, but the complexity is kept 'under the hood'. For example, the power grid works rather well in this regard. Normally, when you go to turn a light on or off it simply works – you don't need to understand how a power station generates electricity, or how the network transmits it. The only concern to you (leaving aside issues of cost) is when you flick the switch and the light doesn't turn on. In such circumstances, beyond the basics of checking the bulb and the fuse box, you still don't need to know how to repair the fault; you just need to know how to get hold of someone with the relevant specialist knowledge to do this.

The problem with the benefits system is that much of the complexity has crept out from under the hood, into the world of the user – people need to be able to understand much of how the system operates in order to be able to use it effectively.

Complexity in the benefits system shouldn't (and can't) be eradicated, but it does need to be pushed back under the hood as much as possible, out of sight of those who just need to get on with their lives, and who don't want or need to understand how it all works. Benefit simplification needs to come from the user's perspective.

There are many approaches that can be taken to achieving this, but reflecting on the following questions when considering a potential change to the benefits system could help to make a start.

Does the change make it more likely that the claimant will be aware of the provision available (or receive it anyway, even if they aren't aware)?

Too often claimants do not receive the support to which they are entitled simply because they are unaware that it exists. For example, in their report on the effectiveness of the localisation of the Discretionary Social Fund, the National Audit Office (NAO) suggested that one reason councils may have been under-spending resources available for establishing Local Welfare Assistance schemes was a lack of public awareness of their existence.[1]

In Chapter 22, it was suggested that Local Welfare Assistance should continue (on top of an improved national loans scheme) in order to provide a final safety net for people facing crisis. If this is to work effectively, it is crucial that these schemes are advertised effectively, both at a national and local level. For example, infuriatingly, there is almost no information about local welfare provision on the gov.uk website. Changes like this would be an easy way to provide a better benefits system.[2]

The ideal scenario is perhaps that everyone automatically receives their full and correct entitlement to benefits (leaving aside vexing cases where receipt of a benefit leaves the claimant worse off, which we will return to in a moment). A good example of this is the Warm Home Discount for low-income pensioners (a passported benefit to help with heating costs, provided as a discount on the claimant's energy bill), which is applied automatically, so eligible claimants neither need to know about it nor apply.

Strangely, while many low-income working-age people may also be eligible for the Warm Home Discount, unlike pensioners, they need to apply to their supplier (who decides about provision on a largely discretionary basis). There doesn't appear to be a strong logic for this; it should be changed to align the way support is provided for those of working age with that for older people.

Does the change make it easier for claimants to provide the information necessary to receive the right entitlement, or improve the likelihood that this information will be correctly recorded?

On the assumption that the claimant is aware of those benefits to which they are entitled, the next stage is for them to provide the information they need to, in order to successfully make a claim. This may be harder than it sounds.

For example, in Chapter 16, it was shown how correct payment of Tax Credits can rely on estimates of income for the year ahead – which can be very difficult to provide. In the early years of Tax Credits this led to high levels of benefit overpayments. Changes were made to the level of income disregards, which meant that claimants were substantially less likely to receive an overpayment, making the system simpler and fairer. In recent years, decisions to reverse these measures have introduced additional complexity (and rising rates of overpayments) back into the Tax Credits system. Faced with this, the government should reverse the cuts to income disregards in Tax Credits introduced in recent years.

Similarly, Chapter 16 showed how a lack of backdating in Universal Credit makes it harder for claimants to receive their correct entitlement, by giving them no leeway for delay should they not be aware of, or have difficulty claiming,[3] the help to which they are entitled. For example, many claimants will first come on to Universal Credit entitlement at the date on which their first child is born – but it is unclear whether there is any flexibility for delay, to recognise that they are unlikely to be making a claim on this date! One month's backdating should be provided as standard in Universal Credit – this would bring it into line with current provision through Tax Credits (backdating of which has also become less generous in recent years), and make sure that even if there is a short delay before someone makes a claim for support, they can still receive their full entitlement.

Another area of particular concern is the ease with which claimants are able to provide the correct information for disability or sickness assessments. As shown in Chapter 15, long delays, poor assessments of evidence provided, and in some cases, even difficulties accessing assessment centres, have all made it harder for claimants to supply the evidence they need to, and to get their needs correctly assessed. Better administration of disability and sickness assessments, and training of those undertaking them, is clearly required, in order to ensure that claimants are able to access the support that they need. If the claimant gives their permission, it should also automatically be the case that their GP – or another health professional who knows them – should be asked for a summary of their health condition or impairment, any hospital treatment, and any views they have on the impact of the sickness or disability on the patient's daily life.

Does the change help to ensure that if a claimant applies for support, and correctly provides all the information that they need to, they receive the support they require, at the time they need it?

In some cases the operation of the benefits system can mean that even if the claimant does everything that they have to do, they still don't get the support they need at the time they need it.

The delay between claiming Universal Credit and the point at which payment is provided is an example of this, where the claimant will face a wait of six weeks or more after claiming Universal Credit after leaving employment, before they receive their first payment. Recommendations for avoiding lengthy delays in payments of Universal Credit on leaving employment were given in Chapter 22.

A similar problem with Universal Credit is the payment of help with childcare costs in arrears. As highlighted in Chapter 16, paying support with childcare costs in this way will leave many low-income families moving into work having to find the money for childcare upfront, which may push them into debt (or keep them out of employment altogether). By paying childcare costs upfront, Universal Credit could do much more to make sure that claimants receive the help they need, at the time it is required.

Does the change ever leave claimants worse off on account of claiming an additional 'entitlement' or making a claim at the wrong time?

In a simple benefits system, claiming an additional entitlement to support will never leave a claimant worse off overall. This is because a claimant would not need to understand how the system works in order to receive their maximum support; they would just need to claim their full entitlement.

That there are circumstances where claimants may receive benefits that leave them worse off indicates the profound problems with the current system.

As highlighted in previous sections, the most notable example of this concerns the provision of contribution-based benefits, where in some cases the combination of pound for pound deductions from means-tested benefit entitlements, plus the payment of Income Tax, mean that claimants can be significantly worse off as a result of these additional 'entitlements'. In order to prevent this, suggestions for changes to how the contribution-based benefits system interacts with income-based benefits and the tax system were made in Chapter 24.

Equally, no one should have to do a complex calculation to work out *when* to claim a benefit. Universal Credit cannot be described as a simple benefit when claimants may be faced with losing hundreds of pounds of entitlement simply by claiming at the wrong time. For example, the problem (highlighted in Chapter 16) of final payments from employment affecting a claimant's first month of Universal Credit entitlement can currently be avoided by making a claim timed to start *after* the final wages from employment are paid. This is unnecessarily complex and confusing for claimants.

Does the change make it easier for the claimant to put things right if something goes wrong?

No matter how efficiently a complex system works, sometimes things will go wrong. A simple system will limit the consequences of this, and ensure that things are put right again as quickly as possible.

One area in which this is particularly important is in the reconsideration of poor decisions – for example, in assessments of ill health and disability (where decision-making has often been found to be particularly poor).

However, many of the changes introduced to the benefits system in recent years make the process of challenging a poor decision considerably harder. For example, the introduction of mandatory reconsideration of Employment and Support Allowance (ESA) claims prior to appeal (as discussed in Chapter 15), combined with non-payment of ESA during these periods, creates unnecessary difficulty for someone asking for a decision about their claim to be looked at again. Reconsideration of decisions can be good for everyone when properly carried out, but the government should scrap the provision that ESA cannot be paid during this time; similarly, those on Universal Credit should not be facing full work-related conditionality during the period of reconsideration and appeal.

In some cases, where something goes wrong, specific and technical knowledge is needed to resolve a problem – if your lights won't turn on, you will probably check the bulb and the fuse box, but beyond this, you are likely to need to call an electrician. Similarly, if things go wrong with someone's benefit claim, and can't easily be put right, it is important that there is someone whom they can ask for support. Sadly, too often, limited provision of welfare rights advice makes it difficult for claimants to get the support they need in order to navigate the complexities of the benefits system.

The removal of welfare rights advice from the scope of legal aid provision is a particular concern, with Citizens Advice warning that this has created an 'advice gap', with appeals failing as a result of claimants being unable to access specialist advice, or to gather medical evidence to support a challenge.

Welfare rights advice is a difficult, specialist profession and shouldn't be otherwise. Support is needed to help the most vulnerable claimants with accessing provision, and for dealing with the most problematic cases. Reductions in the provision available make the system more complex and difficult to navigate.

Does the change make it easier for the claimant to make 'real world' decisions?

If it is to be truly 'simple' from the claimant's perspective, the benefits system needs to make it as easy as possible for them to make decisions about their lives. To enable them to do so, claimants need to be able to understand the kind of behaviours that the benefits system will financially support, and by how much, and those that it will not.

A key example of this is decisions about moving into work and taking on extra hours. Universal Credit was meant to provide smooth, clear work incentives for claimants, so that they could rest assured that if they took on extra work, they would be better off as a result. The reality is rather different. For example (and as discussed in the previous chapter), depending on what decisions are made about the future of free school meals under

Universal Credit, many families could be at risk of being left worse off on earning more.

Similarly, claimants in a loving relationship should know that if they move in with their partner, their family won't be left significantly worse off as a result. The last government believed in this so strongly that they put it at the heart of the so-called 'family test'. However, again, the reality differs from the rhetoric – with the benefit cap and the 'two-child limit' introducing some of the largest couple penalties there have ever been in the benefits system.

Recommendations on both of these issues were outlined in the previous chapter. By addressing some of these contradictions between the kind of behaviours that the government *say* they would like to promote through the benefits system, and those that the system *actually* promotes, social security would be made simpler and more comprehensible to claimants.

Conclusion

For too long, policy-makers have obsessed about how the benefits system can be made simpler – but have focused on simplicity from the perspective of the designers rather than from the perspective of the claimant. This is the wrong way around, and has led to policy changes which (while they may make the benefits system simpler in some 'objective' sense) make it more complicated for claimants to navigate. In some cases, the viewpoints of designer and claimant will align; in other cases they will not. Where they do not, simplicity for the claimant is always to be preferred.

Unlike the claimant, the designer should be able to work 'under the hood' – understanding the mechanics of the benefits system, and the way in which these interact with, and affect, people's lives.

The drive for simplicity from a design perspective may, in part, be the result of a lack of technical understanding of the benefits system among those involved in designing it. Sometimes such technical, mechanistic knowledge of systems can be seen as, in some respects, inferior to broader-brush, social and economic understanding of the role and operation of such systems in society.

In contrast, there is a whole industry built around the detailed knowledge of tax systems. Perhaps this is simply because there is more money in it.

If such a gap in technical knowledge exists, this needs urgent correction. While it is important to understand the 'bigger picture' of the role of the benefits system in society, design of a system larger than the National Health Service is incredibly complex and needs to be undertaken by people who understand it in detail – including how its different parts operate independently, and interact with each other.

Regardless of how, or by whom, the benefits system is next reformed, this set of questions give a starting point for evaluating policy changes from the perspective of creating a simpler, smoother system for the user.

Alongside work to rebuild the safety net; respond flexibly to differences in household need; and more consistently promote socially desirable behaviours, we also need to reform social security in order to make it simpler from the perspective of the claimant. Addressing these four areas together could help to fix our broken benefits system.

26

Conclusion

The benefits system wasn't working as it should in 2010, and in 2020 it will be more dysfunctional still. The safety net has been punched full of holes; it is increasingly unresponsive to variations in household need; it frequently punishes behaviours which (even by the standards set by the government of the day) ought to be rewarded; and, in many respects, it is becoming increasingly complex for claimants to navigate.

Yet despite all this, it should be a system in which we take pride. Amidst all the problems, it is easy to forget that it is the benefits system that every day keeps millions of people from destitution, and enables those with additional needs to play a full role in society.

I have already presented a number of immediate recommendations that aim to help improve this ever-evolving system. Regardless of whether or not those immediate changes are implemented, I want to conclude with some wider themes that emerge from this book, that may help to direct future reform.

There is more than one goal to the benefits system

The benefits system is often presented as being a 'safety net' for preventing destitution. Of course, it does provide this (although too often fails at it), but this is not the only reason it exists.

As suggested over the course of this book, there are at least two more reasons for providing benefits – to equalise inequalities of need, and to reward behaviours deemed socially desirable.

A benefits system that only provided a minimum safety net and nothing else would be very partial and inefficient. It would be one that did not provide additional support to address variations in need (such as children or disabilities) for households living above a minimum threshold. It would also be one that failed to provide incentives for low-paid work (since those whose earnings only reached the minimum threshold of need would be left no better off than those receiving that minimum level of support through welfare).

This misconception of the role of the benefits system can lead to misunderstandings about how best to fix it. For example, some think that the key question is how to increase pay to the point where we no longer need benefit top ups (at least for working claimants). A better question to ask is how the benefit system can be effectively integrated with the labour market, in order to provide financial support *alongside and as a supplement to* earnings for those with higher levels of need.

Cuts tend to make the system less efficient, and undermine the process of reform

Cuts to the benefits system have made it simply work less well. For example, as we saw in Chapter 16, reductions in income disregards in Tax Credits have significantly increased the complexity of the system and the level of overpayments.

Similarly, 'trimming' around the edges of the benefits system in order to reduce costs has undermined reforms which, properly funded, would have the potential to deliver positive outcomes. The clearest example of this is the introduction of Universal Credit. The new system was supposed to make the system fairer, and provide clearer, smoother work incentives. However, chronic underinvestment has meant that, for many households, it achieves the reverse. For example, reductions in work allowances under Universal Credit have significantly undermined the additional work incentives originally planned for the new system (particularly since, in the end, the same reductions were not made to Tax Credits). In this case, rather than Universal Credit being used as an opportunity to improve work incentives and encourage the 'right' behaviours, it was being used as a way of deferring the introduction of cuts to provision, where the immediate introduction through Tax Credits was proving politically difficult.

Reductions in support for disabled people in work have similarly undermined work incentives. In particular, as shown in Chapter 13, the removal of the limited capability for work element in Universal Credit significantly reduces in-work provision for disabled people.

The government has also so far failed to make a long-term decision about the future of free school meals under Universal Credit, to avoid creating one of the largest 'cliff edges' in entitlements for low-income working claimants that the benefits system has ever seen. This seems to be driven by unwillingness to make the investment that would be needed to address this problem by extending free school meals to all families in receipt of Universal Credit.

Intergenerational inequality is an issue, but not so much of an issue as economic inequality

Yes, intergenerational inequality is an issue – much of the money saved from cuts to working-age provision has simply been shifted across to paying for rapid increases in the value of the State Pension. However, crucially, we have seen that not all older people are gaining. In particular, low-income older people in their early- to mid-sixties (and older people on a low income living in a 'mixed age couple') are losing out by effectively being reclassified as 'working age'.

This is principally an issue of economic inequality. At the same time as inequalities in life expectancy are widening, it is some of the most socially disadvantaged who are seeing their effective retirement age increase the most. Furthermore, even when those on a low income do reach retirement age, if they have a younger partner, they may be denied any retirement income until their partner also reaches that age.

Meanwhile, those who gain the most from the rapid escalation of the value of the State Pension are those pensioners with a high level of independent income (placing them outside of the means-tested benefits system), who are also disproportionately likely to have a long life expectancy at retirement. In combination, this means that this group are likely to gain the most, both from increases in the value of the State Pension, and from the length of time it is paid.

We have moved a *long way* from an insurance-based system

As discussed in Chapter 2, the founders of the post-war benefits system believed that it should, first and foremost, be built on insurance-based provision. However, decisions that were made early on sowed the seeds for means-tested provision to dominate. These included the decision not to vary contribution-based benefits to reflect regional differences in housing costs, and the decision (hotly contested at the time) to limit unemployment insurance payments to around six months.

Recent decisions have further undermined insurance-based provision. These include the introduction of a restriction on the period of entitlement to contribution-based Employment and Support Allowance (ESA) for those in the work-related activity group (which, as we showed in Chapter 15, is probably the biggest single factor contributing to the overall decline in sickness benefit claimants in the last few years).

Crucially, the decision to consider most contribution-based benefits as 'unearned income' for the purposes of Universal Credit, and to deduct them in full from entitlements, means that contribution-based benefits are worth nothing for increasing numbers of benefit claimants. Additionally, where such benefits are also taxable, claimants can be left worse off as a result of receiving them instead of their means-tested counterparts. This is fundamentally unfair to those who have paid into the system through National Insurance Contributions.

It is important to understand that the problem with contribution-based benefits today cannot be addressed simply by increasing their value – to do so would be to misunderstand their interaction with the means-tested benefits system and the tax system. Such a change within the current context would risk leaving many of the poorest claimants either not gaining at all (while better-off households see their incomes increase), or at worst, it may even leave them *worse off than before*.

No one government can be held solely responsible for problems with the benefits system – all political parties need to have a better understanding of how the system works

While cuts to provision introduced since 2010 have made many problems worse, it is important to recognise that many of the most fundamental problems within the benefits system have developed over many years.

For example, the problem of some contribution-based benefits being deducted in full from means-tested provision, and then taxed, is also not a new one – although the introduction of Universal Credit makes the problem significantly worse.

Similarly, the decision to increase the Pension Credit age in line with the equalisation of the State Pension age for women – which has trapped many low-income older people on working-age unemployment or sickness benefits – was made well before 2010 (although it began to be introduced in that year).

Across all political parties, better understanding of social security policy is needed in order to make the benefits system work better.

Simplifying the benefits system shouldn't be the goal – simplifying it for the claimant should be

Finally, and as explored in the last chapter, claimants don't need a simple system – they need a system that is *simple to use*. It is an important difference, and one that is poorly recognised by policy-makers.

Someone needs to understand the mechanics of the system, but too often among policy-makers, researchers and lobbyists, this knowledge seems to be missing (and may even contribute to the desire for system simplification).

If we are going to fix this creaky, often unloved, but utterly vital machine, we have to try to understand its internal workings. It is a hard job, but I hope this book will make a small contribution to it.

Notes

Chapter 1

[1] Department for Work and Pensions (2010) *Universal Credit: Welfare that works*. London: Department for Work and Pensions.

[2] Hood, A. and Waters, T. (2017) *Living Standards, Poverty and Inequality in the UK: 2016–17 to 2021–22*. London: Institute for Fiscal Studies.

[3] £7974 in 2016-17 – based on Department for Work and Pensions (2017) *Benefit expenditure and caseload tables*, https://www.gov.uk/government/collections/benefit-expenditure-tables

[4] Spending on the benefits system is expected to be £215 billion in 2017/18. This is based on Department for Work and Pensions (2017) *Benefit expenditure and caseload tables*, https://www.gov.uk/government/collections/benefit-expenditure-tables. Based on Budget 2017, health spending is expected to total £149 billion. Spending on education is expected to be £102 billion, defence £48 billion, and public order and safety £34 billion (a total of £184 billion) – from HM Treasury (2017) *Budget 2017*. London: HM Treasury.

[5] Osborne, G. (2012) *Autumn Statement 2012: Chancellor's statement.*

[6] Osborne, G. (2015) *Chancellor George Osborne's Summer Budget 2015 speech.*

[7] Hodge, M. (2014) *Implementation of Personal Independence Payments nothing short of fiasco.*

[8] These are the child components of Universal Credit, Child Tax Credit and child additions in Income Support. The latter of these started to be phased out in 2003 when Tax Credits were introduced, but the transition from the first system had still not been completed at the point that Universal Credit began to be introduced!

[9] *Broken Benefits* addresses the benefits system that exists in practice across the UK. It should be noted that Northern Ireland has its own benefits legislation, but in the main part this mirrors the UK system. Whilst Scotland does not have fully devolved responsibility over welfare provision, it has similarly started to have some devolved responsibilities. Issues of devolution and the benefits system are discussed in a little more detail at the start of Chapter 4.

Chapter 2

1 Beveridge, W. (1942) *Social insurance and allied services*. Cmd 6404. London: The Stationery Office.

2 Schweinitz, K. (1961) *England's road to social security: From the statute of labourers in 1349 to the Beveridge report of 1942*. Philadelphia, PA: University of Pennsylvania Press, p 17.

3 Ibid, p 17.

4 Ibid, p 15.

5 Ibid, p 19.

6 Chesterman, M. (1979) *Charities, trusts and social welfare*. London: Weidenfeld & Nicholson, p 15.

7 Ibid, p 17.

8 Jordan, W. (1959) *Philanthropy in England 1480 to 1660*. London: Russell Sage Foundation, p 83.

9 Ibid, p 88.

10 Act for Punishment of Sturdy Vagabonds and Beggars 1536 Henry VIII, statute 27; c. 25.

11 Schweinitz, K. (1961) *England's road to social security: From the statute of labourers in 1349 to the Beveridge report of 1942*. Philadelphia, PA: University of Pennsylvania Press, p 25.

12 Ibid, p 28.

13 Beveridge, W. (1942) *Social insurance and allied services*. Cmd 6406. London: The Stationery Office, p 211, Appendix B.

14 Gray, B. (1967) *A history of English philanthropy from the dissolution of the monasteries to the taking of the first census*. London: Frank Cass, p 7.

15 Bruce, M. (1961) *The coming of the welfare state*. New York: B.T. Batsford, p 25.

16 See, for example, Fraser, D. (1984) *The evolution of the British welfare state: A history of social policy since the Industrial Revolution*. London: Macmillan, p 31.

17 Cunningham, H. and Innes, J. (1998) *Charity, philanthropy and reform: From the 1690s to 1850*. Basingstoke: Macmillan, p 30.

18 Jordan, W. (1959) *Philanthropy in England 1480 to 1660*. London: Russell Sage Foundation, p 141.

19 Ibid, p 88.

20 Jones, K. (1991) *The making of social policy in Britain, 1830-1990*. London: Atlantic Highlands, p 2.

21 Ibid.

22 Thane, P. (1978) 'Women and the Poor Law in Victorian and Edwardian England.' *History Workshop Journal*, vol 6, no 1, pp 29-51.

23 Ibid, p 29.

24 Roberts, D. (1963) 'How cruel was the Victorian Poor Law?' *The Historical Journal*, vol 6, no 1, pp 97-107.

25 Jones, K. (1991) *The making of social policy in Britain, 1830-1990*. London: Atlantic Highlands.

26 Blackden, S. (2007) *Scottish Poor Law after 1845*. Poor Law Workshop, 27 April, Oxford Brookes.

27 Owen, D. (1964) *English philanthropy: 1660-1960*. London: Oxford University Press, p 217.
28 Jones, K. (1991) *The making of social policy in Britain, 1830-1990*. London: Atlantic Highlands.
29 Ibid.
30 Beatrice Webb, 'My apprenticeship', p 207, cited in Owen, D. (1964) *English philanthropy: 1660-1960*. London: Oxford University Press, p 504.
31 Thane, P. (1996) *Foundations of the welfare state*. New York: Addison Wesley Longman, p 16.
32 Ibid, p 42.
33 'Education (Provision of Meals) Act 1906', www.legislation.gov.uk/ukpga/1906/57/enacted
34 Office for National Statistics (2011) *'Pension trends', Chapter 1: Pensions legislation: An overview*, http://webarchive.nationalarchives.gov.uk/20160105160709/http://www.ons.gov.uk/ons/rel/pensions/pension-trends/chapter-1--pensions-legislation---archived/chapter-1--pensions-legislation---archived-.pdf
35 Beveridge, W. (1942) *Social insurance and allied services*. Cmd 6404. London: The Stationery Office, p 211, Appendix B.
36 Rose, M.E. (1986) *The relief of poverty: 1834-1914*. 2nd revised edn. Basingstoke: Macmillan, p 48.
37 Timmins, N. (2001) *The five giants: A biography of the welfare state*. Revised edn. London: HarperCollins.
38 Ibid, p 18.
39 Beveridge, W. (1942) *Social insurance and allied services*. Cmd 6404. London: The Stationery Office, p 14.
40 Fraser, D. (1984) *The evolution of the British welfare state: A history of social policy since the Industrial Revolution*. London: Macmillan, p 226.
41 Report of the Ministry of National Insurance 1944-1949, p 5, cited in Fraser, D. (1984) *The evolution of the British welfare state: A history of social policy since the Industrial Revolution*. London: Macmillan, p 226.
42 Ibid, , p 227.
43 Kendall, J. and Knapp, M. (1996) *The voluntary sector in the United Kingdom*. Manchester: Manchester University Press, p 52.
44 Beveridge, W. (1942) *Social insurance and allied services*. Cmd 6404. London: The Stationery Office, p 57.
45 Ibid, p 128.
46 Ibid, p 163.
47 Ibid, p 158.
48 Chapman, R. (1991) '*The development of policy on family allowances and National Insurance in the United Kingdom, 1942-1946.*' MPhil thesis. London: London School of Economics and Political Science.
49 The National Archives, 'Short-term benefit.' The Cabinet Papers, www.nationalarchives.gov.uk/cabinetpapers/themes/short-term-benefit.htm

50 Beveridge, W. (1942) *Social insurance and allied services*. Cmd 6404. London: The Stationery Office, p 77.

51 Ibid, p 83.

52 Her Majesty's Government (1952) *National Assistance: Memorandum by the Ministry of National Insurance*, http://filestore.nationalarchives.gov.uk/pdfs/small/cab-129-50-c-52-96-46.pdf

53 Ibid.

54 Kennedy, S. (2011) *Disability Living Allowance reform*. London: House of Commons Library, Standard Note SN/SP/5869.

55 Thatcher, M. (1963) *Oral answers to questions – Pensions and National Insurance*, www.theyworkforyou.com/debates/?id=1963-03-04a.19.1

56 Beveridge, W. (1942) *Social insurance and allied services*. Cmd 6404. London: The Stationery Office, p 17.

Chapter 3

1 Beveridge, W. (1942) *Social insurance and allied services*. Cmd 6404. London: The Stationery Office, p 14.

2 Seebohm Rowntree, a son of Joseph Rowntree, was himself very involved in the Beveridge Report, including as a member of a sub-committee set up to make recommendations on what might represent a subsistence level of income during a period of unemployment or disability. See Beveridge, W. (1942) *Social insurance and allied services*. Cmd 6404. London: The Stationery Office, p 77.

3 Poverty lines for different household types, compared to minimum 'safety net' benefit rates, can be explored using a calculator on The Children's Society website, at www.childrenssociety.org.uk/news-and-blogs/our-blog/use-our-new-calculator-track-shifting-poverty-line

4 Although, as shown in Chapter 5, because they are individual entitlements, contribution-based benefits are treated somewhat differently.

5 Beveridge, W. (1942) *Social insurance and allied services*. Cmd 6404. London: The Stationery Office, p 77.

6 Rowntree, B.S. (1901) *Poverty: A study of town life*. London: Macmillan.

7 Hirsch, D. (2007) 'Gordon Brown's "progressive universalism" is a nice idea but it may come unstuck', August, www.donaldhirsch.com/grants.htm

8 Or £66,000 if they also received the baby addition to the family element on account of having a child under the age of one.

9 HM Revenue and Customs (2012) *Child and Working Tax Credits Statistics, Finalised Annual Awards, 2010-11*. Cardiff: National Statistics.

10 Beveridge, W. (1942) *Social insurance and allied services*. Cmd 6404. London: The Stationery Office, p 154.

11 Ibid, p 12.

12 Riley-Smith, B. (2015) 'Child tax credit reforms "will teach parents that children cost money"', says Iain Duncan Smith, *The Telegraph*, 6 October, www.telegraph.co.uk/news/politics/conservative/11915653/Child-tax-credit-reforms-will-teach-parents-that-children-cost-money.html

¹³ Assuming their rent and Council Tax are both covered in full, as shown in Chapter 18, this is not always the case. All modelled case studies are examples only; they are not based on real people.

¹⁴ Beveridge, W. (1942) *Social insurance and allied services*. Cmd 6404. London: The Stationery Office, p 154.

¹⁵ £2.10 is equivalent to the £64 gain, split over 30 hours of work.

Part II

¹ Child Poverty Action Group (2017) *Welfare benefits and tax credits handbook - 2017/18*. London: Child Poverty Action Group.

Chapter 4

¹ People who have saved towards their retirement may also receive an additional component as part of their Pension Credit called Savings Credit. This additional component is being phased out from April 2016 with the introduction of the new State Pension (discussed in Chapter 5).

² Technically there is a difference between whether the claim is made jointly or whether one person is the claimant but their level of support is affected by their partner. Which of these applies depends on the claimant's circumstances; we will not explore this further here.

³ For a small number of Income Support claimants, support that would normally be provided through Child Tax Credit is made as additional payments through Income Support, but this is becoming increasingly rare.

⁴ Important, for example, in cases of shared parenting between a separated couple – in such cases, rules set out to which family Child Tax Credit should be paid on account of a particular child.

⁵ All sums have been rounded to the nearest pound throughout the book.

⁶ See Valuation Office Agency (updated 2016) *Understanding Local Housing Allowance rates and broad rental market areas*, www.gov.uk/government/publications/understanding-local-housing-allowances-rates-broad-rental-market-areas

⁷ https://www.gov.uk/government/publications/local-housing-allowance-lha-rates-applicable-from-april-2017-march-2018

⁸ Unlike the private rented sector, there is no upper limit on household size.

⁹ It is important to note that receipt of contributory JSA/ESA should not lead to a claimant missing out on SMI if they don't have a partner or their partner has no income – they should receive SMI within their underlying entitlement, leading to an income-based 'top up' to their contribution-based benefit entitlement. However, the rules around this are not at all clear for claimants.

¹⁰ However, they can only receive each at one rate (so a claimant receiving the high-rate care component of DLA won't receive the low and middle rates as well).

¹¹ DCLG (Department for Communities and Local Government) (2015) *The provisional Local Government Finance Settlement 2016-17 and an offer to councils*

for future years. London: DCLG, Clause 1.4 notes:'The Government will also consider giving more responsibility to councils in England, and to Wales, to support older people with care needs – including people who, under the current system, would be supported through Attendance Allowance. This will protect existing claimants, so there will be no cash losers, and new responsibilities will be matched by the transfer of equivalent spending power.'

12 Javid, S. (2017) 'Supporting local government', www.gov.uk/government/speeches/supporting-local-government

13 The disabled child element is normally paid for children receiving DLA or PIP. The severely disabled child element (paid in addition to the disabled child element) is for children receiving the high-rate care component of DLA or PIP equivalent.

14 Her Majesty's Government (2012) *Welfare Reform Act 2012, Chapter 5.* London: The Stationery Office.

15 DWP (Department for Work and Pensions) (2010) *Universal Credit: Welfare that works.* London: The Stationery Office, p 22.

Chapter 5

1 It is also worth noting that the 'ESA in youth' provision was also scrapped in 2012. This used to enable sick or disabled young people to be treated as if they had built up sufficient contributions to claim ESA(C), regardless of their contributions record.

2 This section only deals with those reaching State Pension age since 2010; entitlements may vary for those who reached pension age before this date.

3 Category C pensions were paid to widows of men aged over 65 in July 1948, and have now disappeared entirely.

4 HM Treasury (2016) 'New State Pension for millions of new pensioners', www.gov.uk/government/news/new-state-pension-for-millions-of-new-pensioners

5 Gov.uk (2017) *The new State Pension,* https://www.gov.uk/new-state-pension/how-its-calculated

6 It is assumed that Glen is not affected by the loss of the limited capability for work component of Universal Credit.

Chapter 6

1 The claimant's own earnings are also treated in a similar way for contributory JSA, but their partner's earnings are ignored.

2 Although normally only £5 per week of earnings are disregarded, even if the claimant is in a couple or is a single parent.

3 This assumes June claimed after April 2017 and is not entitled to the Work Related Activity Component.

4 In the case of couples, it is important to remember that while income-based benefits are paid jointly, and cannot be claimed if either partner in a couple works too many hours, contribution-based benefits are claimed

individually, and someone can continue to claim their entitlement even if their partner is in full-time work.

5   Called the '30-hour element'.

6   In some cases an individual's personal allowance may be enhanced by the 'marriage allowance'. This allows someone whose earnings are below their own personal allowance to transfer up to £1,150 of their allowance to their husband, wife or civil partner (so long as the higher earning partner's income is below a certain threshold).

7   Known as the 'primary threshold'.

8   Receipt of the family element is based on at least one of their children being born before April 2017.

9   Based on the author's analysis of Valuation Office Agency (2016) *Private rental market statistics – May 2016*, www.gov.uk/government/uploads/system/uploads/attachment_data/file/524007/160519_Publication_AllTables.xls

10 Author's analysis of DCLG (Department for Communities and Local Government) (2017) *Table 701: Local authority average weekly rents, by country, United Kingdom, from 1998*, www.gov.uk/government/uploads/system/uploads/attachment_data/file/499056/LT_701.xlsx

11 Some Council Tax Reduction schemes may have removed this disregard.

12 Deductions from earnings for in-work benefit claimants can be higher than this 'peak' rate in certain circumstances. Also, as highlighted earlier in the chapter, EMTRs for claimants working less than 16 hours and in receipt of Income Support/JSA can be higher than this, since, above small disregards, deductions are at 100% of additional earnings.

13 Reduced rather than removed because (as outlined in Chapter 5) out-of-work contribution-based benefits are not incorporated into Universal Credit.

14 Assuming he is still entitled to the higher rate of support for the oldest child (which is being phased out for new claimants).

15 Where it applies, the level of the MIF is set at the claimant's relevant Minimum Wage, multiplied by the number of hours they are expected to work – so for a claimant over 25 and with full work-related requirements the level is £7.50 x 35 hours per week.

16 This is not exactly true. Rather than remove Child Benefit as such, the government decided that families could continue to claim it if they chose to do so, but either not receive payment, or return it through a charge on their tax returns (called the high-income Child Benefit charge). So, families with someone earning more than £60,000 can still get Child Benefit, but would see a deduction from their earnings made through their tax return as a result. Strictly speaking we might still call it a universal benefit, but for clarity, let's stick with 'semi-universal'.

Chapter 7

1   Of course, this depends on what 'stuff' you are buying. Inflation can be measured in a number of different ways; here I use Office for Budget

Responsibility (OBR) forecasts for the Retail Prices Index (RPI) (the way in which most benefits increased at the start of the decade).

2   Cracknell, R. (2010) *2011 benefit uprating*. London: House of Commons Library. (The 'Rossi' index, based on RPI, was also used for the uprating of means-tested benefits.)

3   Cited in O'Leary, J. and Sippitt, A. (2015) 'Has the Prime Minister broken a promise on tax credits?', https://fullfact.org/economy/has-prime-minister-broken-promise-tax-credits/

4   Royston, S. (2016) *The future of family incomes*. London: The Children's Society.

5   Royston, S. (2015) *Short changed: The true cost of cuts to children's benefits*. London: End Child Poverty.

6   Thirty per cent of the savings generated by freezing LHA rates rather than uprating them in line with CPI are reinvested through the Targeted Affordability Fund. See Tomlinson, J. (2015) 'Local Housing Allowance: Written question – 15368', www.parliament.uk/business/publications/written-questions-answers-statements/written-question/Commons/2015-11-09/15368

7   ONS (Office for National Statistics) (2015) *Consumer price inflation: October 2015*, www.ons.gov.uk/economy/inflationandpriceindices/bulletins/consumerpriceinflation/october2015

8   DWP (Department for Work and Pensions) (2014) *Monitoring the impact of recent measures affecting Housing Benefit and Local Housing Allowances in the private rented sector – The response of landlords*. London: DWP.

9   Despite the Department for Social Security not having existed since 2001, 'DSS' is still very often used to refer to people receiving Housing Benefit.

10   DWP (Department for Work and Pensions) (2012) *Housing Benefit: Uprating Local Housing Allowance by CPI from April 2013 (Impact Assessment)*. London: DWP.

11   DWP (Department for Work and Pensions) (2012) 'Welfare up-rating Bill introduced', Press release, www.gov.uk/government/news/welfare-up-rating-bill-introduced

12   For example, in order to receive the support component of ESA, the claimant would have to receive their 'personal allowance' (which was not protected). In order to receive the disability element of Working Tax Credit, the claimant would have to receive at least a basic element (which was not protected), and in order to receive the disabled child element of Child Tax Credit, the claimant would have to receive a child element (which again, was not protected).

13   DWP (Department for Work and Pensions) (2013) *Welfare Benefits up-rating Bill (Impact Assessment)*. London: DWP.

14   HM Government (2015) *Policy costings: Summer Budget 2015*. London: HM Government.

Chapter 8

[1] ITV (2015) 'Review of Lords confirmed in wake of tax credit defeat', www.itv.com/news/update/2015-10-27/worst-thing-you-could-do-for-families-is-have-unlimited-welfare/

[2] Despite this, strictly speaking, the benefits system is 'unlimited' in that a variety of benefits can still be paid without limit in many cases (such as Child Benefit, Disability Living Allowance [DLA], and the disability element of Child Tax Credit), meaning that overall maximum benefit entitlement doesn't have a fixed limit.

[3] Riley-Smith, B. (2015) 'Child tax credit reforms "will teach parents that children cost money", says Iain Duncan Smith, *The Telegraph*, 6 October, www.telegraph.co.uk/news/politics/conservative/11915653/Child-tax-credit-reforms-will-teach-parents-that-children-cost-money.html

[4] Walker, P. and Butler, P. (2017) 'Government under fire over new child tax credit form for rape victims', *The Guardian*, 6 April, www.theguardian.com/society/2017/apr/06/government-under-fire-over-new-child-tax-credit-form-for-victims

[5] Defined as those entitled to Working Tax Credit under the current benefits system, and those earning over a fixed income threshold in Universal Credit.

[6] Osborne, G. (2010) 'George Osborne's speech to the Conservative party conference in full', *The Guardian*, 4 October, www.theguardian.com/politics/2010/oct/04/george-osborne-speech-conservative-conference

[7] Meaning the rent of the 30th from the cheapest household of the relevant size, out of each hundred in the local area. As explained in Chapter 7, freezes on LHA rates have gradually reduced entitlements below the 30th percentile.

[8] Based on data from Valuation Office Agency (2015) *Local Housing Allowance (LHA) rates applicable from April 2015 – March 2016*, www.gov.uk/government/uploads/system/uploads/attachment_data/file/399847/FINAL_2015_LHA_RATES.xls

[9] The benefit cap not only affects unemployed claimants but also some of those out-of-work as a result of illness or disability, or because of caring responsibilities for young children. ESA claimants in the work-related activity group (WRAG) are not exempted from the benefit cap unless they also receive DLA or PIP. ESA claimants in the support group are exempted.

[10] Shelter (2015) 'What could be the impact of freezing Local Housing Allowance for four years – and who might be left out in the cold?' Method Note, October. London: Shelter.

[11] Ramesh, R., Stratton, A., Mulholland, H. and Gentleman, A. (2010) *Housing Benefit cap plan will backfire Ministers told*, https://www.theguardian.com/society/2010/oct/28/housing-benefit-cap-plan-backfire

[12] Analysis of caseload statistics from DWP (Department for Work and Pensions) (2016) *Benefit cap: Number of households capped to November 2015*, www.gov.uk/government/uploads/system/uploads/attachment_data/file/497530/benefit-cap-statistics-to-nov-2015-tables.xls

[13] Author's analysis, based on mid-2014 ONS (Office for National Statistics) population statistics from ONS (2016) *Population estimates for UK, England and Wales, Scotland and Northern Ireland*, www.ons.gov.uk/peoplepopulationandcommunity/ populationandmigration/populationestimates/datasets/ populationestimatesforukenglandandwalesscotlandandnorthernireland

[14] HM Treasury and Department for Work and Pensions (2015) *Welfare Reform and Work Bill: Impact Assessment of Tax Credits and Universal Credit, changes to Child Element and Family Element*. London: HM Treasury/ DWP.

[15] Based on the numbers of children in Tax Credit claimant families from HM Revenue and Customs (2015) *Child and Working Tax Credit statistics: Finalised annual awards – 2013 to 2014*, www.gov.uk/government/uploads/ system/uploads/attachment_data/file/430535/cwtc_Finalised_annual_ awards_2013-14.xlsm

Chapter 9

[1] Cameron, D. (2008) 'Yes, we can get the change we really want', http:// conservative-speeches.sayit.mysociety.org/speech/599677

[2] DWP (Department for Work and Pensions) (2014) *Family test: Assessing the impact of policies on families*, www.gov.uk/government/publications/family- test-assessing-the-impact-of-policies-on-families

[3] BBC News (2014) 'David Cameron says policies must pass "family test"', 18 August, www.bbc.co.uk/news/uk-politics-28831242

[4] DWP (Department for Work and Pensions) (2014) *The family test: Guidance for government departments*. London: DWP.

[5] Hood, A. and Waters, T. (2017) *Living standards, poverty and inequality in the UK: 2016–17 to 2021–22*. London: Institute for Fiscal Studies.

[6] HM Treasury (2010) *Spending Review 2010*. London: HM Treasury, www.gov.uk/government/uploads/system/uploads/attachment_data/ file/203826/Spending_review_2010.pdf

[7] HM Treasury (2010) 'Budget statement by the Chancellor of the Exchequer, The Rt Hon George Osborne MP', http://webarchive.nationalarchives. gov.uk/20130129110402/http://www.hm-treasury.gov.uk/junebudget_ speech.htm

[8] HM Treasury (2011) *Autumn Statement 2011 policy costings*. London: HM Treasury.

[9] Grayling, C. (2011) 'Work and Pensions written question – answered on 8 June 2011', www.theyworkforyou.com/wrans/?id=2011-06-08c.57941.h &s=curr+an+section%3Awrans+section%3Awms#g57941.q0

[10] As the Welfare Reform Minister Lord Freud put it during a debate in the House of Lords: 'We firmly believe that aligning the extra amounts payable for disabled children with those of disabled adults is the right and fair thing to do. We are aiming to focus our support for disabled people on their need, not on their age.' Freud, D. (2011) Lords Hansard text for

12 December, www.publications.parliament.uk/pa/ld201011/ldhansrd/text/111212-0002.htm

[11] Royston, S. and Davey, C. (2013) *Single parents and Universal Credit: Singled out?* London: The Children's Society and Gingerbread.

[12] Analysis of Nomis (2017) *Nomis: Official labour market statistics,* https://www.nomisweb.co.uk/query/asv2htm.aspx. This shows that as of November 2016 there were around 99,000 parents under 25 receiving Income Support.

[13] HM Revenue and Customs (2016) *Child and Working Tax Credits statistics April 2016.* London: HM Revenue and Customs.

[14] McVey, E. (2013) 'Work and Pensions written question answered on 15 January 2013', www.theyworkforyou.com/wrans/?id=2013-01-15a.1372 38.h&s=benefit+uprating+section%3Awrans+section%3Awms#g137238. q0

[15] Department for Work and Pensions (2017) *Households below average income: 1994/95 to 2015/16,* https://www.gov.uk/government/statistics/households-below-average-income-199495-to-201516

[16] Money Saving Expert (2016) *Baby checklist,* www.moneysavingexpert.com/family/baby-checklist

[17] DWP (Department for Work and Pensions) (2014) *The Family Test: Guidance for government departments.* London: DWP.

[18] The Scottish Government (2016) *A new future for social security: Consultation on social security in Scotland.* Edinburgh: The Scottish Government.

[19] Author's analysis, based on an additional £22,500 being taken into account as earnings for Tax Credit purposes, and facing a 41% Tax Credit taper rate.

[20] DWP (Department for Work and Pensions) (2014) *The Family Test: Guidance for government departments.* London: DWP.

[21] For this example we also assume that both families get their Council Tax covered in full by their local Council Tax Reduction scheme in all cases.

[22] Church of England et al (2015) *Child Tax Credits and Universal Credit: Limit on support for families with more than two children.* London: Church of England.

[23] Based on the partner also renting a flat costing £150 per week.

[24] Wilson, W. (2016) *The benefit cap.* Briefing Paper Number 06294. London: House of Commons Library.

Chapter 10

[1] Claimants may also receive the Enhanced Disability Premium, even if they are not in the ESA support group, if they receive the highest rate of the care component of DLA or daily living component of PIP.

[2] DWP (Department for Work and Pensions) (2015) *Welfare Reform and Work Bill: Impact assessment to remove the ESA work-related activity component and the UC limited capability for work element for new claimants.* London: DWP.

[3] Notably, he later corrected his comment at www.facebook.com/StephenCrabbPembs/posts/1123686301014718?pnref=story; the original quote is reported in Butler, P. and Asthana, A. (2016) 'Stephen Crabb under pressure over support for cut in disability aid', *The Guardian,* 21 March,

www.theguardian.com/politics/2016/mar/21/crabb-under-pressure-over-support-for-cut-disability-aid

4   'Removing … the UC LCW [Universal Credit limited capability for work] element for new claims is supportive of the Life Chances legislation in that this policy will gradually build the incentive for people to make the choice to move into work. Removing … the UC LCW element for new claims will increase the gains from moving into employment as the difference between the potential income from earnings and income from benefits grows.' DWP (Department for Work and Pensions) (2015) *Welfare Reform and Work Bill: Impact assessment to remove the ESA work related activity component and the UC limited capability for work element for new claims.* London: DWP.

5   DWP (Department for Work and Pensions) and DH (Department of Health) (2016) *Work, health and disability Green Paper: Improving lives,* www.gov.uk/government/consultations/work-health-and-disability-improving-lives/work-health-and-disability-green-paper-improving-lives

6   Mirza-Davies, J. and Brown, J. (2016) *Key statistics on people with disabilities in employment.* London: House of Commons Library.

7   Kennedy, S. (2012) *Time limiting of contributory Employment and Support Allowance from 30 April 2012.* London: House of Commons Library.

8   Again, excluding 'National Insurance credits only' claimants.

9   Since 2012 there has been a consistent increase of about 50,000 in the number of claimants receiving 'National Insurance Credits only' claims to sickness benefit, compared to the period prior to 2012. This will not represent all of those moved off contribution-based ESA, since without receiving any cash entitlement, many of those who would otherwise have received ESA(C) are likely not to claim the benefit for National Insurance credits only.

10   Without a non-disabled adult in the household, or another person receiving Carer's Allowance to look after them.

11   Royston, S., Royston, S., Rodrigues, L. and Coyle, N. (2012) *Holes in the safety net: The impact of Universal Credit on disabled people and their families.* London: The Children's Society, Citizens Advice and Disability Rights UK.

12   Ibid.

13   Duncan Smith, I. (2015) 'House of Commons, oral answers to questions – Work and Pensions', www.publications.parliament.uk/pa/cm201516/cmhansrd/cm150622/debtext/150622-0001.htm

Chapter 11

1   Thurley, D. (2010) *Pension uprating – Background.* London: House of Commons Library.

2   Thurley, D. and Keen, R. (2017) *State Pension triple lock.* London: House of Commons Library.

3   Osborne, G. (2010) 'June Budget 2010' (speech), www.publications.parliament.uk/pa/cm201011/cmhansrd/cm100622/debtext/100622-0007.htm

[4] HM Treasury (2010) *Budget 2010 (June 2010)*. London: HM Treasury, para 1.107.

[5] Measured by the RPI.

[6] HM Treasury (2015) *Summer Budget 2015*. London: HM Treasury.

[7] The Conservative and Unionist Party (2017) *Forward, together. Our plan for a stronger Britain and a prosperous future: The Conservative and Unionist party manifesto 2017*. London: The Conservative Party.

[8] Stewart, H. (2015) 'Scrap triple lock that protects State Pensions, says thinktank chief', *The Guardian*, 20 October, www.theguardian.com/money/2015/oct/20/pensions-state-scrap-triple-lock-protect-paul-johnson-ifs

[9] Ibid.

[10] Hood, A. and Waters, T. (2017) *Living standards, poverty and inequality in the UK: 2016–17 to 2021–22*. London: Institute for Fiscal Studies.

[11] OBR (Office for Budget Responsibility) (2015) *Welfare trends report, June 2015*. London: OBR.

[12] Lewis, P. (2015) 'GAD paper on the triple lock', http://paullewismoney.blogspot.co.uk/2015/10/gad-on-triple-lock.html

[13] Holehouse, M. (2015) 'What if pensioners paid the Bedroom Tax?', *The Telegraph*, 26 February, www.telegraph.co.uk/news/politics/conservative/11436320/What-if-pensioners-paid-the-bedroom-tax.html

[14] The largest cut was 33% in East Dorset and in Craven, North Yorkshire. See Adam, S. and Browne, J. (2012) *Reforming Council Tax Benefit*. London: Institute for Fiscal Studies.

[15] If claiming after the abolition of the work-related activity component.

[16] Webb, S. (2015) 'Steve Webb: Yes, pensioners have never had it so good – but they still deserve the "triple lock"', *The Telegraph*, 22 October, www.telegraph.co.uk/finance/personalfinance/pensions/11947401/Steve-Webb-Yes-pensioners-have-never-had-it-so-good-but-they-still-deserve-the-triple-lock.html

Chapter 12

[1] Barrett, M. (2012) 'CCHQ launches attack ad in marginal constituencies contrasting "hardworking families" with "people who don't work"', 16 December, www.conservativehome.com/thetorydiary/2012/12/cchq-launches-attack-ad-in-marginal-constituencies-hardworking-families-vs-people-who-dont-work.html

[2] Osborne, G. (2012) 'Autumn Statement 2012: Chancellor's statement', www.gov.uk/government/speeches/autumn-statement-2012-chancellors-statement

[3] Montgomerie, T. (2013) 'New Tory poster – Labour are voting to increase benefits by more than workers' wages', www.conservativehome.com/leftwatch/2013/01/new-tory-poster-labour-are-voting-to-increase-benefits-by-more-than-workers-wages.html

4   Boffey, D. and Urquhart, C. (2013) 'Soldiers, teachers, cashiers and nurses: Faces of the benefit cuts', *The Guardian*, 5 January, www.theguardian.com/politics/2013/jan/05/benefits-cap-shirkers-scroungers

5   Royston, S. (2011) 'Hurting the working through 21 welfare cuts', 16 February, http://touchstoneblog.org.uk/2011/02/hurting-the-working-through-21-welfare-cuts

6   Islam, F. (2015) 'Tory MPs express "concern" over Tax Credits', 29 October, http://news.sky.com/story/1578577/tory-mps-express-concern-over-tax-credits

7   Dominiczak, P. (2015) 'David Cameron: Firms which do not pay minimum wage will be fined up to £20,000', *The Telegraph*, 31 August, www.telegraph.co.uk/news/politics/11835743/David-Cameron-Firms-which-do-not-pay-minimum-wage-will-be-fined-up-to-20000.html

8   Author's analysis of HM Treasury (2016) *Budget 2016: Policy costings*. London: HM Treasury.

9   Based on official figures indicating that 39% of the 13.6 million people in poverty in 1997/98 were in working families and 54% of the 13.5 million people in poverty in 2014/15.

Chapter 13

1   DEP (Department for Work and Pensions) (2010) *Universal Credit: Welfare that works*. London: DWP.

2   As the Universal Credit White Paper notes, 'the highest Marginal Deduction Rate for low-earning workers would be reduced from around 96 per cent to 65 per cent for those earning below the personal tax threshold and to around 76 per cent for basic rate taxpayers.' DWP (Department for Work and Pensions) (2010) *Universal Credit: Welfare that works*. London: DWP, p 15.

3   Miller, M. (2011) 'Universal Credit, Work and Pensions written question, answered on 18 July 2011', www.theyworkforyou.com/wrans/?id=2011-07-18d.66178.h

4   Centre for Social Justice (2009) *Dynamic benefits: Towards welfare that works*. London: Centre for Social Justice.

5   Such as through the Access to Work scheme.

6   Royston, S., Royston, S., Rodrigues, L. and Coyle, N. (2012) *Holes in the safety net: The impact of Universal Credit on disabled people and their families*. London: The Children's Society, Citizens Advice and Disability Rights UK.

7   Duncan Smith, I. (2015) 'Speech on work, health and disability', www.reform.uk/publication/rt-hon-iain-duncan-smith-mp-speech-on-work-health-and-disability/

8   Paid as a loan from 2018.

9   Cameron, D. (2015) 'Speech on welfare', http://press.conservatives.com/post/111947329085/david-cameron-speech-on-welfare

10 Author's calculations, based on average school lunch cost of £2.04 and 190 days in the school year, based on Wollny, I. et al (2015) *School lunch take-up survey 2013 to 2014, Research report*. London: Department for Education.

[11] DWP (Department for Work and Pensions) (2010) *Universal Credit: Welfare that works.* London: DWP.

[12] Gyimah, S. (2016) 'Free school meals, Department for Education written question, answered on 20 June 2016', www.theyworkforyou.com/wrans/?id=2016-06-09.40159.h&s=%22free+school+meals%22+%22universal+credit%22#g40159.q0

[13] 'Universal Credit makes it easier to start work if you're a parent, with increased help towards registered childcare costs, no matter how many hours you work.' DWP (Department for Work and Pensions) (2013) *Universal Credit guides,* www.gov.uk/government/uploads/system/uploads/attachment_data/file/491027/uc-and-your-family-jan16.pdf

[14] Asthana, A. (2016) 'Stephen Crabb urged to overhaul "salami-sliced" universal credit system', *The Guardian,* 29 March, www.theguardian.com/society/2016/mar/29/stephen-crabb-urged-overhaul-universal-credit-system-labour-owen-smith-welfare?CMP=share_btn_tw

[15] Royston, S. and Hounsell, D. (2012) *The parent trap: Childcare cuts under Universal Credit.* London: The Children's Society.

[16] Citizens Advice (2014) *Delivery of support for childcare costs under Universal Credit.* London: Citizens Advice.

[17] Employers for Childcare Charity (2015) *2015 childcare costs report: Key findings.* Lisburn: Employers for Childcare Charity.

[18] titanpaydayloan.co.uk (2016) 'Payday loan FAQ', www.titanpaydayloan.co.uk/payday-loan-faq/

[19] For claimants under Pension Credit age; for older people different rules apply.

[20] For those with an income over the relevant Tax Credit income threshold.

[21] Sainsbury, R. and Corden, A. (2013) *Self-employment, tax credits and the move to Universal Credit.* London: Department for Work and Pensions.

[22] Osborne, G. (2015) 'Chancellor George Osborne's Spending Review and Autumn Statement 2015 speech', www.gov.uk/government/speeches/chancellor-george-osbornes-spending-review-and-autumn-statement-2015-speech

[23] And so received the higher rate of work allowance.

[24] Based on figures given in the Autumn Statement 2015.

Chapter 14

[1] CPAG (Child Poverty Action Group) (2016) *Welfare benefits and Tax Credits handbook 2016/17.* London: CPAG, p 687.

[2] In Wales and Scotland, prescriptions are universally free.

[3] For example, for housing costs or for the cost of children (the equivalent to what would currently be provided through Child Tax Credit). Higher-income earners are excluded from passported benefit entitlements through the introduction of earnings thresholds (earnings points above which the claimant can no longer keep their passported benefit entitlement).

4 Although notably this means that actual entitlements (over the course of a year) for JSA claimants who move back into work may be rather less than one might think – both for income-based and for contribution-based JSA claimants.

5 Although the claimant may get some of this back, since lower net income as a result of the additional deductions will in itself *increase* their Universal Credit entitlement.

6 This would be significantly higher, but the additional tax paid is then deducted from the claimant's earnings – reducing their net income for the purposes of calculating their Universal Credit.

7 The Bereavement Support Payment has its own problems, but these are outside the scope of this chapter.

8 This is not necessarily the case for a couple, since two full old Basic State Pensions, or two new State Pensions, can exceed the value of Pension Credit. In addition, under the old system, a couple each receiving a Basic State Pension in full may receive a Pension Credit top up known as Savings Credit, designed to provide some additional help to lower-income pensioners who had saved towards their retirement.

9 As well as other forms of unearned income, such as occupational pensions.

Chapter 15

1 Duncan Smith, I. (2015) 'House of Commons, oral answers to questions – Work and Pensions', 22 June, www.publications.parliament.uk/pa/cm201516/cmhansrd/cm150622/debtext/150622-0001.htm

2 Duncan Smith, I. (2016) 'Resignation letter', *The Guardian*, 18 March, www.theguardian.com/politics/2016/mar/18/iain-duncan-smith-resignation-letter-in-full

3 Pearlman, V., Royston, S. and Silk, C. (2012) *Right first time?* London: Citizens Advice.

4 Gentleman, A. (2012) 'Third of incapacity benefit claimants ruled fit for work', *The Guardian*, 15 March, www.theguardian.com/society/2012/mar/15/third-of-incapacity-benefit-claimants-ineligible

5 Royston, S. (2010) *Not working: CAB evidence on the ESA Work Capability Assessment*. London: Citizens Advice.

6 Pearlman, V., Royston, S. and Silk, C. (2012) *Right first time?* London: Citizens Advice.

7 Gentleman, A. (2011) 'New disability test "is a complete mess" says expert', *The Guardian*, 22 February, www.theguardian.com/politics/2011/feb/22/new-disability-test-is-a-complete-mess

8 Viney, M. (2014) 'Work Programme adviser: "Almost every day one of my clients mentioned feeling suicidal"', *The Guardian*, 5 November, www.theguardian.com/society/2014/nov/05/work-programme-adviser-box-ticking-sanctioning-sick-people

9 DWP (Department for Work and Pensions) (2012) 'Grayling: Statistics show our benefit reforms are justified', www.gov.uk/government/news/grayling-statistics-show-our-benefit-reforms-are-justified

[10] Gentleman, A. (2012) 'Third of incapacity benefit claimants ruled fit for work', *The Guardian*, 15 March, www.theguardian.com/society/2012/mar/15/third-of-incapacity-benefit-claimants-ineligible

[11] Including ESA, Incapacity benefit, Severe Disablement Allowance and Income Support for sickness or disability.

[12] And to remove 'ESA in youth', an entitlement to contribution-based ESA for young people with disabilities, without them needing to build up a National Insurance Contribution record.

[13] Claimants appealing a decision about being placed in the 'limited capability for work' group rather than the support group could continue to receive ESA.

[14] Such as Income Support. As the Welfare Reform Minister Lord Freud put it in the House of Lords: 'At the moment, if someone appeals a refusal of ESA, it can continue to be paid pending the appeal being heard; this is not changing. What is changing is that there can be no appeal until there has been a mandatory reconsideration. So there will be a gap in payment. In that period ... the claimant could claim Jobseeker's Allowance or Universal Credit.... Of course, he or she may choose to wait for the outcome of the application and then, if necessary, appeal and be paid ESA at that point.' Freud, D. (2013) *Universal Credit, Personal Independence Payment, Jobseeker's Allowance and Employment and Support Allowance (Decisions and Appeals) Regulations 2013: Motion to approve*, www.publications.parliament.uk/pa/ld201213/ldhansrd/text/130213-0003.htm

[15] Citizens Advice (accessed 2016) *Your money and benefits during an ESA reconsideration*, www.citizensadvice.org.uk/benefits/sick-or-disabled-people-and-carers/employment-and-support-allowance/while-youre-getting-esa/esa-money-and-benefits-during-reconsideration/

[16] DWP (Department for Work and Pensions) (2014) *Mandatory reconsiderations, requests and decisions to October 2014, Great Britain: Experimental official statistics*, www.gov.uk/government/uploads/system/uploads/attachment_data/file/387871/MR_adhoc_final.pdf

[17] IMDB (2017) *I, Daniel Blake (2016) quotes*, www.imdb.com/title/tt5168192/quotes?item=qt3307344

[18] Citizens Advice (2014) *Rebalancing Universal Credit: Making it work for disabled people.* London: Citizens Advice.

[19] Guy, G. (2014) 'Nowhere to turn: Citizens Advice speaks out on impact of legal aid cuts', 8 July, www.citizensadvice.org.uk/about-us/how-citizens-advice-works/media/press-releases/nowhere-to-turn-citizens-advice-speaks-out-on-impact-of-legal-aid-cuts/

[20] Green, A. (2014) *Citizens Advice submission to the Justice Select Committee Inquiry into the impact of changes to civil legal aid under the Legal Aid, Sentencing and Punishment of Offenders Act 2012.* London: Citizens Advice.

[21] 'Many people going through the ESA claims process are unhappy with the way they are treated and the decisions which are made about their fitness for work. The current provider of the WCA, Atos, has become a lightning rod for all the negativity around the ESA process and DWP and

Atos have recently agreed to terminate the contract early.' Begg, A. (2014) 'Employment and Support Allowance needs fundamental redesign say MPs', www.parliament.uk/business/committees/committees-a-z/commons-select/work-and-pensions-committee/news/esa-wca-report-substantive/

22   Bartlett, E. (2014) 'Controversial "fit-for-work" firm Atos quits £500million government contract', Metro, 27 March, http://metro.co.uk/2014/03/27/controversial-fit-for-work-firm-atos-quits-500million-government-contract-4680301/

23   DWP (Department for Work and Pensions) (2012) *Disability Living Allowance reform – Impact assessment.* London: DWP.

24   House of Commons Committee of Public Accounts (2014) *Personal Independence Payment – First report of session 2014-15.* London: House of Commons.

25   DWP (Department for Work and Pensions) (2012) *Disability Living Allowance reform – Impact assessment.* London: DWP.

26   DWP (Department for Work and Pensions) (2016) *Personal Independence Payment: April 2013 to July 2016,* www.gov.uk/government/statistics/personal-independence-payment-april-2013-to-july-2016

27   House of Commons Committee of Public Accounts (2014) *Personal Independence Payment – First report of session 2014-15.* London: House of Commons.

28   Gray, P. (2014) *An Independent Review of the Personal Independence Payment Assessment,* www.gov.uk/government/uploads/system/uploads/attachment_data/file/387981/pip-assessment-first-independent-review.pdf

29   The Committee chair, Margaret Hodge, scathingly noted: 'The Department's failure to pilot the scheme meant that the most basic assumptions, such as how long assessments would take and how many would require face-to-face consultations, had not been fully tested and proved to be wrong. This resulted in significant delays, a backlog of claims and unnecessary distress for claimants who have been unable to access the support they need to live, and in some cases work, independently.' Hodge, M. (2014) 'Implementation of Personal Independence Payments nothing short of fiasco', www.parliament.uk/business/committees/committees-a-z/commons-select/public-accounts-committee/news/personal-independence-payments-substantive/

30   Hodge, M. (2014) 'Implementation of Personal Independence Payments nothing short of fiasco', www.parliament.uk/business/committees/committees-a-z/commons-select/public-accounts-committee/news/personal-independence-payments-substantive/

31   Author's analysis based on DWP (Department for Work and Pensions) (2017) *Benefit expenditure and caseload tables,* www.gov.uk/government/collections/benefit-expenditure-tables

32   Ibid.

33   House of Commons Committee of Public Accounts (2014) *Personal Independence Payment – First report of session 2014-15.* London: House of Commons.

[34] DWP (Department for Work and Pensions) (2016) *The Government response to the consultation on aids and appliances and the daily living component of Personal Independence Payment*. London: DWP.

[35] Tomlinson, J. (2016) 'Personal Independence Payment consultation response announced', www.gov.uk/government/news/personal-independence-payment-consultation-response-announced

[36] Ibid.

[37] I use this example because the government's response to their 2012 consultation on PIP assessment criteria mentioned this as an example of an appliance that might be required by a claimant as a result of a health condition rather than out of choice.

[38] DWP (Department for Work and Pensions) (2015) *Consultation on aids and appliances and the daily living component of Personal Independence Payment*. London: DWP.

[39] See http://shop.rnib.org.uk/mobility/canes/guide-canes/85cm-folding-guide-cane-pencil-tip.html

[40] Tomlinson, J. (2016) 'Personal Independence Payment consultation response announced', www.gov.uk/government/news/personal-independence-payment-consultation-response-announced

[41] DWP (Department for Work and Pensions) (2016) *The Government response to the consultation on aids and appliances and the daily living component of Personal Independence Payment*. London: DWP.

[42] Crabb, S. (2016) *Hansard*, 21 March, Column 1268, www.publications.parliament.uk/pa/cm201516/cmhansrd/cm160321/debte

Chapter 16

[1] See Inland Revenue (2001) *New Tax Credits: Supporting families, making work pay and tackling poverty*. London: Inland Revenue.

[2] White, M. (2005) 'Blair apology for Tax Credit chaos', *The Guardian*, 23 June, www.theguardian.com/politics/2005/jun/23/uk.money

[3] Merrick, J. (2005) 'Blair sorry for Tax Credit fiasco', *This is Money*, 23 June, www.thisismoney.co.uk/money/news/article-1591332/Blair-sorry-for-tax-credit-fiasco.html#ixzz40oOk58Xt

[4] RevenueBenefits (2016) *Tax Credits: Understanding the disregards*, http://revenuebenefits.org.uk/tax-credits/guidance/how-do-tax-credits-work/understanding-the-disregard/#History%20of%20the%20income%20disregards

[5] Author's analysis based on HM Revenue and Customs (2016) Child and Working Tax Credits statistics: Finalised annual awards – 2014 to 2015, www.gov.uk/government/statistics/child-and-working-tax-credits-statistics-finalised-annual-awards-2014-to-2015 and HM Revenue and Customs (2016) Child and Working Tax Credits statistics: Finalised annual awards, supplement on payments – 2014 to 2015, www.gov.uk/government/uploads/system/uploads/attachment_data/file/525513/cwtc_awards_sup.xls

6   HM Treasury (2015) *Summer Budget 2015 policy costings.* London: HM Treasury. This measure affects only Tax Credits, not Universal Credit, so savings from this will be expected to fall as claimants are transitioned to the new system.

7   See, for example, the 'Tax Credit Casualties' at www.taxcc.org/

8   Similarly, see Jones, O. (2015) *The Establishment.* London: Penguin Random House, p 300, in which Caroline Lucas recounts how people no longer seemed angry about cuts in support: 'they were just so ground down by it all. It was just like they'd lost the will to fight....'

9   Not Child Benefit, which remains paid separately.

10   This example is from Royston, S. (2012) 'Understanding Universal Credit.' *The Journal of Poverty and Social Justice,* vol 20, no 1, pp 69-86.

11   See for example, Fran Bennett's evidence to the Welfare Reform Bill Committee in 2011: Bennett, F. (2011) *White Paper on Universal Credit, Work and Pensions Committee written evidence,* www.publications.parliament.uk/pa/cm201011/cmselect/cmworpen/743/743we14.htm

12   Some exceptions apply to the seven-day waiting period.

13   Royston, S. (2015) *Waiting for Credit: The delivery of Universal Credit as experienced by Citizens Advice clients in England and Wales.* London: Citizens Advice.

14   Ibid.

Chapter 17

1   Viney, M. (2014) 'Work Programme adviser: "Almost every day one of my clients mentioned feeling suicidal"', *The Guardian,* 5 November, www.theguardian.com/society/2014/nov/05/work-programme-adviser-box-ticking-sanctioning-sick-people

2   Some exceptions to this apply.

3   It started to be applied to the claimant's personal allowance.

4   Although not to disability premiums awarded as part of the entitlement.

5   Butler, P. (2015) 'DWP finally acts to end housing benefit "maladministration" scandal', *The Guardian,* 6 October, www.theguardian.com/society/patrick-butler-cuts-blog/2015/oct/06/dwp-finally-acts-to-end-housing-benefit-maladministration-scandal

6   Figures produced using DWP (Department for Work and Pensions) (2016) *Stat-Xplore,* https://stat-xplore.dwp.gov.uk/ This is final decisions (after reviews and appeals are taken into account).

7   Note that this is the proportion rather than the number of claimants – which we would expect to rise in periods of rising unemployment simply because there are more of them.

8   $r=0.38$; notably, the relationship becomes considerably stronger once you factor in a time lag between the claimant count and the proportion of claimants sanctioned (so, the proportion of claimants sanctioned in August 2010 compared to the claimant count for August 2009). When this is done, $r=0.79$. This suggests that a responsive increase in sanctions-use happens

a short time after an increase in the claimant count; it is possible that this could reflect a delay before the implementation of a new policy direction.

[9] Based on analysis of figures from DWP (Department for Work and Pensions) (2016) *Stat-Xplore*, https://sw.stat-xplore.dwp.gov.uk/webapi/jsf/dataCatalogueExplorer.xhtml

[10] Partly, but not entirely, as a result of increasing numbers of ESA claimants in the work-related activity group.

[11] Rickman, D. and McKernan, B. (2015) 'Sixteen of the most senseless benefit sanction decisions known to man', Independent, http://indy100.independent.co.uk/article/sixteen-of-the-most-senseless-benefit-sanction-decisions-known-to-man--x1dmkd2_Me

[12] Author's analysis of data from DWP (Department for Work and Pensions) (2016) *Stat-Xplore*, https://stat-xplore.dwp.gov.uk/

[13] Ayre, D., Capron, C., Egan, H., French, A. and Gregg, L. (2016) *The cost of being care free: The impact of poor financial education and removal of support on care leavers.* London: The Children's Society.

[14] Douglas, D. (2015) 'Benefit sanctions "linked to food bank use"', *Inside Housing*, 9 April, www.insidehousing.co.uk/benefit-sanctions-linked-to-food-bank-use/7009199.article

[15] Perry, J., Williams, M., Sefton, T. and Haddad, M. (2014) *Emergency use only: Understanding and reducing the use of food banks in the UK.* London: The Child Poverty Action Group, Church of England, Oxfam GB and The Trussell Trust.

[16] Head, D. (2014) 'I was ill with hunger, went to prison for stealing food and became homeless', *The Guardian*, 29 July, www.theguardian.com/society/2014/jul/29/benefits-sanctions-matthew-oakley-report-hunger

[17] Scottish Government (2013) *The potential impacts of benefit sanctions on individuals and households*, www.gov.scot/Resource/0044/00440885.pdf

[18] Griggs, J. and Evans, M. (2010) *Sanctions within conditional benefits systems: A review of evidence.* York: Joseph Rowntree Foundation.

[19] Thompson, G. (2015) '"My mental health deteriorated rapidly": the real impact of benefit sanctions', *The Guardian*, 27 January, www.theguardian.com/society/2015/jan/27/mental-health-benefit-sanctions-work-and-pensions-select-committee

[20] Preece, S. (2015) 'Exclusive: DWP admit using fake claimant's comments in benefit sanctions leaflet', *Welfare Weekly*, 5 February, www.welfareweekly.com/exclusive-comments-used-in-official-benefit-sanctions-leaflet-were-made-up-dwp-admits/

[21] Mason, R. and Butler, P. (2016) 'Labour to refer "groundless" Iain Duncan Smith claim to statistics watchdog', *The Guardian*, 12 March, www.theguardian.com/politics/2016/mar/12/labour-refer-groundless-iain-duncan-smith-claim-statistics-watchdog

[22] See Watts, B. et al (2014) *Welfare sanctions and conditionality in the UK.* York: Joseph Rowntree Foundation; and Griggs, J. and Evans, M. (2010) *A review of benefit sanctions.* York: Joseph Rowntree Foundation.

23 On the assumption that their relevant rate of minimum wage is the National Living Wage (£7.50 per hour at the time of writing).

24 Butler, P. (2016) 'DWP "punishing" low-paid full-time workers under new benefits rule', *The Guardian*, 14 April, www.theguardian.com/society/2016/apr/14/dwp-punishing-low-paid-full-time-workers-under-new-benefits-rule

Chapter 18

1 DWP (Department for Work and Pensions) (2012) *Discretionary Housing Payments: DWP response to the consultation on the Discretionary Housing Payments guidance manual*. London: DWP.

2 DWP (Department for Work and Pensions) (2014) *Evaluation of removal of the spare room subsidy – Interim report*. London: DWP.

3 Wilson, W. (2015) *Discretionary Housing Payments*, Briefing paper number 06899. London: House of Commons Library.

4 Berry, K. (2014) *Discretionary Housing Payments*. Edinburgh: Scottish Parliament Information Centre.

5 Scottish Government (2016) *Discretionary Housing Payments in Scotland: As at 30 September 2016*. Edinburgh: The Scottish Government.

6 Wilson, W., Barton, C. and Keen, R. (2016) *Housing Benefit measures announced since 2010*. Briefing paper number 05638. London: House of Commons Library.

7 Stone, J. (2016) 'Iain Duncan Smith refused to speak during a Bedroom Tax debate and got a junior minister to answer every question', *Independent*, 28 January, www.independent.co.uk/news/uk/politics/iain-duncan-smith-refused-to-speak-during-a-bedroom-tax-debate-and-got-a-junior-minister-to-answer-a6838901.html

8 DWP (Department for Work and Pensions) (2014) 'Benefit cap: 10,000 people find jobs or stop claiming Housing Benefit', www.gov.uk/government/news/benefit-cap-10000-people-find-jobs-or-stop-claiming-housing-benefit

9 Figures in 2013/14 prices.

10 See The Children's Society (2015) 'Thanks to your critical support, the Government reinstated £130 million of funding for local welfare assistance', www.childrenssociety.org.uk/what-you-can-do/campaign-change/local-welfare

11 NAO (National Audit Office) (2016) *Local welfare provision*. London: NAO. Results are based on the 97 councils that provided information to the DWP on spending in 2013-14 and 2014-15.

12 DWP (Department for Work and Pensions) (2012) *Annual Report by the Secretary of State for Work and Pensions on the Social Fund 2011/2012*. London: DWP.

13 Royston, S. and Rodrigues, L. (2013) *Nowhere to turn? Changes to emergency support*. London: The Children's Society.

14 BBC News (2013) 'George Osborne: "No-one will get something for nothing"', 30 September, www.bbc.co.uk/news/uk-politics-24327890

15 The Scottish Government provide additional funding to local authorities to enable them to protect those who were previously receiving Council Tax Benefit from this cut: see www.gov.scot/Topics/Government/local-government/17999/counciltax/CTR

16 LGA (Local Government Association) (2015) *Council Tax Support: The story continues.* London: LGA.

17 Adam, S. et al (2014) *Council Tax support schemes in England: What did local authorities choose, and with what effects?* London: Institute for Fiscal Studies. Previous research had also found that the cut to funding for Council Tax Benefit for working-age claimants was around 19% – presumably this was higher than the cut in entitlement because some councils chose to protect working-age claimants.

18 LGA (Local Government Association) (2015) *Council Tax Support: The story continues.* London: LGA.

19 Adam, S. et al (2014) *Council Tax support schemes in England: What did local authorities choose, and with what effects?* London: Institute for Fiscal Studies.

20 Ibid.

21 LGA (Local Government Association) (2015) *Council Tax Support: The story continues.* London: LGA.

22 Council Tax Support Update (2016) 'Council tax arrears rise fastest where support is cut most', http://counciltaxsupport.org/resources/commentary/council-tax-arrears-rise-fastest-where-support-cut-most/

23 Capron, L. and Ayre, D. (2015) *The wolf at the door – How council tax debt collection is harming children.* London: The Children's Society.

Chapter 19

1 The distinction in the pension age in 1940 was introduced through the Old Age and Widows Pensions Act. The original distinction was made on the basis that husbands tended to be older than their wives – in order to ensure that a married couple could receive their full joint pension when the husband reached 65. Thurley, D. (2012) *State Pension age: Background.* London: House of Commons Library.

2 Thurley, D. (2016) *State Pension age increases for women born in the 1950s.* Briefing paper number cbp-07405. London: House of Commons Library.

3 ONS (Office for National Statistics) (2014) *National life tables, UK: 2013-2015.*

4 DWP (Department for Work and Pensions) (2013) *Long-term State Pension sustainability: Increasing the State Pension age to 67: Impact assessment.* London: DWP.

5 Osborne, G. (2013) 'Chancellor George Osborne's Autumn Statement 2013 speech', www.gov.uk/government/speeches/chancellor-george-osbornes-autumn-statement-2013-speech

6 HM Government (2010) *State of the nation report: Poverty, worklessness and welfare dependency in the UK.* London: Cabinet Office.

7 ONS (Office for National Statistics) (2011) *Trends in life expectancy by the National Statistics Socio-economic Classification 1982-2006.* Newport: ONS.

8   Bennett, J. et al (2015) 'The future of life expectancy and life expectancy inequalities in England and Wales: Bayesian spatiotemporal forecasting.' *The Lancet*, vol 386, no 9989, pp 163-70.

9   Ibid.

10 As mentioned previously, the State Pension age for women is also rising to equalise with that for men. The justification for this is different to the rise in the Pension Credit age, and is not addressed here.

11 This overlaps with the introduction of ESA – it is difficult to know how this is likely to affect the proportion of older people as a proportion of the claimants population at different points; however, the findings seem broadly in line with increases in the proportion of the JSA claimant population.

12 At the time of writing, this would put him above eligibility age for Pension Credit.

13 Based on earnings forecasts of 2.7% and 3.0% in 2018 and 2019 respectively. Based on figures from OBR (Office for Budget Responsibility) (2017) *Economic and fiscal outlook, March 2017*. London: OBR.

14 *Daily Mail* (2011) 'One in five of UK's poorest men "will die before they qualify for State Pension"', 20 April, www.dailymail.co.uk/news/article-1378749/Fifth-UKs-poorest-men-die-qualify-state-pension.html

15 Although the partner over pension-age will be exempted from work-related requirements.

16 Rising from £78 billion in 2017/18 prices in 2010, to £96 billion in 2020/21 – based on DWP (Department for Work and Pensions) (2017) *Benefit expenditure and caseload tables – Outturn and forecast Spring Budget 2017*. London: DWP.

Part V

1   Osborne, G. (2015) 'Chancellor George Osborne's Summer Budget 2015 speech', www.gov.uk/government/speeches/chancellor-george-osbornes-summer-budget-2015-speech

2   Osborne, G. (2015) 'Oral answers to questions Treasury: Tuesday 27 October 2015', www.publications.parliament.uk/pa/cm201516/cmhansrd/cm151027/debtext/151027-0001.htm

Chapter 20

1   Or, from £8,175 to £8,151, when Northern Ireland is included. Note that calculations in this section are for Great Britain (GB) only; this is for consistency, since the split of welfare expenditure outlined in the following section is only available at GB rather than UK level.

2   Rising from £75 billion (in 2015/16 prices) in 2010, to £94 billion in 2020/21.

3   ONS (Office for National Statistics) (2014) *The effects of taxes and benefits on household income, 2013/14 – reference tables (table 7)*, www.ons.gov.uk/file?uri=/peoplepopulationandcommunity/

personalandhouseholdfinances/incomeandwealth/datasets/
theeffectsoftaxesandbenefitsonhouseholdincomefinancialyearending2014

[4] Waters, T. (2017) *Distributional analysis.* London: Institute for Fiscal Studies.

[5] All case studies are based on the following assumptions:

- Household earnings for Tax Credit purposes are the same in 2009 as in 2010 – if earnings were lower in 2009 than 2010, the between-year income disregard would mean that in some of the cases 2010 incomes would be higher than stated.
- Between 2016 and 2020, gross household earnings increase in line with RPI (except in cases of the National Minimum Wage with a worker over the age of 25, where it is assumed that earnings increase to £9 per hour by 2020).
- Overall costs of living for the given household types increase in line with current RPI forecasts. An assumption like this is necessary for simplicity of modelling, but is unlikely to be exactly accurate for two reasons: (1) RPI forecasts are only predictive and (2) individual household types will face variations in increases in costs of living depending on the balance of individual household expenditure.
- RPI forecasts are based on the OBR March 2017 forecasts.
- Families claim Universal Credit in 2020 rather than make a claim through the current Tax Credits and Benefits system – this is a crucial assumption, since the structure of the new system is different.
- 2020 claimants are new claimants – the government has promised that 'cash losers' affected by the transition on to Universal Credit will receive cash protection of their previous entitlement. This is an important provision (although it has limitations since, as noted in Chapter 4, [1] it is only cash protection; [2] it only applies to existing claimants who are transferring across to Universal Credit; and [3] it can be lost as a result of changes in household circumstances). This chapter explores the long-term future of incomes for different household types, and for this reason, it is more useful to consider the situation for new claimants entering the system in 2020 rather than existing claimants moving across.

[6] The change from uprating by RPI to uprating by CPI has meant that DLA has lost some value despite being exempt from benefit freezes.

[7] Assumes that a triple lock is in place – earnings growth forecast to be higher than inflation or 2.5% in 2018/19 and 2019/20, at 2.8%, and 3.0% respectively.

[8] Maximum entitlement = £499 (standard allowance) + £435 (rent). From this the State Pension of £734 is deducted.

Chapter 21

[1] Both the relative and absolute poverty measure can be measured either before or after the deduction of housing costs.

[2] Cameron, D. (2006) 'Tackling poverty is a social responsibility', http://conservative-speeches.sayit.mysociety.org/speech/599937

[3] Measured after housing costs. Hood, A. and Waters, T. (2017) *Living standards, poverty and inequality in the UK: 2016-17 to 2021-22.* London: Institute for Fiscal Studies.

[4] Ibid.

[5] Including the End Child Poverty coalition's 'Now you see them' campaign, www.endchildpoverty.org.uk/now-you-see-them/

[6] Measured as living in households on less than 60% median income before housing costs are deducted.

[7] Hood, A. and Waters, T. (2017) *Living standards, poverty and inequality in the UK: 2016-17 to 2021-22.* London: Institute for Fiscal Studies.

[8] Royston, S. (2015) *Short changed: The true cost of cuts to children's benefits.* London: End Child Poverty.

[9] Forsey, A. (2014) *An evidence review for the All-Party Parliamentary inquiry into hunger in the United Kingdom.* London: The Children's Society.

[10] Freud, D. (2013) *Lords Hansard,* column 1072, 2 July, www.publications. parliament.uk/pa/ld201314/ldhansrd/text/130702-0001.htm

[11] Royston, S. and Rodrigues, L. (2013) *Nowhere to turn?: Changes to emergency support.* London: The Children's Society.

[12] Butler, P. (2014) 'Families turn to food banks as last resort "not because they are free"', *The Guardian,* 20 February, www.theguardian.com/society/2014/feb/20/food-bank-review-undermines-ministers-claim

[13] University of Oxford (2015) 'Study finds greater use of food banks linked to higher unemployment, sanctions and cuts in welfare spending', www.ox.ac.uk/news/2015-04-09-increased-use-food-banks-linked-higher-unemployment-sanctions-and-welfare-cuts

[14] Centre for Regional Economic and Social Research (2014) *Monitoring the impact of recent measures affecting Housing Benefit and Local Housing Allowances in the private rented sector: The response of landlords.* London: Department for Work and Pensions.

[15] Kaur, M. (2017) *Universal Credit progress update: 2016 NFA and ARCH survey findings.* London: National Federation of ALMOs and Association of Retained Council Housing.

[16] Scope (2013) *Disabled people and financial well-being: Credit and debt.* London: Scope.

[17] paydayloansnow.co.uk (accessed 2016) 'As welfare gets cut, payday loans step up', www.paydayloansnow.co.uk/blog/as-welfare-gets-cut-payday-loans-step-up/

[18] Wintour, P. (2014) 'Extended benefit sanctions push up numbers seeking advice on paying bills', *The Guardian,* 14 April, www.theguardian.com/politics/2014/apr/14/extended-benefit-sanctions-jsa-citizens-advice-bills

[19] Royston, S. (2015) *Waiting for credit: The delivery of Universal Credit as experienced by Citizens Advice clients in England and Wales.* London: Citizens Advice.

[20] UCL Institute of Health Equity (2014) *Local action on health inequalities: Fuel poverty and cold home-related health problems.* London: Public Health England.

[21] NHS choices (2016) 'Cause of malnutrition', www.nhs.uk/Conditions/ Malnutrition/Pages/Causes.aspx

[22] BMA (British Medical Association) (2015) *Food for thought: Promoting healthy diets among children and young people.* London: BMA.

[23] Ibid.

[24] Wilkinson, R. and Pickett, K. (2009) *The spirit level: Why more equal societies almost always do better.* London: Allen Lane.

[25] May, T. (2016) 'Statement from the new Prime Minister Theresa May', www. gov.uk/government/speeches/statement-from-the-new-prime-minister-theresa-may

[26] Department for Education (2016) *Revised GCSE and equivalent results in England, 2014 to 2015,* www.gov.uk/government/uploads/system/uploads/ attachment_data/file/494073/SFR01_2016.pdf

[27] Achieving either A/A★s in both assessments, or one B and one A★.

[28] Department for Education (2016) *Revised GCSE and equivalent results in England, 2014 to 2015,* www.gov.uk/government/uploads/system/uploads/ attachment_data/file/494073/SFR01_2016.pdf

[29] May, T. (2016) 'Statement from the new Prime Minister Theresa May', www.gov.uk/government/speeches/statement-from-the-new-prime-minister-theresa-may

[30] The Children's Commission on Poverty (2014) *At what cost? Exposing the impact of poverty on school life.* London: The Children's Society.

[31] DCLG (Department for Communities and Local Government) (2017) *Statutory homelessness and homelessness prevention and relief October to December 2016,* www.gov.uk/government/statistical-data-sets/live-tables-on-homelessness

[32] McCann, K. (2011) 'Grant Shapps criticises media for ignoring homelessness', *The Guardian,* 12 October, www.theguardian.com/housing-network/2011/oct/12/grant-shapps-criticises-media-over-homelessness

[33] Taylor, M. (2015) '"Vast social cleansing" pushes tens of thousands of families out of London', *The Guardian,* 28 August, www.theguardian.com/ uk-news/2015/aug/28/vast-social-cleansing-pushes-tens-of-thousands-of-families-out-of-london

[34] Sense (2015) 'Disabled people face being cut off from society, warns national charity', 9 March, www.sense.org.uk/content/disabled-people-face-being-cut-society-warns-national-charity

[35] See, for example, Action for Children, NCB (National Children's Bureau) and The Children's Society (2016) *Losing in the long run: Trends in early intervention funding.* London: Action for Children, NCB and The Children's Society, for analysis of trends in funding for, and spending on, early intervention services (including children's centres) between 2010 and 2020.

[36] Ridge, T. (2009) *Living with poverty: A review of the literature on children's and families' experiences of poverty.* London: Department for Work and Pensions.

[37] The Children's Commission on Poverty (2014) *At what cost? Exposing the impact of poverty on school life.* London: The Children's Society.

[38] OBR (Office for Budget Responsibility) (2015) *Economic and fiscal outlook, July 2015*. London: OBR.

Chapter 22

[1] Work and Pensions Committee (2014) *Employment and Support Allowance and work capability assessments – First report of Session 2014–15*. London: House of Commons.

[2] Because the rate at which it would be paid (the 'assessment rate') is no higher than the equivalent JSA rate – the only savings would be from those who would be entitled to JSA but who decide not to claim.

[3] Work and Pensions Committee (2014) *Employment and Support Allowance and work capability assessments – First report of Session 2014–15*. London: House of Commons.

[4] PwC (PricewaterhouseCoopers) (2015) *UK economic outlook*. London: PwC.

[5] The amount of support paid for housing costs under Universal Credit would need to be measured by comparing support paid through UC for those with housing costs, to the level of support which *would be paid* if the claimants didn't receive support with housing costs – the difference would be the support provided for housing costs.

[6] Lloyd, T. (2014) 'Are rent caps the answer?' Shelter, 27 February, http:// blog.shelter.org.uk/2014/02/are-rent-caps-the-answer/

[7] DWP (Department for Work and Pensions) (2010) *Universal Credit: Welfare that works*. London: DWP, p 1.

[8] Royston, S. (2015) *Waiting for credit: The delivery of Universal Credit as experienced by Citizens Advice clients in England and Wales*. London: Citizens Advice.

[9] BBC News (2010) 'Budget: Saving Gateway scheme is scrapped', 22 June, www.bbc.co.uk/news/10376543

Chapter 23

[1] For example, pay may vary to some degree depending on where someone lives in the country, reflecting variations in levels of local costs of living.

[2] See www.jrf.org.uk/report/minimum-income-standard-uk-2016

Chapter 24

[1] See Royston, S., Rodrigues, L. and Hounsell, D. (2012) *Fair and square: A policy report on the future of free school meals*. London: The Children's Society. We suggest that in order to pay for the extension of free school meals to working families, part payment for this additional entitlement could come from reducing the income disregards within their Universal Credit entitlement. A reduction in the family's income disregard would mean that

as they move into work, the amount of Universal Credit they receive will begin to be reduced on the basis of earnings at a slightly lower earnings point. However, under our policy proposals these families will continue to receive free school meals as they move into work. We estimated that a reduction in the level of the income disregard of £5 for each child in the household could pay for nearly half of the cost of extending free school meals to working families.

[2] Living Wage Foundation (2016) 'Do you think pay should cover the basic cost of living?', www.livingwagemovement.org/about/. Note that this is currently significantly higher than the statutory National Living Wage.

Chapter 25

[1] NAO (National Audit Office) (2016) *Local welfare provision*. London: NAO.

[2] The only information on gov.uk that I can find for the general public is a note on the budgeting loans pages saying that 'you may be able to get other kinds of support, including help from your local council'. The page does have links to the Scottish and Welsh schemes.

[3] With a small number of exceptions, as previously outlined.

Index